MW01193454

The Poetics of Processing

The Poetics *of* Processing

Memory Formation, Identity, and the Handling of the Dead

EDITED BY

Anna J. Osterholtz

UNIVERSITY PRESS OF COLORADO

Louisville

Published by University Press of Colorado
245 Century Circle, Suite 202
Louisville, Colorado 80027

Manufactured in the United States of America

The University Press of Colorado is a proud member of the Association of University Presses.

The University Press of Colorado is a cooperative publishing enterprise supported, in part, by Adams State University, Colorado State University, Fort Lewis College, Metropolitan State University of Denver, Regis University, University of Colorado, University of Northern Colorado, University of Wyoming, Utah State University, and Western Colorado University.

∞ This paper meets the requirements of the ANSI/NISO Z39.48-1992 (Permanence of Paper).

ISBN: 978-1-64642-060-5 (hardcover)
ISBN: 978-1-64642-061-2 (ebook)
https://doi.org/10.5876/9781646420612

Library of Congress Cataloging-in-Publication Data

Names: Osterholtz, Anna J., editor.
Title: The poetics of processing : memory formation, identity, and the handling of the dead / edited by Anna J. Osterholtz.
Description: Louisville : University Press of Colorado, [2020] | Includes bibliographical references and index.
Identifiers: LCCN 2020028107 (print) | LCCN 2020028108 (ebook) | ISBN 9781646420605 (cloth) | ISBN 9781646420612 (ebook)
Subjects: LCSH: Whitehead, Neil L. | Human remains (Archaeology) | Dead—Social aspects. | Funeral rites and ceremonies, Ancient. | Death—Social aspects. | Violence.
Classification: LCC CC79.5.H85 P64 2020 (print) | LCC CC79.5.H85 (ebook) | DDC 930.1—dc23
LC record available at https://lccn.loc.gov/2020028107

LC ebook record available at https://lccn.loc.gov/2020028108

Cover illustration courtesy of The Cleveland Museum of Art

For those whose bodies we excavate,
Whose bodies we learn from,
Whose names are lost,
May your stories be told.

Contents

Figures

Tables

The Poetics of Processing

1

Introduction

Processing and Poetics, Examining the Model

ANNA J. OSTERHOLTZ

Just as the dead do not bury themselves (Parker Pearson 1999), the dead also do not manipulate or process their own mortal remains. The manipulation of human remains can be seen as a discursive act, communicating cultural information through actions that create social identity and memory. Manipulation of the body embodies symbolism relating to the construction of society, bringing order to the disorder of death, and giving meaning to the change symbolized by death. Though he was discussing violence, Whitehead's poetics model can be applied to this process as well, particularly when we examine processing and body manipulation as "socially constructive cultural performance" (Whitehead 2004b, 60). This volume arose out of a session organized by Anna Osterholtz and Debra Martin at the 2016 Society for American Archaeology in Orlando, Florida. For the session, we asked the contributors to consider postmortem treatment of the physical body through a poetics lens, to examine body-processing as a mechanism for the recreation of cosmology events and the creation of memory. The creation of processed bodies has the capacity to transform space, ritually close and open spaces, and reinforce relationships between the living and the dead. The session and this volume are focused on the processing of the body, in what ways it occurs, and how the physical body (and its manipulation) is used as a social tool. The contributors also focus on how the living manipulate the dead both literally and figuratively, using the physical and metaphorical transformation of their remains as a mechanism for the creation of social stratification and power.

DOI: 10.5876/9781646420612.c001

Whitehead himself examined the role of manipulation of the body as poetic with his exploration of the *kanaimà* complex in Amazonia (Whitehead 2004b), the difference being that his focus is on the violence of the act, not the nature of the body (in that it is dead when the violence happens). This is a shamanistic process involving mutilation of the body. The fluids associated with putrefaction take on specific social meanings depending on the orifice from which they issue. That the victim of this violence is dead is seen as passivity, a lack of desire to stop the violence or mutilation. As Whitehead (2004b, 71) notes, "the poesis involved in the idea of *kanaimà* thus refers to the way in which knowledge of and ideas about *kanaimà* are creatively entangled in a wide variety of indigenous discourse-sexuality and gender, modernity and tradition, Christian religion and native shamanism, interpersonal antagonism and kin relationships, and ultimately human destiny and the cosmos."

THE POETICS MODEL

The focus of the volume centers on applying Whitehead's (2004a, 2004b) concept of poetics to various mortuary and skeletal assemblages. Whitehead famously applied the concept of poetics to the study of violence, noting the power that violence has in "expression and creation of identity" (Whitehead 2004b, 59). Contributors to the present volume look at the manipulation of the physical body as equally important. Whereas Whitehead asked, "Why are we so violent?" we ask, "Why do we manipulate bodies?" Violent interaction and body manipulation share elements that allow for the application of the poetics model to both. Violence can involve physical contact between the aggressor and victim, violence can also be performed in order to influence the behavior of a third group, the witnesses. This three-part model has been used to examine warfare and violence (e.g., Osterholtz 2013), but can also be applied to body-processing. This relationship can also be seen in the example of the *kanaimà*, where the physical contact with the body confers meaning on the processing itself. This physical contact is performed in order to influence the behavior or belief of the witnesses. The poetics model also argues that the performance and ritual components can be synergistic in their impact.

Whitehead argues that violence must be understood as an important cultural system. He says that this involves "recognition that violence is as much a part of meaningful and constructive human living as it is an imagination of the absence and destruction of all cultural and social order" (2007, 41). Violence is not a simple topic, it is both *con*structive and *de*structive. It is used to create social order and social identity as well as to create social differentiations and hierarchies. Processing and body manipulation can also be said to be both *con*structive and *de*structive, or both *de*generative and *re*generative.

Just as Whitehead argued that violence needed to be seen as historically and culturally contingent, the authors in this volume present numerous case studies showing that interpretation of body manipulation must be historically and culturally oriented. In the case of the historic chapters, understanding the context of the remains allows for a richer understanding of the stories these bones tell. Understanding the historicity of the assemblages, as the chapters in the volume show, allows for a robust interpretation of the relationship between the living and the dead.

Poetics, specifically, allows for any cultural activity—in the case of this volume, the processing of the human body—to be seen as regenerative and meaningful. The meaning comes not only from the activity itself but from the involvement of the community or witnesses to the activity. Involving the community or witnesses adds a performative element to the ritual of processing. It is the synergistic combination of ritual and performance that gives processing incredible power to impact social groups and to create social memory or as a "sanctioned means of collective communication and exchange" (Whitehead 2005, 23).

THE BODY AS MATERIAL FOR SOCIAL MEMORY

The idea of the body as a physical object that can be manipulated for social and political ends has been growing as a construct within bioarchaeology over the past several years. Sofaer's *The Body as Material Culture* (2006) takes this quite literally. The body can be viewed materially; this materiality of the body itself allows for the creation of identity and social memory. Social memory is an important element for the power of the model for creating meaning. How does processing the body lead to the creation of social memory? Through the use of physical manipulation, sense memory is created. Community witnessing of or participation in action helps create group identity and memory (Osterholtz and Harrod 2013). The act of processing itself creates legitimacy of the mortuary program and all that it entails (Whitehead 2007). Each is dependent upon the context in which it is used; again, historicity is important. The chapters within this volume offer numerous case studies about how physical manipulation of the body can be used to create social memory. Pérez (2006) also examines the use of the body as a political tool, with manipulation of the body being instrumental in the creation and maintenance of social hierarchy. In particular, his politicization-of-the-dead model has been fruitful for the interpretation of violent assemblages elsewhere (see Campbell, chapter 7, this volume).

The materiality of the body can be examined archaeologically and historically. Mortuary processes are at the heart of identity in many if not most societies. Mortuary treatment is indicative of social beliefs about social order, an afterlife, and the overall relationship between the living and the dead. Burial in perpetuity, as happens commonly in the United States has persisted partly due to the creation through this process of a commemorative location. The processing of the body in preparation for burial and the selection of a coffin, burial clothing, burial plot, memorial stone, and so on create an expectation of future visitation. In keeping individual burial plots in perpetuity, we also acknowledge and honor the dead as individuals, not necessarily as part of a larger collective. This can be compared to modern burial practices in other parts of the world, such as Greece, where burial space is rented for a limited amount of time. At the end of this time, the bones are disinterred and placed in an ossuary with other family members. The focus for future visitation is on the family or community unit, not necessarily the individual.

These two different methods of remembrance would (and do) leave visible archaeological traces. Through a poetics approach, each method of remembrance could be interpreted to highlight different relationships. Why do we concern ourselves with identification of individual graves? Why is this important in American society? It could be argued that due to the particular historicity of American history, we are individualistic and tend to embody individuals with suites of characteristics that other cultures might attribute to groups or communities as a whole. The grave of Susan B. Anthony has long been used as a way to express solidarity with female candidates and feminism in general. In the first national election in which the nominee of a major political party was female, women and men stood in line for hours to place their "I Voted" stickers on her tombstone (figure 1.1). In this way, the creation of memory involved with her burial embodied much grander ideals than just her individual identity.

The use of the body as material with cultural meaning is multifaceted: such uses can be considerate or punitive, or can signal an alternative status. All create social identity and social memory for different reasons and signal different cultural values. Visiting the grave of a loved one reinforces links to family, whereas visiting the grave of a suffragette might reinforce a feeling of connectedness with larger social movements and imagined communities. Stewart and Strathern (1999, 650) note that a sorcerer's corpse would be "dishonored and abused before being returned to its home village, in the same way as might happen to a war casualty." The manipulation of the corpse carried meaning in a punitive way greater than just the return of the body to his or her home village.

This poetics approach is also linked somewhat to what Giddens (1984) described as "structuration." Giddens believed that societies should be viewed not just as large-scale structures but as "dialectics of structures and practices" (Bernbeck 2008, 396). Giddens defines structures as the "intersection of presence and absence [of social relations or social phenomena]; underlying codes have to be inferred from surface manifestations" (1984, 16). Social structures are formed through practice

FIGURE 1.1. Grave of Susan B. Anthony the day after the 2016 election. (Photo by Daniel Penfield, Own work, CC BY-SA 4.0, https://commons.wikimedia.org/w/index.php?curid=53579895.)

and form practice in a feedback loop. In effect, larger social structures can be used to infer practice. However, Bernbeck (2008) cautions against the examination of practice at the expense of considering the constraining effects of cultural structures. The poetics approach as used here examines this relationship between practice and structure as an important generator of identity and social memory.

ORGANIZATION OF THE VOLUME

The individual chapter's authors have taken different elements of poetics, based on the historicity and overall research questions being asked. In this way, they show the breadth of the theoretical paradigm.

There are three sections to the book based on geographic location of the case study. The first section comprises case studies from the Americas. In chapter 2, Beth Koontz Scaffidi examines the transformational power of feline trophy heads in the Majes Valley, Arequipa, Peru, and their inclusion in burials as grave goods.

The creation, use, and disposal of these trophy heads is important in negotiating supernatural dangers undertaken by the makers of human trophy heads. Feline trophy heads can therefore be seen as generative forces for the community. Chapter 3 examines performance and meaning at Paquimé, Chihuahua, Mexico. Kyle Waller and Adrianne Offenbecker discuss the presence of both primary burials and an upper layer of heavily processed individuals. They argue that the possible human sacrifices, as evidenced by the processing of the upper individuals, reflect a potent source of sociocultural power manipulated by ritual elites to reinforce social control and political power.

In chapter 4, Kristin Kuckelman examines patterns of ritual modification at several ancestral Puebloan sites of the northern San Juan region. She traces the movement of groups from pueblo to pueblo, arguing that the ritual processing was used by multiple groups at different times. Chapter 5 focuses on the same geographic region: Debra Martin and Anna Osterholtz examine processing at three different ancestral Puebloan assemblages, showing both the consistency and the changes that were occurring through time in the region. They argue that the extreme processing evident in the site was both regenerative and destructive. They also argue that it created social memory and influenced social behavior on a community level.

The second section of the volume involves case studies from Europe, Eurasia, and Africa. Chapter 6 addresses tomb usage in ancient Aksum, Ethiopia. Here, Dilpreet Singh Basanti argues that stelae served as a longer-lasting "body" for the family of the dead and held a sort of personhood of their own. Chapter 7 looks at violent death and processing in ancient Egypt. Roselyn Campbell examines state-sanctioned violence and the subsequent processing of those remains as indicators of social will and control, arguing that in some ways it was this manipulation that negotiated the power structure between the rulers and the ruled. In chapter 8, Marin Pilloud and colleagues argue that social memory was a key component at the site of Çatalhöyük, Turkey, centering around daily practice and some embodiment of the house as a repository for memory and identity. They believe that postmortem processing added to the already important place that daily practice had in reinforcing social structure and practice. In chapter 9, Megan Perry and Anna Osterholtz examine the use and reuse of tomb space at the Nabataean site of Petra as a way to examine concepts of the body, memory, and group identity.

The final section of the volume centers on historic postmortem processing (anatomization) in the United States as evidence of structural violence. In chapter 10, Christina Hodge and Kenneth Nystrom examine the role of medical students' rites of passage as student physicians in the dissection of cadavers, and how those cadavers were selected for dissection. The choice of groups such as African Americans or almshouse inmates illustrates the degree of structural violence present at the time. These graves were not seen as worthy of protection and those bodies were not sacred: they were Other. In chapter 11, Carlina de la Cova examines the populations making up the Hamann-Todd Collection. The collection is used today by many bioarchaeologists and historians of medicine to understand the course of pathological conditions in human skeletal remains, but it is disproportionately made up of individuals who were impoverished, were deemed insane, or were people of color. As seen in chapter 10 (Hodge and Nystrom), de la Cova demonstrates that overrepresentation of these groups within the study collections illustrates the degree of social power present in those making decisions about inclusion in the collections and processing.

Finally, the concluding chapter by Eric Haanstad presents a social perspective on the creation of meaning through poetics. Written by a student and colleague of Neil Whitehead, this chapter summarizes the chapters within the poetics framework. Haanstad ties together elements of all chapters to highlight the concept that "death processing is not about the dead at all and is clearly focused on manipulating the living" (chapter 12, this volume). Haanstad looks forward and encourages researchers to highlight the tensions between legitimacy and illegitimacy in poetics and amplification of processing as a key to identity formation.

The case studies are broadly distributed, both in terms of geography and time period; the contributions illustrate the varied ways in which manipulation of the body can be incredibly culturally meaningful. Culture change can be spotted (Perry and Osterholtz, chapter 9), and we can see the presence of processing as a socially steadying and regenerative factor across time (Martin and Osterholtz, chapter 5). Processing of the bodies of community members as part of a mortuary ritual reinforces social ties and illustrates the relationship between the living and the dead. The houses of the dead become proxies for the dead themselves (Basanti, chapter 6, Pilloud et al., chapter 8). We can see status and hierarchy (Waller and Offenbecker, chapter 3; Campbell, chapter 7). Processing of the bodies of Others (Hodge and Nystrom, chapter 10; de la Cova, chapter 11), outsiders (Kuckelman, chapter 4), and prisoners of war (Scaffidi, chapter 2) illuminates social hierarchy and access to power. The model is therefore remarkably elastic and allows us to examine deeper meaning than a surface understanding that processing and mortuary processes occur. Through a poetics approach to processing and mortuary programs, we can see how multifaceted these processes really are. Processing and all that go into these complex mortuary programs are discursive and tend toward being recursive as well in that processing and body manipulation are "powerful and performative and [have] the means of creating the conditions of its own verification and therefore its own reinforcement" (Bourdieu 1998, 72). Whitehead described the poetics of violence as a process "whose symbols and rituals are as relevant to its enactment as its instrumental aspects." It is "an indispensable aspect of being able to interpret, and not just condemn, violent acts" (Whitehead 2007, 44). These are not simple processes any more than violence is a simple concept. Violence also tends to act as a justification of violence, so it is also recursive discourse. The same could be said of the poetics of processing.

POETICALLY MOVING FORWARD

The chapters in this volume show just how diverse poetic interpretations can be, depending on research questions and additional theoretical perspectives employed by the authors. Poetics offers a way to examine the synergistic effect of practice and structure, the role that action has in group identity and social memory. The model has a significant amount of flexibility and is contingent upon the historical and cultural contexts of the group examined.

REFERENCES

Bernbeck, Reinhard. 2008. "Structural Violence in Archaeology." *Archaeologies: Journal of the World Archaeological Congress* 4 (3): 390–413.

Bourdieu, Pierre. 1998. *Practical Reason: On the Theory of Action*. Stanford, CA: Stanford University Press.

Giddens, Anthony. 1984. *The Constitution of Society: Outline of the Theory of Structuration*. Berkeley: University of California Press.

Osterholtz, Anna J. 2013. "Hobbling and Torture as Performative Violence: An Example from the Prehistoric Southwest." *Kiva* 78 (2): 123–144.

Osterholtz, Anna J., and Ryan P. Harrod. 2013. "Warrior, Soldier, Big Man: Warrior Ethos, Identity Formation and the Negotiation of Social Roles in Multicultural Settings." 78th annual meeting of the Society for American Archaeology, Honolulu, HI.

Parker Pearson, Michael. 1999. *The Archaeology of Death and Burial*. College Station: Texas A&M University Press.

Pérez, Ventura R. 2006. "The Politicization of the Dead: An Analysis of Cutmark Morphology and Culturally Modified Human Remains from La Plata and Peñasco Blanco (AD 900–1300)." Unpublished PhD dissertation, Anthropology, University of Massachusetts Amherst.

Sofaer, Joanna R. 2006. *The Body as Material Culture: A Theoretical Osteoarchaeology*. Cambridge, UK: Cambridge University Press.

Stewart, Pamela J., and Andrew Strathern. 1999. "Feasting on My Enemy: Images of violence and Change in the New Guinea Highlands." *Ethnohistory* 46 (4): 645–669.

Whitehead, Neil L. 2004a. "Introduction: Cultures, Conflicts, and the Poetics of Violent Practice." In *Violence*, edited by N L. Whitehead, 3–24. Santa Fe, NM: SAR Press.

Whitehead, Neil L. 2004b. "On the Poetics of Violence." In *Violence*, edited by Neil L. Whitehead, 55–78. Santa Fe, NM: SAR Press.

Whitehead, Neil L. 2005. "War and Violence as Cultural Expression." *Anthropology News* 46 (5): 23–26. doi: 10.1525/an.2005.46.5.23.1.

Whitehead, Neil L. 2007. "Violence and the Cultural Order." *Daedalus* 136 (1): 40–50. doi: 10.2307/20028088.

PART I

The Americas

2

Power, Mediation, and Transformation

Dismembered Heads from Uraca (Majes Valley, Peru) and the Andean Feline-Hunter Myth

BETH KOONTZ SCAFFIDI

TROPHY HEADS, AGENCY, AND RITUAL PRACTICE

Social bioarchaeologists have shifted away from viewing the dead body as a fixed, pre- or postsocial being—a mere palimpsest upon which meaning is inscribed by surviving mourners (*sensu* Connerton 1989). According to Crandall and Martin, this shift is beginning to reveal "the ways that the border between living and dead, corpse and person, social agent, and biological entity are fluid, sometimes liminal, and often subject to constant cultural negotiation" (Crandall and Martin 2014, 430). While the body is a natural metaphor that orders the beliefs and cosmologies of a society (Douglas 2004; Scheper-Hughes and Lock 1987), focusing on the dead body as a powerful but ultimately inert object risks obfuscating the very culturally entrenched meanings that inform and necessitate deeply visceral interactions with dead bodies in the first place.

Practice-minded approaches interrogate borders between the living and dead, but can also contemplate the dead body as agentive in its own right. Following Tung (2014a) and Sofaer (2006), it is proposed here that dead bodies have "effective" (Robb 2004, 132) or "secondary" (Gell 1998, 7) agency, in that they can limit and elicit certain behaviors from the living. Recognizing this agency is fundamental to understanding how beliefs about the boundaries between life and death structured trophy manufacturing and use. By animating trophy heads, their poetics, or the way these powerful signs and symbols are "used performatively through time" (Whitehead 2002, 2), become more apparent. Viewing the practices of

DOI: 10.5876/9781646420612.c002

trophy-head manufacture through the lens of animistic cosmologies offers insights into the meanings and motives for cutting, slicing, ripping, burning, and filing down skeletal elements. These animated heads cease to be merely "the fleshy vehicles of Cartesian minds, but cultural bodies, both marked and materially inscribed by physical harm but also sentient and articular, searching for a way to reoccupy themselves" (Whitehead 2004a, 20–21). Here it is argued that trophy manufacturing and display practices were informed not only by culturally informed symbolism, but also by anxieties concerning the actual agency of dead trophy victims and the physical dangers of handling both animas (i.e., the spirit or soul) and flesh (or bodies) of communal outsiders. The poetics of trophy processing can be viewed as a complex negotiation between actors and observers in natural, spiritual, and physical realms to achieve the proper balance of life forces, rather than a merely symbolic performance.

Trophies are corporeal elements removed from the body and crafted into objects conveying ritual or political meaning. Trophies would have been imbued with effective agency by those who had visceral interactions with them, and also by community members who may not have interacted with them physically but would have felt and responded to the power and presence of the enemy's dangerous vital force. Transformation of these heads from living people to relics, to communal energies, would have impacted community order in deeply meaningful ways throughout the phases of their use lives from processing, to presentation, to interment. Through a study of human trophy heads from the cemetery of Uraca in the Majes Valley, Arequipa, Peru, the iconographic and bioarchaeological evidence for trophy-taking as violent performance is considered. First, the contexts of trophy-taking within the context of Andean animism is discussed. Then archaeological context and the Uraca trophies are described, along with evidence of the various ways the Uraca trophies were cut, defleshed, and sculpted. Cumulatively, these data are used to argue that trophies were used in dynamic performance rituals that mitigated the volatility of dead enemy spirits. Finally, Whitehead's (2004b) poetics model is applied, emphasizing how trophy-processing reconfigures the liminal realms between life and death and between outsider and insiders, politicizing the dead body and reinforcing messages of dominance (Pérez 2012), while generating new social meanings through this creative reconfiguration of the body (Whitehead 2004b, 2007). This framework, along with a description of feline trophy-head iconography from the region, is offered as a scheme for understanding trophy-taking as violent performance, comprising complex constructions and deconstructions of socio-spiritual identity for human and animal trophy victims, ritual participants, and observers.

Andean Trophy-Taking

The use of various human and nonhuman animal body parts as ritual objects is common throughout the world (see Chacon and Dye 2007). The tradition of decapitating, dismembering, and curating heads is particularly well-known in the Andes and Amazon through ethnographic and ethnohistoric accounts, and in the prehistoric Andes by the rich iconographic, sculptural, and bioarchaeological record. Trophy-taking was practiced throughout the region as far back as the Preceramic and Early Horizon. Most documented specimens date to the Early Intermediate Period (EIP, ca. AD 1–750) in the Nasca region and the Middle Horizon (AD 600–1000) in the Wari heartland and some hinterland regions (Tung 2007). Andean trophy heads are typically characterized by postmortem modifications, showing that they were displayed, worn, or otherwise used in ritual. This includes a variety of body parts modified for display, such as skulls modified into bowls and teeth with modified roots reported in Moche contexts on the North Coast (Verano et al. 1999), occipital-bone portions and phalanges drilled with holes found in Wari imperial contexts (Tung 2007), and skullcaps used by the Inca for consuming beverages (Ogburn 2007).

Bioarchaeologists have distinguished between fleshed trophy heads and defleshed trophy skulls (Verano 1995). Ethnohistoric drawings by Guaman Poma (ca. 1613) depict trophy heads: Inca warriors hold freshly decapitated heads by the hair, with ligaments and muscles attached to the neck, closed eyes, and liquids dripping from the nose; a warrior presents an enemy head decorated with headdress and facial adornments to an Inca ruler (Nielsen 2009; Ogburn 2007). In similar scenes painted half a century earlier, Wari warrior gods hold fleshed heads with intact cervical vertebrae, still wearing the face paint and headdress reflecting their ethnic identities (Tung 2014b, 247). These scenes show fleshy trophy heads retaining their idiosyncratic facial features, hairstyles, and traditional garb. Trophy heads are contrasted with defleshed trophy skulls, which are fully or mostly skeletonized, with cut marks along muscle and ligament attachment sites that show musculature was cut or burned away before flesh was removed (Kellner 2006; Tung 2007; Verano 2008).

Making Nasca and Wari Trophy Heads

Generally, trophy-makers chopped the head from the body at the cervical vertebrae, enlarged the foramen magnum to remove internal tissues, stripped away muscles and tendons, removed portions of the occipital and parietal, and then drilled or perforated the cranial vault to thread a toggled carrying cord through the hole (Kellner 2006; Verano 1995). The carrying cords were woven of reeds, textiles, or human hair, attached to a wooden toggle (Proulx 1999; Verano 1995, 2003;). Kellner (2006) and

Tung (2007) classify trophy-head styles based on the location of the perforation and the extent of posterior cranial-bone breakage. In the Wari style, the trophy-maker removed the inferior occipital and bored a hole at the bregma, enabling the head to dangle upright (Tung 2007, 2008, 2012). This standardized manufacturing suggests a few individuals oversaw trophy manufacture in the Wari heartland. In contrast, Nasca-style heads display a wide range of variation in the location of the perforation and the extent of posterior breakage. Perforations are located in various places along the frontal bone, and posterior breakage ranges from none to completely removed, creating a mask (Kellner 2006; Williams, Forgey, and Klarich 2001). This variation suggests that Nasca trophies were taken in a different social context than in the Wari heartland, and that trophy-makers were a less-specialized group of people.

In the Wari and Nasca examples, artisans carefully preserved the countenance of the decedent, albeit to varying degrees. Scenes on Nasca and Wari pots depict hair, face paint, headdresses, and other identifying features preserved, at least for the initial phase of the trophy's use-life (Proulx 2001, 2006; Tung 2007, 2012). The Wari examples were eventually burned and skeletonized, but iconographic evidence supports that they began their use-life fully fleshed (Tung 2007, 2012). In contrast, in many Nasca examples, the facial tissues are completely untouched, and even the eyelids, eyebrows, and hair are completely preserved. In other cases, facial tissues and muscles were cut off, and in some cases, reapplied (Verano 1995). In some examples from coastal Arequipa, eyebrows, beards, carefully braided hair, and feathered headdresses are still preserved.

The mouth, eyes, and tongue received special treatment: lips were often pinned shut with *huarango* (cactus) spines, eyes were cut out and stuffed with cotton, and tongues were removed and attached to the carrying cord (Sotil Galindo 2009; Verano 2003; Williams, Forgey, and Klarich 2001). It is unclear whether Wari heads had their eyes removed and mouths shut, but ceramic scenes depict the heads gritting their teeth with spread and snarling lips (Tung 2012), suggesting their mouths were not closed during that phase of ritual display. In Nasca examples, the mandible is sometimes tied to the zygomatic, while in others, the mandible is not preserved (Sotil Galindo 2009; Verano 1995; Williams, Forgey, and Klarich 2001). In some coastal Arequipa specimens, the mouth is not closed with cactus spines, but the eyelids are pulled taut over globular bulbs of cotton, forming a new eye that projects from the face (Sotil Galindo 2009, 36).

Ethnohistoric analogy can explain why the head was targeted for removal, and why the mouth and eyes were manipulated. In many cultures, the head and the hands are considered the center of a person's essence (Scheper-Hughes and Lock 1987). In the Andes, this essence is called *camaquen* (Bray 2009), *sami* (Allen 1988), or *upani* (Lau 2008). It can be understood as a volatile soul, life-force, or "forceful spirit" (Salomon 1995, 323), or an essential vitality, which can be harnessed for its destructive or productive forces. Arnold and Hastorf (2008) present compelling evidence from Andean archaeological and ethnographic studies that the eyes, tongue, and mouth were targeted because they were the loci of volatile enemy spirits. Handling these dangerous elements would have required the performance of specific rituals to mediate the danger of the enemy's volatile, but generative, life force.

There may also have been practical reasons for the removal of the eyes and closure of the mouth in trophy-head processing. The Huarochirí Manuscript, a late sixteenth-century indigenous narrative of the Spanish cleric Francisco de Ávila, describes the use of *huayos*, trophy masks made from skin and bones of men captured in warfare. The enemy head was first flayed, then danced with in public ceremonies, and then strung up along with food offerings to be transported to the spirit realm (Salomon and Urioste 1991, 120–121). A myriad of Nasca (Proulx 2000, 2006), Paracas (Paul 1990), and Wari (Tung 2007, 2008, 2012) scenes depict trophies worn by ritual participants, either hung from the belt or shoulders, or around the neck. This, along with the Huarochirí account, shows that trophies were used as props or costumes in ritual dances and displays. The delicate tissues of the eyes, mouth, and hair would have needed to be secured to prevent loss during ritual processions, movements, and dances.

TROPHIES AND ANIMISTIC AND POLITICAL BODY RITUALS

Animism, broadly, is the belief that all entities have animating forces dwelling within (Tylor 1913). Andean cosmologies have animistic components, focusing on balancing the nonhuman and human ancestral life forces that inhabit animals, objects, and places (Bird-David 1999; Duviols 1978; Sillar 2009). Ethnohistoric accounts of Andean and Amazonian animism can inform interpretations of prehistoric ritual (e.g., Alberti and Bray 2009; Groleau 2009; Lau 2008; Weismantel 2015). Andean animism emphasizes engagement with ancestral spirits dwelling in *apus* (mountain gods) and *huacas* (durable places and objects inhabited by spirits). *Huacas* include landscape features, stones, temples, tombs, mummy bundles, dolls, ceramic vessels, and hardened everyday objects, like potatoes (Allen 1988; Bray 2009; Salomon 1995; Sillar 2009). Animated things and places are understood to have their own agendas, and sacrifices are carried out to placate the spirits and achieve desired outcomes. Trophy heads, when viewed through the lens of animism, are likely to have been regarded as *huacas* where powerful human or animal spirits resided, requiring specific ritual practices and performances to harness or shield the community from those powers.

Viveiros de Castro's (1998) concept of perspectivism describes how nonhuman spirits have human forms hidden beneath their outwardly visible shells.

Animistic practices emphasize fluidity between human and nonhuman spirits, and between human spirits, as a means of aggregating vitality. For example, among the Amazonian Wari, new life and "productive relationships" are generated by traversing and exchanging across spiritual boundaries, such as between predator and prey (Conklin 2001, 203–204). Among the Amazonian Kayabi, vitality is generated by traversing between enemy and Kayabi perspectives during mourning rituals for loved ones (Oakdale 2005, 118). This fluidity transforms enemy or animal spirits into new persons, but it also creates a danger that the living might follow the deceased into death. Many Amazonian communities practice mortuary rituals focused on dismantling the image of the deceased (e.g., see Fausto 1999; Oakdale 2005), burning and consuming body parts (Conklin 2001), or mutilating the victim's orifices before consuming the "juices of putrefaction" (Whitehead 2002, 14–15) as a means of ritually consuming the victim's life force. In the Andes, ethnographic accounts emphasize the feeding of Mother Earth through sacrifice and food offerings, a reciprocal act through which new life is generated (Allen 1988; Bastien 1978; Gose 1994; Isbell 2005; Sallnow 1987). In both contexts, deceased and unborn spirits linger just beyond the human realm, intervening in the human world of their own volition, or waiting to be summoned through appropriate rituals. Bodily exuviae, like heads, hairs, nails, and even entire corpses, are used in rituals to achieve desired outcomes (Bloch 1992; Bloch and Parry 1982).

Body parts can be used as objects in animistic rituals to simultaneously signify political meaning. Arnold and Hastorf's work (2008) considers the various functions that Andean trophy-taking rituals may have served. In the Foucauldian sense, they are bodies that have been made docile, or emblems that "symbolize and generate the breakdown of the social body of victim communities," as empires and states manipulate the body politic (Tung 2012, 201). The accumulation of trophy heads can be seen as a type of commodity fetishism of "kingly things" (Appadurai 1986, 22), which aggregated prestige for the trophy-taker and community (Arnold and Hastorf 2008; Becker and Alconini 2015). Trophy heads could also be viewed as palimpsests (Connerton 1989) or objects facilitating memory pathways (Abercrombie 1998), as their display would have retold communal tales of important battles and enemies overcome. Trophy-taking rituals simultaneously reified the taker's power over death, the enemy, the enemy's community, and the forces of nature, while reifying social hierarchies, religious beliefs, and masculine and military ideals. Understanding the Uraca trophies as animated objects demonstrates how ritual performances mediated and transformed the potentially polluting and destructive forces of dismembered heads, while destroying and reconfiguring the identities of the victim, trophy-takers and -makers, and donor and recipient communities.

ARCHAEOLOGICAL CONTEXT AND URACA TROPHIES

Uraca is a cemetery site in the lower Majes Valley, Arequipa, Peru, located southeast of Nasca cultural and ceremonial centers during the Early Intermediate Period and southwest of the Wari capital in the south-central highlands, the imperial heartland during the Middle Horizon (figure 2.1). Uraca artifacts show influence from both cultures, even though very little points to direct interaction with Nasca or Wari agents. Uraca is the closest cemetery to *Toro Muerto*, an enormous petroglyph site where carvings on more than 500 boulders depict feasting, llama sacrifices, dancing in elaborate headdresses and wigs, ancestral mummy worship, and hunting (Linares Málaga 2004; Núñez Jiménez 1986; Van Hoek 2010). The *Toro Muerto* petroglyphs portray violent acts, including warriors with decorated tunics and shields, and feline beasts and human-animal creatures holding human trophy heads (Linares Málaga 2004; Núñez Jiménez 1986) (figure 2.2).

Uraca's artifact assemblage suggests that the ritual practices depicted at *Toro Muerto* were performed in real-life (Scaffidi 2018; Scaffidi and García Márquez 2015). For example, the large quantity of flutes and whistles recovered confirm the importance of music and dance in Uraca rituals. An enormous quantity of feathered headdresses and braided wigs of human hair suggest costumes played an essential role in rituals for the living and the dead. Raptor talons, llama burials, and human and feline trophies excavated from Uraca may have been used as elements of ritual costume that helped shamans and participants shift between animal, ancestral, and enemy perspectives during rituals.

Trophy Heads at Uraca

HUMAN TROPHY-HEAD VICTIMS AND STYLES

In all, 12 trophy heads or defleshed crania were recovered from looted mortuary contexts at Uraca, along with seven defleshed mandibles that could not be matched to crania. These individuals presented cut marks that showed that muscles and ligaments had been removed, perforations were made in various locations, and occipital and parietals were removed to varying degrees. An additional adult male cranium was defleshed like the trophy heads, but without the perforation or removal of the occipital. This individual is counted among the trophy heads due to this extensive defleshing.

All defleshed crania were young to middle adult males who suffered at least one cranial injury.[1] Of the 15 injuries documented, 12 healed prior to death. Injuries

[1] Except for individual 7006, the posterior cranial vault bones could not be observed, so this fracture rate is probably an underestimation of actual violence-related trauma.

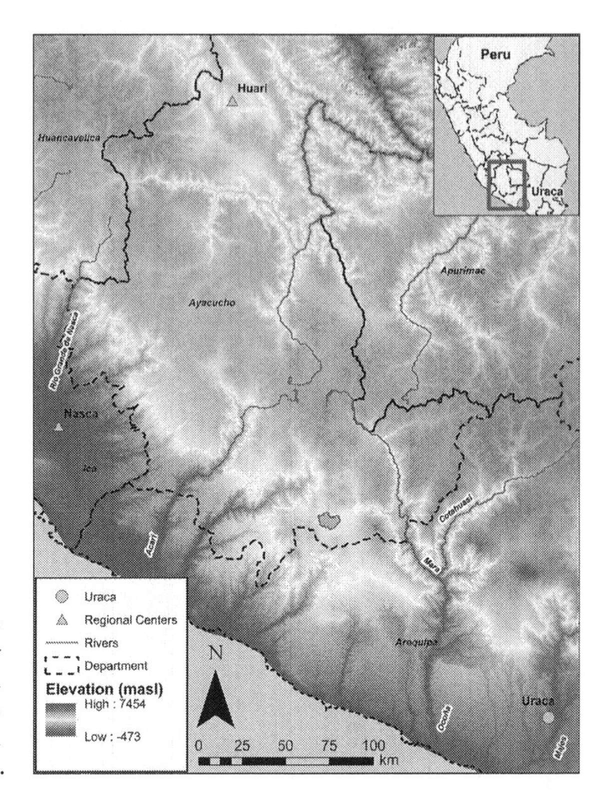

Figure 2.1. Uraca site location relative to Early Intermediate Period (Nasca) and Middle Horizon (Huari) cultural centers.

Figure 2.2. Petroglyphs from Uraca: (a) anthropomorphic figure holding trophy head in its right hand; (b) feline holding human trophy head from its mouth; (c) human warrior holding trophy head in his right hand. (Images processed using the DStretch Plug-in for ImageJ by John Harmon.)

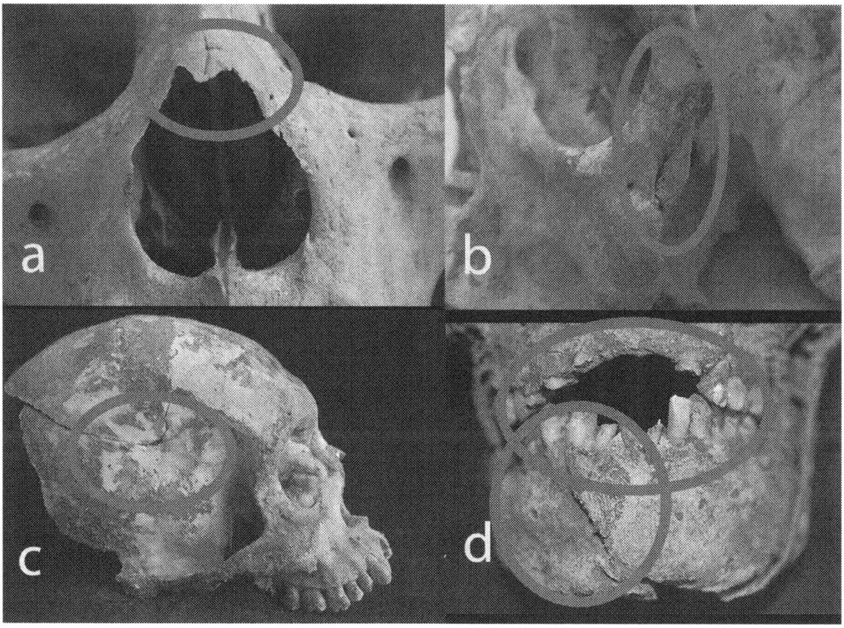

FIGURE 2.3. Trophy-head fractures: (a) healed nasal fracture (Individual 7003); (b) perimortem hinging on left zygomatic process of the maxilla and (c) possible sharp-force trauma to the right parietal (Individual 7004); and (d) antemortem trauma to the anterior teeth and perimortem fracture to the left mandible (Individual 7010).

were most commonly broken noses (figure 2.3a) and blunt-force trauma or depression fractures to the cranial vault. Two of the trophy victims suffered multiple violent encounters during their life: one suffered two perimortem injuries, a hinged fracture to the left eye socket (figure 2.3b), sharp-force injury on the right parietal (figure 2.3c), and an antemortem fracture to the left nasal bones; another suffered a perimortem blow that cleaved the mandible in two, as well as trauma to the anterior incisors that was in the process of healing prior to this fatal encounter (figure 2.3d). Preliminary biogeochemical analysis of lead and strontium isotopes suggests that at least four of the victims grew up in nearby valleys before ultimately being interred at Uraca (Scaffidi et al. 2016). The demographic profile, injury pattern and recidivism, and the reconstruction of isotopic life histories suggest that the victim heads were taken in hostile intergroup conflict, not from revered ancestors within the community.

Variants of what Kellner (2006) and Tung (2007) construe as Nasca- and Wari-style trophies were preserved at Uraca. There were five Nasca-style face-mask skulls with perforations in various locations on the frontal bone, and with most of the occipital and parietals removed. One Wari-style skull was recovered, with a perforation at the bregma and minimal removal of the occipital. Two other trophy skulls were horizontally oriented half-masks (Kellner 2006), where all but the bones of the splanchnocranium were chopped away. Six of these trophy skulls showed evidence of burning at the perforation or along the broken parietals. The remaining three mummified Nasca-style heads presented completely preserved facial musculature and hair, without any evidence of burning. The masseter muscle is preserved in these three men, showing the mandible was intentionally left intact.

FELINE TROPHY HEAD

In association with the three mummified heads was a fleshed feline cranium, half of a mandible, and four paws. Although cut marks are not visible due to the preservation of fur, the posterior cranial bones were sliced away, and the eyes cut out in a similar fashion to the human trophies, as discussed below. The size and shape of the skull suggests this is an Andean pampas cat (*Leopardus colocolo*), a feline the size of a domestic cat, indigenous to the Andean coast.

Ritual Performance with Uraca Trophies

The Uraca trophy victims show extensive evidence of postmortem processing. This methodical removal of cranial tissues would have required visceral interactions between trophy-maker and victim, while evidence of retouching shows the trophies were continuously used and recrafted by the recipient community. The intentional removal of the tissues of the eye and mouth orifices suggests the trophies were made to be moved with during ritual displays. The "poetics" of this ritual processing and ritual movement would have reinforced expressions of dominance over the enemy, generating new meanings and identities for observers, participants, and the conquered, thus "amplifying" the force of these violent acts and messages (Whitehead 2007, 7).

RETOUCHING AND REUSE

The two horizontal half-masks have unique perforation patterns showing that they were retouched and reused through time. Individual 7000 presents one perforation drilled on the left sphenoid, another penetrating the endocranial bone on the left frontal (figure 2.4a), and another on the right temporal at the mastoid process (figure 2.4b). After the frontal perforation broke, cord was retied through the left eye orbit (figure 2.4a). Similarly, individual 7001 presents a charred perforation that is fractured at the superior edge. Like for individual 7000, ritual participants

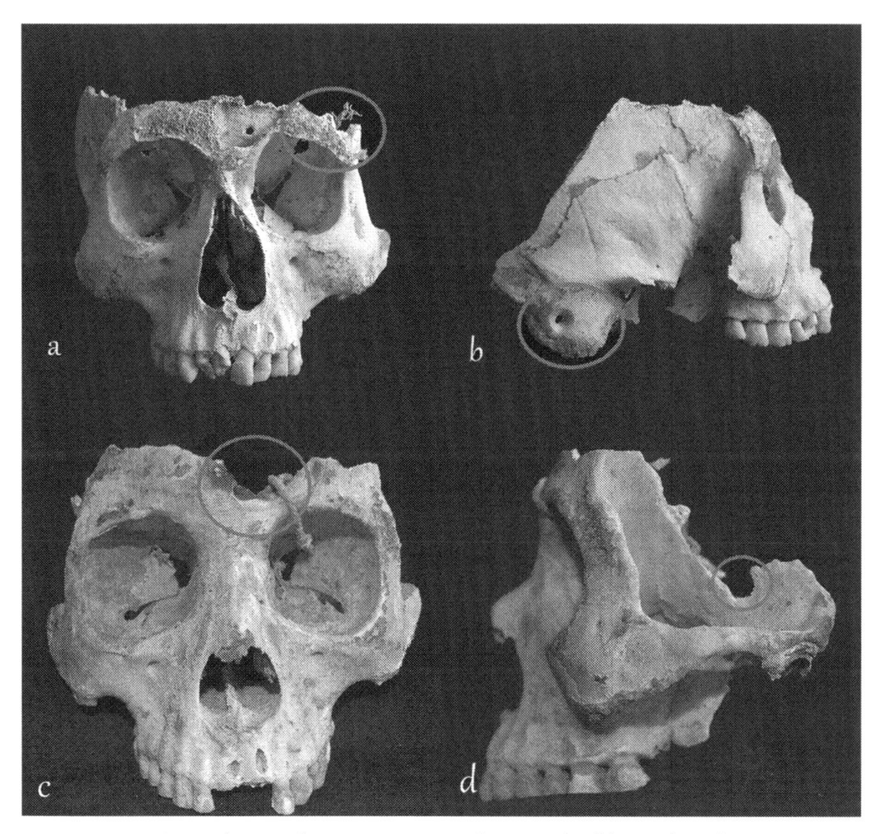

FIGURE 2.4. Retouching and reuse. Top: retouching, with additional perforations through (a) the left eye orbit and (b) the right mastoid process (Individual 7000). Bottom: (c) adult male trophy with retouched perforation threaded through the left eye orbit and (d) perforation on left temporal (Individual 7001).

threaded a cotton cord through the left eye socket after the original perforation broke away (figure 2.4c). At some point in its use-life, the left temporal was also perforated (figure 2.4d). Because these two trophy skulls show signs of retouching and repair, they must have been used in ritual for many years, even after the flesh had decomposed.

Two trophies returned AMS dates that were much older than either the non-trophy or trophy subsamples. Individual 7006, the Wari-style skull, lived from approximately 136 BC to AD 21, while Individual 7010, a mummified Nasca-style head, dated to approximately 137 BC–AD 115 (Scaffidi 2018). These heads could represent trophies taken by ancestral Uracans, preserved until their interment alongside the communal deceased. Or, they could represent trophies from ancestral Uracans or enemy groups, captured in raids against other communities. In either case, the age of these heads shows the persistence of this practice over half a millennium, demonstrating the significance of this violent practice in the ongoing (re)configuration of community identity.

REMOVAL OF THE EYES

Two trophy skulls show intense small cut marks (< 1 mm) around the eye orbits, suggesting the eyes were intentionally removed (figure 2.5). The eye cut marks along the frontal process of the zygomatic bone and eye orbits are similar to those reported in three trophies from the Kallawaya territory of Bolivia (Becker and Alconini 2015). The authors argue that the eyes may have been extracted during life, perhaps during torture, as depicted in scenes of Inca captains removing the eyes of rebels illustrated in the Spanish chronicles (Guamán Poma de Ayala 1613). Like the Kallawaya trophies, it is not possible to determine whether these cut marks are evidence of eye extraction *in vivo* or of cutting through the orbicularis oculi or ocular palpebra to remove the eyeballs postmortem. These cut marks could also have been produced during attempts to cut through the temporalis muscle to remove the mandible while leaving internal orbital tissues intact.

RE-CREATING THE EYES

Two trophy skulls displayed eye orbits stuffed with cotton (others may once have been stuffed before the cotton fell out), without associated orbital cut marks. This suggests the eye tissues decomposed naturally before being removed and replaced with cotton. The three trophy heads displayed intensive reworking of the eyes, but without visible cut marks. In these three cases, the trophy-maker punched through the palpebral tissue and removed only the eyeball. Next, the maker stuffed the inside with cotton and then stretched either the palpebral tissue, leather, or a vegetal skin back over the cotton to reform an eyeball (figure 2.6a).

The feline head received a similar treatment to these three human trophy heads. The head and paws were removed, and the cat's eyes were removed and recrafted, but with red fringed wool cord instead of cotton. The cat's eyes may have decomposed naturally or may have been extracted as part of a ritual performance. This treatment hints that human and animal bodies were endowed by ritual participants with similar traits, requiring similar types of curative dismemberment.

MANIPULATION OF THE MOUTH

Five of the trophies showed abnormal dental wear patterns, with the buccal cusps worn down at an oblique angle (figure 2.7). The fact that each tooth of the maxilla

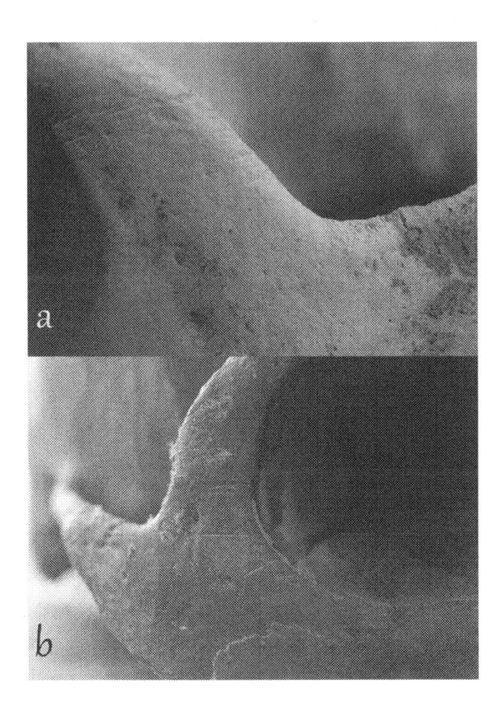

FIGURE 2.5. Removal of the ocular tissues: with cut marks (a) to the anterior and posterior edge of the frontal process of the zygomatic bone (Individual 7000), and (b) along the orbital margins of the frontal process of the zygomatic (Individual 7011).

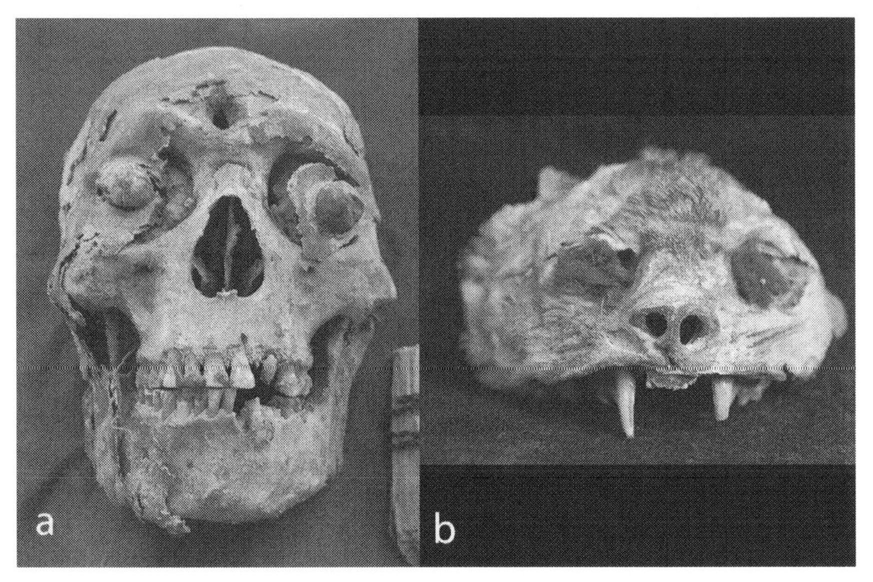

FIGURE 2.6. Re-creation of the eyes: (a) with eyes removed and recrafted from cotton (Individual 7011), and (b) pampas cat with red-wool textile substituted for eyes.

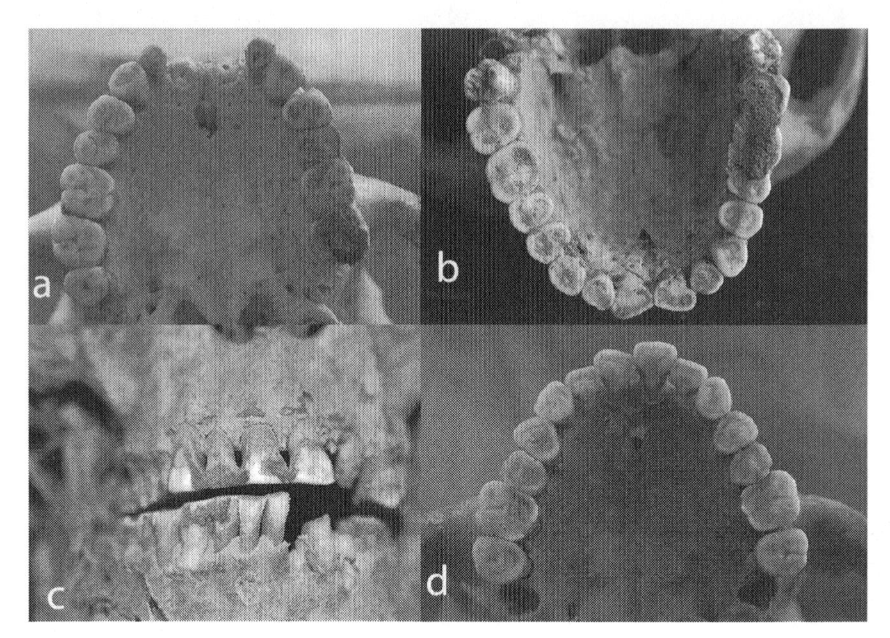

FIGURE 2.7. Abnormal dental wear: (a) Individual 7001 and (b) Individual 7003, both with filed buccal cusps and clay-like substance on occlusal surfaces; (c) Individual 7008, showing filed-down appearance of maxillary and mandibular teeth; and (d) Individual 7011 with filed or worn buccal cusps.

and mandible is worn suggests that the teeth may have been filed down rather than used as a third hand in craft production, where only a few teeth would be affected (figure 2.7c). Also, the teeth are often partially covered by a thick, brownish-gray substance the color of local clay. It is possible the teeth were ground down before going into battle as a rite of passage. However, given how perfectly the teeth fit together even after the tissues around the mouth have decayed, it is more likely that trophy-makers filed the teeth down after death and cemented the mouth shut. No evidence of sealing the mouth with cactus spines or tying the mandible on with cord was observed at Uraca, unlike in Nasca examples.

This sealing of the mouth may have served practical and ritual purposes. Verano argues that mouths and eyes of Nasca trophies were shut with cactus spines or stuffed to prevent the facial tissues from retracting during decomposition (Verano 1995). Perhaps mouth-closing and eye removal also served a practical purpose at Uraca—keeping the mandible attached and the head in one piece while it was used in ritual dances or displays. This may also have sealed the volatile enemy spirit inside the head, unable to harm Uraca inhabitants.

Feline Hunters and Trophy-Head Prey

Understanding Andean trophy-taking as a cultural system (Whitehead 2007) requires an examination of feline and trophy-head themes in cosmology and iconography. The pampas cat is commonly depicted in Nasca art, with its characteristic striped bands and spots, pointed ears, and flat forehead. The association of human trophies with the feline trophy skull, along with the petroglyphs depicting human and feline trophy-takers at *Toro Muerto* (figure 2.2b), shows that Uraca mortuary ritual was influenced by religious themes from Nasca and Paracas, where the "mythical spotted cat theme" is associated with power, fertility, violence, and trophy-taking (Paul 1990; Proulx 2001; Wolfe 1981). Anthropomorphic beings with mixed human-feline traits are often depicted flying with trophy heads, wearing human trophy heads attached to their belts, hands, or shoulders, or "tasting" human heads (Paul 1990; Proulx 2000).

For example, a painted textile fragment from the Norweb Collection at the Cleveland Museum of Art depicts a striped and spotted anthropomorphized pampas cat wearing an elaborate headdress and with decorated hair and beard ornaments. It holds a human head by the hair in its left hand and a knife in its right hand, while its tail terminates in another head (Sawyer 1973) (figure 2.8). Further associations between the pampas cat and violence are evident in a *Spondylus*-shell artifact from the Cleveland Museum of Art. It is inlaid with a pampas cat figure, holding a club or gourd in its right front paw, and wearing a headdress (figure 2.9). The feline's eyes glow red like the feline trophy from Uraca, representing the feline's supernatural power.

Pampas cats, with and without trophy-head associations, are found in rock-art scenes from the Majes and the neighboring Siguas Valley. There is no evidence of pampas-cat imagery on ceramics in the region, but the feline theme might extend to textiles. Many of the woven belts or head wrappings recovered from Uraca have an alternating dot, zig-zag, and stripe pattern. The woven pattern is like the unique markings on the pampas cat—these belts may have been worn by shamans, warriors, or the trophy-makers themselves, to mark their power over the enemy, the enemy's community, and the afterlife. The presence of the feline head in association with human trophies and its similar treatment suggests that the flesh and animas of humans and enemies were powerful forces that had to be transformed into generative communal forces through ritually appropriate techniques.

DISCUSSION: FELINE SPIRITS AND TROPHY-HEAD PROCESSING

Death ruptures the social fabric, requiring rites of passage to transition the volatile life force of the deceased to the community of ancestral spirits (Hertz 1960).

FIGURE 2.8. Cloth with Procession of Figures, 100 BC–700 AD. Central Andes, South Coast, Nasca people, 100 BC–AD 700, Early Intermediate Period, 1–650. Cotton and pigment (field); camelid fiber (borders and fringe); overall: 69.80 × 280.70 cm (27 7/16 × 110 1/2 inches); mounted: 81.28 × 6.35 cm (32 × 2 1/2 inches). The Cleveland Museum of Art, The Norweb Collection 1940.530.

FIGURE 2.9. Shell with Inlaid Feline, 100 BC–700 AD. Peru, South Coast, Nasca style (100 BC–AD 700). *Spondylus* shell with shell, stone, and gold inlay; overall: 7.50 × 7.40 cm (2 15/16 × 2 7/8 inches). The Cleveland Museum of Art, in memory of Mr. and Mrs. Henry Humphrey's gift of their daughter 1950.567.

Van Gennep's tripartite division of rites of passage into separation, marginality, and aggregation phases has been used to explain how the living cope with the dangerous liminal phases of death (e.g., Parker Pearson 1999; van Gennep 1960). Here, the roles of felines and trophy manipulation in the performance rituals and the reconfiguration of identity during the liminal phase are considered. These rituals symbolically create order and disorder (Whitehead 2005) during uncertain liminal times.

Trophy-Head Processing as Ritual Performance

During the liminal phase, the dead, killer, and community are in an ambiguous state: the souls of the dead and the killer are still volatile, untamed, and unclean (Douglas 1966). Proulx argues that this liminal danger, in part, motivated the processing of enemy heads by the Nasca. He analogizes that the Amazonian Jívaro pinned the lips of trophy victims to keep the vengeful spirits from exiting from the mouth while waiting for the enemy life force to dissipate (Proulx 1999, 5). The iconographic evidence of Andean trophy manipulation and the bioarchaeological evidence of processing the Uraca heads shows that they were powerful symbols and signs that would have alluded to past events (Whitehead 2004b) in violent performances that would have structured behavior and meaning for witnesses and participants alike (Osterholtz 2012; Riches 1986). The feline identity may have been adopted by trophy-takers and -makers to assert their authority and power during this visceral, treacherous process of bodily manipulation.

Trophy-processing, in some cases, may have begun before the victim was killed. The two individuals with orbital cut marks may have been tortured via eye extraction during life. There is no way to test whether these two men were alive or dead at the time the eye tissues were removed, but if alive, onlooker witnesses from the enemy group would have perceived a violent spectacle that "created massive psychological trauma for the survivors" (Pérez 2012, 20). Mutilation of the eyes may have been the first in a series of symbolic acts to show the complete domination of the victor over the dominated victim.

Next, the eye and mouth orifices were ritually closed, respectively, by removing the ocular tissues and stuffing the eyes with cotton, and either by removing the flesh around the lips or by filing down the teeth and pasting the mouth shut. This mutilation and ritual closing of the orifices may have served several purposes. First, removal of the eyes and possibly the tongue, and closing the mouth, may have been symbolic ways of killing the victim again, while community participants looked on. Second, the mutilation of these organs may have been a way of protecting the trophy-maker and the recipient community from the volatile enemy life force. Third, removing these organs before they could naturally decay would have deprived the victim's community of their customary burial rites and the natural disposition of life forces. By controlling the time and location of the removal of these vital organs, the Uraca trophy-makers controlled how the enemy's life force was relegated to the afterlife or transformed into a generative force for their own community. The fact that the feline's eyes were removed and recrafted like three of the trophy victims shows that the feline's life force needed to be controlled and transformed in a similar way.

(Re)configuring Identities through Trophy-Head Manipulation

The fact that some of the Uraca heads had their facial tissues and hair painstakingly preserved, while others were completely defleshed and continuously whittled away through time, strongly suggests a complex, changing discursive relationship between the maker, the victim, and witnesses. At least during the initial phases of its use life, the identity of an Uraca head was carefully preserved so that the victim's face was identifiable. While the victim's identity and personhood were still intact, the victim (and by extension, his natal community) would be humiliated and physically punished, demonstrating the power and authority of the taker's community over a specific enemy (and their community). Enemy heads were like macabre little puppets, awaiting reanimation during ceremonial dances and ritual reenactments of important battles. While a victim's identifying features were preserved, trophy-head performances would have narrated important battle victories to community onlookers, possibly generations after the event. In this way, domination over the trophy-victims' identities would have been crucial in defining the trophy-taker and recipient community's identity: as Whitehead (2005, 1) argues, violent mutilation of these identifiable victims would have served as a "sanctioned means of communication and exchange," so that the "enemy" became integral to group identity.

Iconographic evidence supports that trophy heads were used in ritual dances or displays—heads are commonly depicted as part of ritual costume or props in Nasca and Wari iconography, or are held in the hands or worn as necklaces in displays of warrior prowess. (Ochatoma Paravicino and Cabrera Romero 2002; Proulx 1999, 2000, 2001; Tung 2007, 2008). Nasca scenes show heads being worn in dances or carried as sacrifices to an ancestral mummy bundle (Proulx 2000, 2006). All but one of the Uraca trophy heads have perforations for the carrying cord, and most have their toggles and cords preserved, showing that Uraca ritual participants displayed their trophies in similar ways. Except for the Wari-style head, the complete removal of the occipital and parietal bones would have enabled the trophies to be worn as masks, perhaps attached to headdresses or hats, or even dangled from belts so that the empty endocranial space would lie flush against the leg muscles or waist of the wearer during ritual movements.

The feline trophy and the two human half-masks would have been easily woven into a headdress or incorporated into a hat or headband. In the process of enrobing themselves in the victim's flesh, the trophy-wearer would have further displayed domination over the victim's body, while signifying the transformation of the victim from a powerful warrior of a subjugated enemy group into a generative force for the taker's community. Donning the feline costume may have endowed the wearer with the power and authority of ancestral leaders, so that the trophy-wearer's body became the mitigating force between the spiritual power of the ancestors and the polluting forces of the enemy's life force. The transformation of an enemy head into a ritual artifact would have been an intimate and emotional endeavor. Quilter reminds us that "participating in or watching fellow human beings transformed into chunks of rotting flesh, flayed skins, and dismembered carcasses" would have been terrifying (2002, 172). "Putting on" the powerful mask of an enemy trophy would have simultaneously reinforced the notion of the enemy as a powerful warrior, with sufficient bravery to complete the task, while communicating the enemy's new identity as a subjugated object controlled by the wearer.

At some point, all but the three mummified Nasca-style heads were completely defleshed. The two half-masks were whittled down further, apparently after the original perforations were damaged, possibly through extensive use. Identifying features were intentionally removed or had decomposed. As Viveiros de Castro argues in the case of the Tupian Araweté, this kind of incorporation of enemies into the group may have been a crucial phase in the regeneration of society (Viveiros de Castro 1992). The processing of the enemy dead is a means of consuming the enemy's life force and transforming it into fertility for the recipient community. Through this process, the victim's original identity is literally and metaphorically stripped away, leaving only an anonymized ancestor.

Scenes in Paracas, Nasca, and Uraca art seem to show this incorporation. Many Nasca scenes show a feline or raptor spirit consuming the head and passing the head through the body to the tail (Proulx 2000, 2006), as in a ritual digestion. Some of the Majes and Siguas petroglyphs show the incorporation of the trophy victim into the pampas cat's body, as the trophy head hangs from the feline's tail. The painted textile in figure 2.8 shows the entire cycle. An anthropomorphized pampas cat with its characteristic markings stands on two legs. It has decapitated a head with the knife in its right hand, and dances, dressed in a ritual tunic and headdress, presenting the head in its left hand. The four cats depicted have digested other heads, as evidenced by the heads emanating from their tails, while a flying spirit whisks heads away to the spiritual realm, grasped between its talons. This scene illustrates a key point: in artistic depictions, the trophy victims are identifiable, while the taker's identity is obscured. These feline impersonations may communicate the taker's "transmutation" to a spiritual being (Nielsen 2009, 235), or may allude to ancestral heroes (Paul 1990). In either case, Whitehead's poetics model enables the view that the manipulation of human and feline trophies at Uraca were components of publicly visible ritual processing that simultaneously communicated historical events and reconfigured individual and collective identity for the victim, for the trophy-takers, -makers, and -wearers, and for their respective communities.

CONCLUSION: TROPHY-TAKING AS GENERATIVE PERFORMANCE

In sum, the processing of Uraca trophy heads—when viewed considering the feline mythology displayed in Nasca and Wari local art, as well as concepts of Andean animism and perspectivism—can be viewed as a violence performance that communicated the ideal of feline domination and reconfigured identities through the process of continually displaying and modifying heads.

Cut marks, dental filing, and other postmortem modifications of the Uraca heads show the trophies were continuously modified, while AMS dates from two of the oldest trophies show at least two of the heads were in use for hundreds of years. The retooling or repair marks on the half-mask trophies show the trophies were continuously used long after the flesh had decayed. These may have been passed down through generations, through the families of important chiefs or shamans, as the volatile life-force of the enemy soul was tamed, reanimated, and conquered again in ritual reenactments. The breakage and burning away of most of the parietal and occipital bones, the sealing of the mouth and eyes, and the rich Paracas-, Nasca-, and Wari-era iconography showing trophies being worn, strongly suggest that the heads were worn at Uraca in dance and rituals that served to mediate the dangerous liminality imposed by the presence of the enemy spirit.

After decapitation, Uraca trophy-takers removed the flesh and eyes, shut the mouth, sculpted new eyes, and wore and displayed the head. These intensely visceral interactions with the dead victim may have taken place over the course of many years, as discursive signs and symbols (Whitehead 2004b). The accumulation of heads and the intricate manipulation of flesh and bone would have communicated spiritual and physical conquest to observers, shifting the identity of the trophy-taker to feline authority, while "ritually producing" (Whitehead, 2004b, 71) and shifting the identities of the victims from conquered warriors to a generative force for the trophy-taker's community. Understanding Uraca (and Andean) trophy-taking in this way shows that violent dismemberment and rituals with trophies should not be relegated to "senseless" violence, or mere masculine displays of dominance (Whitehead 2004a), but rather, as deeply imbedded within a cultural and historical framework that necessitated the performance of these rituals as vital to the continuation of life itself.

REFERENCES

Abercrombie, Thomas Alan. 1998. *Pathways of Memory and Power: Ethnography and History among an Andean People*. Madison: University of Wisconsin Press.

Alberti, Benjamin, and Tamara L Bray. 2009. "Introduction." *Cambridge Archaeological Journal* 19 (03): 337–343.

Allen, Catherine J. 1988. *The Hold Life Has: Coca and Cultural Identity in an Andean Community*. Smithsonian Series in Ethnographic Inquiry. Washington, DC: Smithsonian Institution Press.

Appadurai, Arjun. 1986. *The Social Life of Things: Commodities in Cultural Perspective*. Cambridge UK and New York: Cambridge University Press.

Arnold, Denise Y., and Christine A. Hastorf. 2008. *Heads of State: Icons, Power, and Politics in the Ancient and Modern Andes*. Walnut Creek, CA: Left Coast Press.

Bastien, Joseph William. 1978. *Mountain of the Condor: Metaphor and Ritual in an Andean Ayllu*. The American Ethnological Society Monograph 64. St. Paul, MN: West.

Becker, Sara, and Sonia Alconini. 2015. "Head Extraction, Interregional Exchange, and Political Strategies of Control at the Site of Wata Wata, Kallawaya Territory, Bolivia, during the Transition between the Late Formative and Tiwanaku periods (AD 200–800)." *Latin American Antiquity* 26 (1): 30–48.

Bird-David, Nurit. 1999. "'Animism' Revisited: Personhood, Environment, and Relational Epistemology 1." *Current Anthropology* 40 (S1): S67–S91.

Bloch, Maurice. 1992. *Prey into Hunter: The Politics of Religious Experience*. The Lewis Henry Morgan Lectures 1984. New York: Cambridge University Press.

Bloch, Maurice, and Jonathan P. Parry. 1982. *Death and the Regeneration of Life*. New York: Cambridge University Press.

Bray, Tamara L. 2009. "An Archaeological Perspective on the Andean Concept of Camaquen: Thinking through Late Pre-Columbian Ofrendas and Huacas." *Cambridge Archaeological Journal* 19 (03): 357–366.

Chacon, Richard J., and David H. Dye. 2007. "Introduction to Human Trophy Taking: An Ancient and Widespread Practice." In *The Taking and Displaying of Human Body Parts as Trophies by Amerindians*, edited by Richard J. Chacon and David H. Dye, 5–31. New York: Springer.

Conklin, Beth A. 2001. *Consuming Grief: Compassionate Cannibalism in an Amazonian Society*. Austin: University of Texas Press.

Connerton, Paul. 1989. *How Societies Remember: Themes in the Social Sciences*. New York: Cambridge University Press.

Crandall, John J., and Debra L Martin. 2014. "The Bioarchaeology of Postmortem Agency: Integrating Archaeological Theory with Human Skeletal Remains." *Cambridge Archaeological Journal* 24 (03): 429–435.

Douglas, Mary. 1966. *Purity and Danger: An Analysis of Concepts of Pollution and Taboo.* London: Routledge and Kegan Paul.

Douglas, Mary. 2004. *Natural Symbols: Explorations in Cosmology*. London: Routledge.

Duviols, Pierre. 1978. "'Camaquen, upani': un concept animiste des anciens Péruviens." In *Amerikanistische Studien: Festschrift für Hermann Trimborn*, edited by R. Hartmann and U. Oberem, 132–144. Collectanea Instituti Anthropos 20. Switzerland: St. Augustin.

Fausto, Carlos. 1999. "Of Enemies and Pets: Warfare and Shamanism in Amazonia." *American Ethnologist* 26 (4): 933–956.

Gell, Alfred. 1998. *Art and Agency: An Anthropological Theory*. Oxford: Clarendon Press.

Gose, Peter. 1994. *Deathly Waters and Hungry Mountains: Agrarian Ritual and Class Formation in an Andean Town*. Vol. 4. Toronto: University of Toronto Press.

Groleau, Amy B. 2009. "Special Finds: Locating Animism in the Archaeological Record." *Cambridge Archaeological Journal* 19 (03): 398–406.

Guaman Poma de Ayala, Felipe. 2006 [1613]. *The First New Chronicle and Good Government*, abridged and edited by David Frye. Indianapolis, IN: Hackett Publishing Company.

Hertz, Robert A. 1960 [1907]. *Death and the Right Hand: A Contribution to the Study of the Collective Representation of Death*. Translated by Rodney Needham and Claudia Needham. Glencoe, IL: The Free Press.

Isbell, Billie Jean. 2005. *To Defend Ourselves: Ecology and Ritual in an Andean Village.* Prospect Heights, IL: Waveland Press.

Kellner, Corina. 2006. "'Trophy' Heads in Prehistoric Peru: Wari Imperial Influence on Nasca Head-Taking Practices." In *Skull Collection, Modification and Decoration*, edited by Michelle Bonogofsky, 101–111. Oxford: Archaeopress.

Lau, George F. 2008. "Ancestor Images in the Andes." In *The Handbook of South American Archaeology*, edited by Helaine Silverman and William Isbell, 1025–1043. New York: Springer.

Linares Málaga, Eloy. 2004. *Arte repuestre en Arequipa y el sur del Perú*. Arequipa, Peru: Universidad Católica Santa María.

Nielsen, Axel E. 2009. "Ancestors at War: Meaningful Conflict and Social Process in the South Andes." In *Warfare in Cultural Context: Practice, Agency, and the Archaeology of Violence*, edited by Axel E. Nielsen and William H. Walker, 218–243. Tuscson: University of Arizona Press.

Núñez Jiménez, Antonio. 1986. *Petroglifos del Perú: Panorama mundial del arte rupestre.* 2a ed. 4 vols. Vol. 4. Ciudad de La Habana: Proyecto Regional de Patrimonio Cultural y Desarrollo PNUD/UNESCO con la colaboración del Instituto de Cooperación Iberoamericana y el Centro de Estudios Económicos y Sociales del Tercer Mundo: Editorial Científico-Técnica.

Oakdale, Suzanne. 2005. "Forgetting the Dead, Remembering Enemies." In *Interacting with the Dead: Perspectives on Mortuary Archaeology for the New Millennium*, edited by Gordon F.M. Rakita, Jane E. Buikstra, Lane A. Beck, and Sloan R. Williams, 107–123. Gainesville: University Press Florida.

Ochatoma Paravicino, José, and Martha Cabrera Romero. 2002. "Religous Ideology and Military Organization in the Iconography of a D-shaped Ceremonial Precint at Conchopata." In *Andean Archaeology II: Art, Landscape, and Society*, edited by Helaine Silverman and William H. Isbell, 225–247. New York: Kluwer Academic.

Ogburn, Dennis E. 2007. "Human Trophies in the Late Pre-Hispanic Andes." In *The Taking and Displaying of Human Body Parts as Trophies by Amerindians*, edited by R. J. Chacon and D. H. Dye, 505–522. New York: Springer.

Osterholtz, Anna J. 2012. "Hobbling and Torture as Performative Violence: An Example from the Prehistoric Southwest." *Kiva* 78 (2): 123–144.

Parker Pearson, Michael. 1999. *The Archaeology of Death and Burial, Texas A&M University Anthropology Series*. College Station: Texas A&M University Press.

Paul, Anne. 1990. *Paracas Ritual Attire: Symbols of Authority in Ancient Peru*. The Civilization of the American Indian Series, No. 195. Norman, OK: University of Oklahoma Press.

Pérez, Ventura R. 2012. "The Politicization of the Dead: Violence as Performance, Politics as Usual." In *The Bioarchaeology of Violence*, edited by Debra L., Martin, Ryan P. Harrod, and Ventura R. Pérez, 13–28. Gainesville: University Press of Florida.

Proulx, Donald A. 1999. "Nasca Headhunting and the Ritual use of Trophy Heads." In *Nasca: Geheimnisvolle zeichen im alten Peru*, edited by Judith Rickenbach, 79–87. Zurich: Museum Rietberg Zurich.

Proulx, Donald A. 2000. "Nasca Ceramic Iconography: An Overview." *Studio Potter* 29 (1): 37–42.

Proulx, Donald A. 2001. "Ritual Uses of Trophy Heads in Ancient Nasca Society." In *Ritual Sacrifice in Ancient Peru*, edited by Elizabeth P. Benson and Anita G. Cook, 119–136. Austin: University of Texas Press.

Proulx, Donald A. 2006. *A Sourcebook of Nasca Ceramic Iconography: Reading a Culture Through Its Art*. Iowa City: University of Iowa Press.

Quilter, Jeffrey. 2002. "Moche Politics, Religion, and Warfare." *Journal of World Prehistory* 16 (2): 145–195.

Riches, David. 1986. *The Anthropology of Violence*. Oxford, UK, and New York: Blackwell.

Robb, John. 2004. "The Extended Artefact and the Monumental Economy: A Methodology for Material Agency." In *Rethinking Materiality: The Engagement of Mind with the Material World*, edited by Elizabeth DeMarrais, Chris Gosden, and Colin Renfrew, 131–139. Cambridge, UK: McDonald Insitute for Archaeological Research.

Sallnow, Michael J. 1987. *Pilgrims of the Andes*. Washington, DC: Smithsonian Institution Press.

Salomon, Frank. 1995. "'The Beautiful Grandparents': Andean Ancestor Shring and Mortuary Ritual as Seen through Colonial Records." In *Tombs for the Living: Andean Mortuary Practices: A Symposium at Dumbarton Oaks*, edited by Tom D. Dillehay, 315–353. Washington, DC: Dumbarton Oaks Research Library and Collection.

Salomon, Frank, and Geogre L. Urioste. 1991. *The Huarochirí Manuscript: A Testament of Ancient and Colonial Andean Religion*. Austin: University of Texas Press.

Sawyer, Alan R. 1973. "Painted Nasca Textiles." The Junius B. Bird Pre-Columbian Textile Conference. Washington, DC: The Textile Museum and Dumbarton Oaks, Trustees for Harvard University.

Scaffidi, Beth K. 2018. "Networks of Violence: Bioarchaeological and Spatial Perspectives on Structural and Physical Violence in the Pre- and Early-Wari Era in the Lower Majes Valley, Arequipa, Peru." PhD, Department of Anthropology, Vanderbilt University, Nashville, TN.

Scaffidi, Beth K., and Manuel García Márquez. 2015. "Informe Final para el Ministerio de Cultura: Proyecto Arqueológico Uraca, Valle de Majes, 2014."

Scaffidi, Beth K., George Kamenov, Ashley Sharpe, and John Krigbaum. 2016. "Making Enemies, Making Places: Geographic Origins of Trophy Heads from Uraca, Arequipa, Peru." 9th World Congress on Mummy Studies, Lima, Peru, August 10, 2016.

Scheper-Hughes, Nancy, and Margaret Lock. 1987. "The Mindful Body: A Prolegomenon to Future Work in Medical Anthropology." *Medical Anthropology Quarterly* 1: 6–41.

Sillar, Bill. 2009. "The Social Agency of Things? Animism and Materiality in the Andes." *Cambridge Archaeological Journal* 19 (03): 367–377.

Sofaer, Joanna R. 2006. *The Body as Material Culture: A Theoretical Osteoarchaeology*. Cambridge, UK: Cambridge University Press.

Sotil Galindo, Raúl. 2009. *Las cabezas ofrenda de la cultural Nasca*. Lima, Peru: Universidad a Las Peruanas.

Tung, Tiffiny A. 2007. "From Corporeality to Sanctity: Transforming Bodies into Trophy Heads in the Pre-Hispanic Andes." In *The Taking and Displaying of Human Body Parts as Trophies by Amerindians*, edited by Richard J. Chacon and David H. Dye, 481–504. New York: Springer.

Tung, Tiffiny A. 2008. "Dismembering Bodies for Display: A Bioarchaeological Study of Trophy Heads from the Wari Site of Conchopata, Peru." *American Journal of Physical Anthropology* 136: 294–308.

Tung, Tiffiny A. 2012. Violence, Ritual, and the Wari Empire: A Social Bioarchaeology of Imperialism in the Ancient Andes. Gainesville: University Press of Florida.

Tung, Tiffiny A. 2014a. "Agency, 'Til Death Do Us Part?' Inquiring about the Agency of Dead Bodies from the Ancient Andes." *Cambridge Archaeological Journal* 24 (03): 437–452.

Tung, Tiffiny A. 2014b. "Making Warriors, Making War: Violence and Militarism in the Wari Empire." In *Embattled Bodies, Embattled Places: War in Pre-Columbian America*, edited by A. K. Scherer and J. W. Verano, 229–258. Washington, DC: Dunbarton Oaks Library.

Tylor, Edward Burnett. 1913. *Primitive Culture: Researches into the Development of Mythology, Philosophy, Religion, Language, Art, and Custom*. London: Murray.

Van Gennep, Arnold. 1960. *The Rites of Passage*. Chicago, IL: University of Chicago Press.

Van Hoek, Maarten. 2010. "'Trophy' Heads in the Rock Art of the Majes Valley, Perú: Exploring their Possible Origin." *RUPESTREWEB*.

Verano, John W. 1995. "Where Do They Rest? The Treatment of Human Offerings and Trophies in Ancient Peru." In *Tombs for the Living: Andean Mortuary Practices*, edited by Tom D. Dillehay, 189–227. Washington, DC: Dumbarton Oaks Research Library and Collection.

Verano, John W. 2003. "Mummified Trophy Heads from Peru: Diagnostic Features and Medicolegal Significance." *Journal of Forensic Sciences* 48 (3): 525–530.

Verano, John W. 2008. "Trophy Head-Taking and Human Sacrifice in Andean South America." In *The Handbook of South American Archaeology*, edited by Helaine Silverman and Willam H. Isabell, 1047–1060. New York: Springer.

Verano, John W., Santiago Uceda, Claude Chapdelaine, Ricardo Tello, Maria Isabel Paredes, and Victor Pimentel. 1999. "Modified Human Skulls from the Urban Sector of the Pyramids of Moche, Northern Peru." *Latin American Antiquity* 10 (1): 59–70.

Viveiros de Castro, Eduardo. 1998. "Cosmological Deixis and Amerindian Perspectivism." *Journal of the Royal Anthropological Institute* 4 (3): 469–488.

Viverios de Castro, Eduardo. 1992. *From the Enemy's Point of View: Humanity and Divinity in an Amazonian Society*. Chicago, IL: University of Chicago Press.

Weismantel, Mary. 2015. "Seeing like an Archaeologist: Viveiros de Castro at Chavín de Huantar." *Journal of Social Archaeology* 15 (2): 139–159.

Whitehead, Neil L. 2002. *Dark shamans: Kanaimà and the Poetics of Violent Death*. Durham, NC: Duke University Press.

Whitehead, Neil L. 2004a. "Introduction: Cultures, Conflicts, and the Poetics of Violent Practice." In *Violence*, edited by Neil L. Whitehead, 3–24. Santa Fe, NM: SAR Press; Oxford: James Currey.

Whitehead, Neil L. 2004b. "On the Poetics of Violence." In *Violence*, edited by Neil L. Whitehead, 55–78. Santa Fe, NM: SAR Press; Oxford: James Currey.

Whitehead, Neil L. 2005. "War and Violence as Cultural Expression." *Anthropology News* 46 (5): 23–26. doi: 10.1525/an.2005.46.5.23.1.

Whitehead, Neil L. 2007. "Violence and the Cultural Order." *Daedalus* 136 (1): 40–50. doi: 10.2307/20028088.

Williams, Sloan R., Kathleen Forgey, and Elizabeth Klarich. 2001. "An Osteological Study of Nasca Trophy Heads Collected by A. L. Kroeber during the Marshall Field Expeditions to Peru." *Fieldiana* 33 (1516): 1–104.

Wolfe, Elizabeth Farkass. 1981. "The Spotted Cat and the Horrible Bird: Stylistic Change in Nasca 1–5 Ceramic Decoration." *Ñawpa Pacha* 19 (1): 1–62.

3

The Politics and Poetics of Performance Violence at Casas Grandes, Chihuahua, Mexico

KYLE D. WALLER AND ADRIANNE M. OFFENBECKER

Perimortem and postmortem manipulation and processing of human skeletal remains has long been implicated in the ritual practices of the inhabitants of Paquimé, Chihuahua, Mexico. The site's excavator, Charles Di Peso, compared the highly variable mortuary patterns to Mesoamerican codices, and suggested that these patterns resulted from Mesoamerican-style cult institutions (Di Peso, Rinaldo, and Fenner 1974). Rakita (Rakita 2001, 2008, 2009) alternatively suggests that this processing may be the result of ancestor veneration. Suggestions from other researchers include anthropophagy, interpersonal violence, or human sacrifice (Casserino 2009).

In this chapter, a comprehensive bioarchaeological analysis of burial tomb 44-13, one of the most potent loci of ritual practices at Paquimé, is used to examine evidence of perimortem trauma and postmortem processing, and to differentiate between competing hypotheses for these patterns. Skeletal evidence revealed extensive corpse-processing of older subadults and young females consistent with patterns of human sacrifice noted amongst the Maya (Tiesler 2007). The context of sacrifice suggests a violent death, which—when combined with relatively low frequencies of traumatic injuries at Paquimé generally (Casserino 2009; Kohn 2008, 2011) and their poor health when compared to the rest of the Paquimé assemblage—supports Di Peso's contention that these individuals were part of a ritual focused on two high-status males buried below them. By emphasizing the "poetic" elements of violence (Whitehead 2004, 2007), we suggest that this processing may have been a

DOI: 10.5876/9781646420612.c003

cultural performance intended to create a spectacle, as part of strategies to centralize social control. Comparison with other ritual loci at Paquimé that involved the manipulation of human remains suggests that several different ritual strategies were pursued by elite individuals.

REGIONAL BACKGROUND

The intersection of violence and ritual behaviors has become a significant focus of archaeological research in the prehistoric North American Southwest. Theoretical and methodological developments have allowed bioarchaeologists to move beyond merely counting cut marks and checklist taphonomy (Pérez 2006). Instead, emphasizing the variability in bioarchaeological indicators of violence, and processing and combining this with local and regional archaeological data, has demonstrated that violence has extensive time depth and took many forms, ranging from postmortem skeletal processing to massacres (see review in Martin 2016).

Deciphering meaning from the ample variation in form and function of violence requires a theoretical perspective that extends beyond commonly applied processual and ecological explanations, such as raiding, resource stress, and sociopolitical intimidation (e.g., LeBlanc 1999; Lekson 2002). As other chapters in this volume readily demonstrate, emphasizing the "poetics" of violence—how violence and its associated signs and symbols were used through time—provides an alternative theoretical perspective well suited to bioarchaeological analyses of violence and corpse-processing (Whitehead 2004, 68). The core of the poetics model is that violence and its associated performances and impacts are based upon historically contingent forms of symbolism and ideology. In this view, violence has a culturally informed logic, the same as any other aspect of culture (Springer 2011, 93). Violence isn't merely a means to end or an outcome, it is performed and experienced (Whitehead 2004). Such performances are imbued with potent signs and symbols that must be readily interpretable by potential audiences, if violent actions are to be understood (Whitehead 2004, 68). These signs and symbols give acts of violence their culturally specific meaning, and are what actors manipulate and allude to during such performances.

For bioarchaeologists, the poetics model is readily applicable and intuitive for interpreting prehistoric violence. Whitehead (2007, 6) provides an operational definition for poetics: "Mapping how cultural conceptions of violence amplify and extend the social force of violent acts, and how those acts produce shared violent meanings." The symbols and signs discussed by Whitehead (2004) are a core component of analyses of prehistoric ritual and religion and can be linked to the cultural and contextual information derived from biocultural approaches to human skeletal remains. It is this contextual analysis of the performance that leads to corpses with cut marks, blunt-force trauma, and postmortem processing that is the strength of the poetics model. This model allows bioarchaeologists a way to extend their inferences of violence beyond the mere physical acts of harm to consider the cultural meaning and motivation in violent activities (Whitehead 2004, 68).

Whitehead (2004, 59) builds upon previous inferences that view violence as a social action constructed through the participation of perpetrators, victims, and witnesses by highlighting the fact that this participation can happen at both individual and collective scales. Viewing multiple perspectives is crucial for bioarchaeological applications of poetics, as bioarchaeologists typically emphasize the perspective of the victims, for their bones are the lens through which the presence of violence is inferred. However, this perspective minimizes or ignores the motivations of perpetrators and the impact of the performance of violence upon witnesses. Considering the experiences of witnesses, and the meaning understood by them, is crucial for inferring the motivation of performance violence and its social impact.

Cross-cultural reviews of performance violence demonstrate a wide range of motivations. For example, Kantner reviewed 35 archaeological and ethnographic examples of societies that inflicted severe trauma to a person, and found that in 65 percent (23/35) of cases, social control was the primary motivation for extreme violence and anthropophagy (Kantner 1999). One of the most common forms of social control was political intimidation, in which violence was used to terrify enemies and political rivals, or to control subordinates (Kantner 1999, 4).

Alternatively, the presence of skeletal trauma may be caused by a culture's normative mortuary practices. In 28.5 percent (10/35) of cases, mortuary rituals produced marks consistent with perimortem processing (Kantner 1999). These activities included dismemberment, defleshing, burning, smashing and breaking bones, and burial in pits or pots (Kantner 1999, 10). Notably, in cases where mortuary ritual produced trauma to skeletal remains, the corpse would be buried in a formal locus, and the form of the preparation would follow a standardized pattern recognizable to members of the society, even if limited individuals received that treatment (Kantner 1999, 12).

Several recent case studies from the North American Southwest demonstrate how careful bioarchaeological analysis and consideration of archaeological context can be used to tease apart causal explanations for performance violence (Anderson 2014; Anderson, Martin, and Thompson 2012; Osterholtz 2012, 2013). An example of performance violence comes from Osterholtz's (2012, 2013) analysis of human skeletal remains from the Pueblo I Sacred Ridge site in Southwestern Colorado. A minimum of 33 individuals were discovered in two unique pit features along the southern ridge of the site. Some of these individuals received repeated injuries to the feet, including blows to the ankles and the tops and bottoms of feet to hobble and torture individuals. These individuals were then heavily processed and commingled after death. Osterholtz (2013) suggests that these examples of torture may have been used in enforcing normative behavior during a period of cultural instability and change. Additionally, the use of violence in a highly visible context may have been a strategy employed by the perpetrators as a tool to minimize social tensions arising from scalar stress.

Other examples of performance violence may include forms of intra- and intergroup violence, ancestor veneration, or mortuary rituals (Chinchilla Mazariegos et al. 2015; McAnany 2013; Medina Martín and Sánchez Vargas 2007; Ogilvie and Hilton 2000; Watson and Phelps 2016). Ogilvie and Hilton (2000) present a case study from Ram Mesa, an ancestral Puebloan site in northeastern New Mexico. They demonstrate that the pattern of cut marks, blunt-force trauma, and extreme fragmentation is consistent with Southwestern ethnographies showing the punishment and execution of witches (Darling 1998; Walker 1998).

Contextual approaches demonstrate that multiple processes leaving skeletal signatures of violence and processing may be operating simultaneously. Recent research with the skeletal remains from La Quemada (AD 500–900), a frontier Mesoamerican site in south-central Zacatecas, Durango, Mexico, provides a clear example of the co-occurrence of multiple forms of skeletal trauma with distinctly different social meanings (Nelson, Darling, and Kice 1992; Nelson and Martin 2015; Pérez, Nelson, and Martin 2008). Bones inside a temple have shallow, V-shaped cut marks near proximal and distal ends of long bones, suggesting defleshing of desiccated corpses. Using archaeological context and Huichol ethnographic analogies, Nelson and Martin (2015) infer that these remains reflect ancestor worship. In contrast, bone discovered in open areas around a patio displayed a wider variety of processing techniques. These include crania drilled for display as trophies, deep V-shaped cut marks suggesting perimortem defleshing and dismemberment, and pot polish. Nelson and Martin conclude that the bones in open areas reflect dominance and triumph in warfare. Both examples illustrate the use of corpses and bones to communicate a range of complex symbolic meanings.

BIOCULTURAL CONTEXT

The site of Paquimé is on the west bank of the Rio Casas Grandes, on the eastern flank of the north–south trending Sierra Occidental mountains (figure 3.1). The site is in a comparatively well-watered part of the region, making it amongst the best places in the North American Southwest for irrigation agriculture (Minnis, Whalen, and Howell 2006).

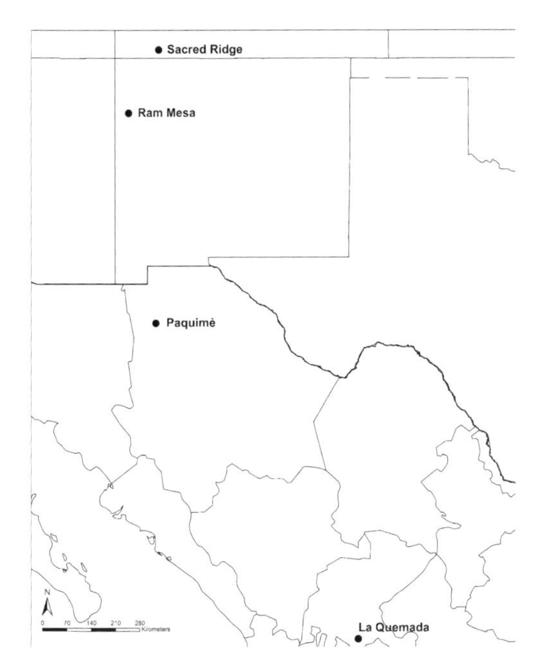

FIGURE 3.1. Location map of Paquimé.

Paquimé is a large, multistory adobe complex, nearly 1 km^2 in size, that was occupied during the Medio Period (AD 1200–1450). Habitation complexes are located along the eastern end of the site, while ritual architecture, such as platform and effigy mounds, are concentrated on the western edge of the site. The site was home to an estimated 2,000–5,000 people (Di Peso 1974; Whalen, MacWilliams, and Pitezel 2010;). Much of the discussion of Paquimé, and the Casas Grandes region generally, has focused on Southwest–Mesoamerican interactions (e.g., Bradley 1999; Foster 1999; Kelley 1986, 2000; Lekson 2015, Punzo and Villalpando 2015). Cultural features in the form of I- and T-shaped ballcourts, colonnades, animal-effigy mounds, macaw husbandry, ceramic iconography, gene flow, and trophy skulls all attest to nonlocal influences. The site possesses nearly 1-m-thick adobe walls, extensive irrigation agriculture and a water reservoir, over a ton of marine shell procured from the Gulf of California, a walk-in well with a human calvarium embedded in the floor, and substantial storerooms containing utilitarian items, such as manos and metates (Di Peso 1974).

Public and private ritual and religious performance was likely one of the core methods by which Paquimeño elites acquired and maintained status differentiation, as well as providing events emphasizing social cohesion (e.g., Rakita 2009). In addition to other functions, Paquimé appeared to be a pilgrimage site (VanPool and VanPool

2018; Whalen 2013). The site itself was visually impressive, with massively overbuilt walls, and a location on a rise that made it seem even larger than it was (VanPool and VanPool 2018; Whalen, MacWilliams, and Pitezel 2010). Large agave-roasting ovens may have been used to process sweet agave and possibly alcohol (e.g., King et al. 2017) for ceremonial feasts. Highly visible public spaces, such as centrally located, highly visible platform mounds and open ballcourts were likely loci of public ritual activity. Public ceremonies were likely performed by ritual specialists wearing elaborate ceremonial garb, which is depicted in both rock art and ceramics as including jewelry, serpent and macaw headdresses, and distinctive sandals (VanPool and VanPool 2007; VanPool and VanPool 2018). These ceremonies would have incorporated imagery and symbolism related to horned plumed serpents, a significant symbol of religion and authority in the Casas Grandes region (e.g., VanPool and VanPool 2007).

Theatrical public performances, such as those that occur during pilgrimages, are an important community integrative mechanism. They communicate and enforce existing community norms, while helping to define the political reality of people experiencing them (Inomata 2006). Such spectacles are designed to display a sense of community and group identity (Inomata 2006). These ceremonies at Paquimé would have been used to foster community cohesion, while also allowing status competition and aggrandizing behaviors between ritual actors (e.g., Rakita 2009). VanPool and VanPool (2018) note that the site and its associated rituals would have been a tremendous, possibly overwhelming sensory experience for pilgrims.

One significant form of ritual imagery involved using human bodies and bones to communicate symbolic meanings. There are a number of cases of the manipulation of bones and bodies at Paquimé. For example, long bones from three high-status urn burials found in a hidden room in the central Mound of the Offerings may have been manipulated as part of public and private rituals, as part of rites of ancestor worship (Rakita 2009). Several "trophy" skulls located in a private, cross-shaped room elsewhere at the site had circular drill holes near the sagittal and squamosal sutures, suggesting that they were suspended vertically in a manner similar to Chalchihuites *tzompantli* (Waller 2017). Bioarchaeological analyses of the Paquimé skeletons have demonstrated extensive postmortem processing as part of mortuary rituals (Casserino 2009; Kohn 2008, 2011; Offenbecker 2018; Waller 2017). Other examples of ritual applications of manipulated human skeletal remains include a skullcap embedded in the stairs on the path to a ritually significant walk-in well, a necklace made of phalanges found with the urn burials, and musical rasps made from human bones. Thus, like La Quemada, it is likely that human bodies and bones were used to communicate a wide range of symbolic meanings at Paquimé.

Violence may also have been used to communicate symbolic meanings. Di Peso suggested that human sacrifice was performed during ritual activities. The authors classified 10 burials as human sacrifices (burial Type 8), seven of which were interred beneath a ceremonial ballcourt (Di Peso 1974). These interments were perhaps the most notable cases of human corpse manipulation, as two of the three subcourt burial pits contained disarticulated human extremities (Di Peso, Rinaldo, and Fenner 1974, 397). The multiple burial at the north end of the ballcourt contained an extra pair of articulated feet, while the south end of the court consisted of two young adult females, one of which was pregnant and another whose severed arm was found draped over her shoulder. Di Peso argued that the Paquimé burials with severed extremities mirrored Mesoamerican rituals associated with the ballcourt cult. Another suspected sacrifice was found in Unit 8, where a child was found wrapped around a roof support beam and is thought to have been placed there as part of a dedicatory ritual during construction (Di Peso 1974).

Di Peso recovered a minimum of 576 human skeletons during excavations of Paquimé (Di Peso 1974). There was tremendous variability in location, facility, mortuary furniture, and processing and handling of corpses. Burial facilities included both sealed and unsealed pits, features with removable coverings, tombs, and urn burials. Burials were most commonly interred beneath residential room floors and plazas but were also found in a diversity of other contexts, including room fill, abandoned rooms, and beneath a ceremonial ballcourt. Twenty-seven percent of burials were multiple interments, which contained between two and 14 individuals.

There have been two previous systematic studies of the Casas Grandes mortuary program. Ravesloot's (1988) analysis used a representationist Binford-Saxe-Brown perspective to assess evidence of social ranking (Binford 1971; Brown 1995; Saxe 1970). Using standard mortuary characteristics such as burial location, mortuary furniture, and corpse position and orientation, he used multivariate statistical techniques to identify three distinct clusters of burial types. As the high-status burial types included both adults and subadults, he suggested that Paquimé was characterized by vertical status differentiation, and that this status was ascribed rather than achieved. Burial tomb 44-13 (the focus of this chapter), was one of the "high status" interments identified by the authors.

Rakita built upon Ravesloot's analysis by emphasizing the role of ritual specialists and ceremonial practices for the emergence of sociopolitical complexity at Paquimé (Rakita 2001, 2008, 2009). Using standard anthropological definitions for cult institutions, Rakita examines mortuary variability and nonmortuary ritual behavior and identifies two distinct cults: a political cult and an earth/fertility cult. According to Rakita, the political cult manipulated human remains and other potent symbols as part of public and private ritual performances, in an attempt to solidify their social status and institutionalize inequality (Rakita 2009). Rakita cites the urn burials and necklace of human phalanges found in Unit 4, as well as the previously mentioned sacrifices, and an effigy of a hand carved from cranial bone as ritual objects for the ancestor cult. The presence of human-bone objects in numerous ritual contexts suggests that the use and manipulation of human bodies and bones would have been a widely recognizable element of Casas Grandes ritual practices, and a symbol that could be manipulated by ritual elites (Rakita 2009).

In contrast, he suggests that the earth/fertility cult emphasized community bonds and social cohesion, such as world renewal, agricultural fertility, and community well-being. The rituals would have emphasized unified sets of beliefs. The same elites would conduct both political and earth/fertility rituals. During the earth/fertility rituals, the elites would set aside their aggrandizing strategies to conduct rituals for the good of the community, even as leading these rituals reinforced their status.

Recent bioarchaeological analyses by Kohn and Casserino have included the examination of postmortem processing, human sacrifice, and cannibalism in the Paquimé skeletal assemblage (Casserino 2009; Kohn 2008, 2011). Kohn (2008, 2011) argues that in addition to the 10 human sacrifices suggested by Di Peso, there were additional sacrificed individuals, who were characterized by extreme peri- and postmortem processing, such as scalping, defleshing, dismemberment, cooking, burning, and fracturing for marrow extraction (Di Peso 1974). Furthermore, she argues that these cases of skeletal processing fit the criteria set forth by White (1992) and by Turner and Turner (1999) for identifying cannibalism in the archaeological record. According to Kohn (2011), cannibalism at Paquimé was likely the result of Mesoamerican influence and was a socially sanctioned component of the religious system at the site.

As part of his study of violence and body-processing, Casserino also addressed the hypothesis of whether human sacrifice and cannibalism were practiced at Paquimé. Of the 126 individuals that Casserino examined, postmortem modification was found on 36 skeletons, with the majority of remains being highly fragmented and incomplete (Casserino 2009). The types of postmortem processing observed were cut marks, burning, scalping, percussion marks, anvil abrasions, decapitation, fracturing and pot polish. To evaluate whether sacrifice and cannibalism were practiced at Paquimé, Casserino compared the types and patterns of trauma and postmortem processing present in the Paquimé skeletal assemblage to those encountered at sites where cannibalism has been argued (Mancos, Cowboy Wash, Castle Rock, Polacca Wash, and Burnt Mesa) (Casserino 2009). He found that there were striking similarities between these assemblages and the Paquimé skeletal remains, leading him to conclude that human sacrifice and cannibalism were practiced by the site's inhabitants. Casserino further suggests that cannibalism was practiced throughout the Medio Period and that it likely took multiple forms (Casserino 2009). More specifically, postmortem processing found on interred specimens likely represented endo- or ceremonial cannibalism, whereas similar processing on non-interred (unburied) individuals was likely due to exo-cannibalism (consumption of outsiders, such as enemies) or gustatory cannibalism (i.e., for nutrition).

It should be noted, however, that Casserino did not provide a case-by-case assessment of the 36 individuals with postmortem processing to determine which individuals may or may not have been cannibalized (Casserino 2009). Instead, he considers the skeletal remains collectively to reach his conclusion that cannibalism was practiced at the site. He eliminates warfare and massacre as explanations for the pattern of skeletal trauma and processing present in the Paquimé skeletal assemblage but does not consider corpse-processing due to mortuary ritual as an alternative explanation. Kohn also fails to present and convincingly eliminate alternative explanations for the postmortem processing observed in the Paquimé skeletal assemblage; however, she does base her conclusion about cannibalism on the osteological evidence from specific burials and contexts (Kohn 2011). While cannibalism may have been practiced at Paquimé, alternative explanations or the co-occurrence of multiple activities, such as ancestor veneration or mortuary corpse-processing, are certainly possible as well. As such, more nuanced analyses of corpse-processing at Paquimé are needed.

THE HOUSE OF THE DEAD

Burial 44-13 is a unique tomb in Unit 13 at Paquimé. The unit was named the "House of the Dead" because it contained the most human burials (n = 117 individuals) recovered from any unit at the site, as well as the majority of ceramic hand drums and decapitated turkey remains, which may have been associated with death cults (Di Peso 1974; Rakita 2009). Most interments in Unit 13 were subfloor room burials; however, the most elaborate and complex burial in this unit, and at the entire site, was a tomb that contained at least 12 individuals: seven primary articulated burials and at least five disarticulated individuals scattered about the uppermost layer of the grave (figure 3.2). The tomb had a shelf built into one end, which was covered with wood planking, and contained an exceptional amount of grave goods.

The bottommost layer, which represents the first burial event, consists of two adult females, 44F and 44G, buried in sitting, flexed positions. A large number of grave goods were interred with these individuals, including several Ramos Polychrome vessels, shell tinklers, beads, and pendants, as well as stone beads and pendants. The next burial layer consists of two individuals, 44E, a robust adult male, whom Di Peso suggested was the most important individual in the tomb, and 44D, an adult female (Di Peso 1974). Individual 44E was buried in a supine position with

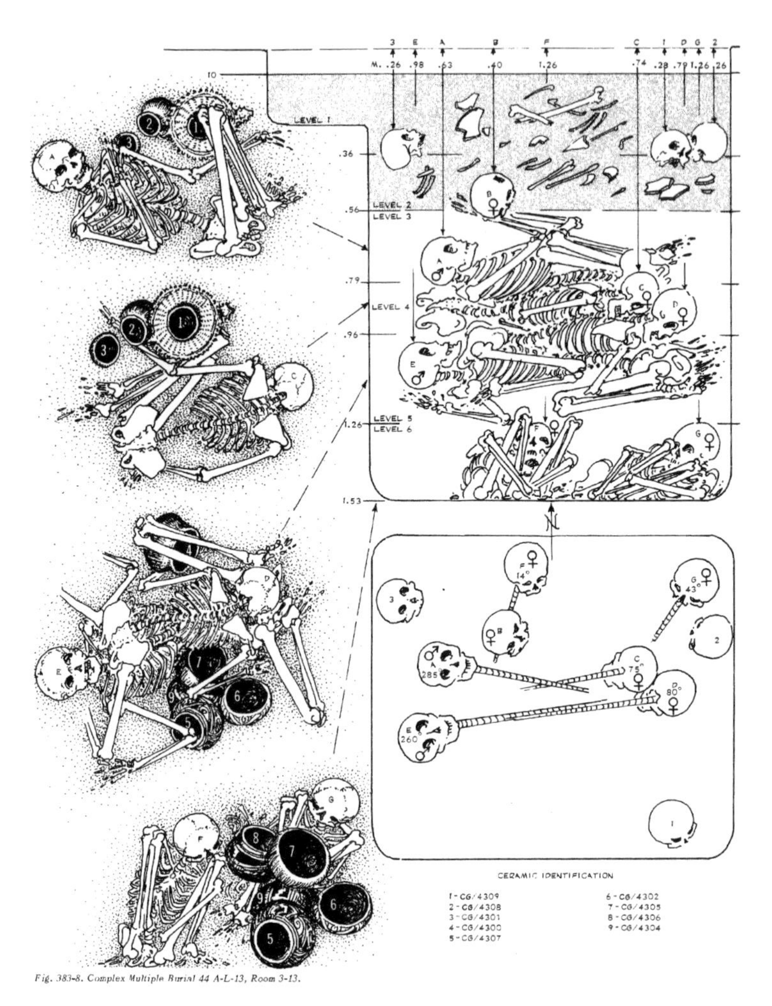

FIGURE 3.2. Schematic of Burial 44-13. (Adapted from Di Peso, Rinaldo, and Fenner 1974, 389; original linework by Alice Wesche.)

his legs frogged apart and was accompanied by several ceramic vessels of varying types, shell tinklers, a stone pendant, and unidentified food remains. The female (44D) was buried suggestively with her face resting on the pelvis of 44E and her pelvis resting near the cranium of 44E. This individual in particular was alluded to as a potential retainer burial (Di Peso 1974). The next burial layer consists of one adult female, 44C, who was placed in a flexed position on her right side. The final layer of articulated human remains consists of burials 44A and 44B, an adult male and female, respectively. Burial 44A was placed in a flexed supine position with his arms flexed across his pelvic region and was accompanied by several types of ceramic vessels, including Ramos Black, Ramos Polychrome, and Villa Ahumada Polychrome, as well as shell beads, pendants and tinklers, turquoise, a red slate ring, obsidian projectiles, turkey remains, and a ceramic hand drum. The skull of the female, 44B, was resting near the hands of burial 44A and was found with shell and stone beads, as well as a stone pendant. This individual also exhibited mild occipital flattening.

The uppermost layer of the tomb consists of at least five disarticulated and fragmentary individuals, burials 44H–L. Burial 44H is a young adult and possibly female, but the remains are too fragmentary to confidently assign a sex. Burials 44I–L are children/adolescents between the ages of 7 and 16. These remains were found in association with a number of artifacts, including jewelry and fragments of ceramic hand drums (Di Peso, Rinaldo, and Fenner 1974). The impermanence of the wood covering, and the general disorganization of the top layer of the burial, has led various researchers to suggest that Burial 44-13 was the site of ongoing ritual activities that continued well after the first individuals were interred (Casserino, 2009; Rakita 2001, 2009). According to Di Peso, the top layer of disarticulated and fragmentary remains was a sacred offering to the individuals below, who were high-status members of the community and possibly part of an elite lineage (Di Peso 1974). Various studies have demonstrated that several of the objects recovered from Burial 44-13, particularly the headless turkey and intentionally smashed ceramic hand drums, were ritually charged symbols of rank and authority (Ravesloot 1988; VanPool and VanPool 2007). Finally, both Kohn (2008, 2011) and Casserino (2009) have interpreted the presence and type of postmortem processing among the fragmentary and disarticulated individuals as reflective of anthropophagy of elite lineages in an endocannibalistic ritual.

ANALYTICAL METHODS

All skeletons were placed in anatomical position, and commingled elements were reassociated where possible. Complete osteological inventories were recorded, and were used to calculate a minimum number of individuals, using the counts of repeated elements (Buikstra and Ubelaker 1994). The sex of the six adults was estimated using standard ordinal features of the os coxa and cranium (see methodologies presented in Buikstra and Ubelaker 1994; Phenice 1969). Subadult age-at-death was estimated using Moorrees and colleagues' dental development sequence (Moorrees, Fanning, and Hunt 1963). Dental scores from multiple teeth were combined to obtain a median age-at-death estimate, using the methods from Shackelford and colleagues (Shackelford et al. 2012), and an R script made available by Lyle Konigsberg (http://tiny.cc/sbp01x). Adult age-at-death estimation was calculated via transition analysis, a Bayesian method that minimizes the effect of reference sample mimicry and results in more-precise age-at-death estimates for older adult individuals (Boldsen et al. 2002; Milner and Boldsen 2012). Age-at-death estimates from the pubic symphysis and auricular surface were used where available, but were obtained from the first rib (DiGangi et al. 2009) and sacral closure methods (Ríos, Weisensee, and Rissech 2008) where os coxae data were unavailable.

Following criteria outlined by Tiesler, all individuals were examined for evidence of perimortem trauma and postmortem skeletal processing (Tiesler 2007). Cut marks were photographed and recorded as presence/absence data. Other indicators of peri- and postmortem skeletal processing, such as burning, anvil abrasions (Turner and Turner 1999), and rounding of skeletal elements reflecting "pot polish" were recorded as well (White 1992). Finally, indicators of postdepositional taphonomy, such as root etching and rodent gnawing, were noted.

Results

Demography

Results of the demographic analysis are presented in table 3.1. According to our sex estimations, the articulated burials consisted of two adult males and five adult females. These estimates are consistent with those reported by Di Peso and colleagues (Di Peso, Rinaldo, and Fenner 1974). Paleodemographic analyses of Paquimé show adult mean age at death was approximately 40 years of age: 41 years for males and 38 years for females (Waller 2017). There does not appear to be a significant difference in age-at-death and overall life expectancy for the articulated skeletons when compared with the population as a whole (table 3.1). It is interesting to note, however, that the point estimate of one of two prominent male burials (44A) exceeds the average life expectancy by approximately seven years, while four of the five female burials died at least a decade earlier than the average female at Paquimé.

In contrast, the demographic profile of the disarticulated remains is highly distinct from that of the articulated burials; four of the five individuals were adolescents between the ages of seven and 15. The remaining individual was a young adult female (44H), for whom, however, a more precise age could not be estimated, due to the extremely fragmentary nature of the remains. There are no other burials at Paquimé that contain as many subadults (Di Peso, Rinaldo, and Fenner 1974; Waller 2017). This distinct age-related pattern suggests that their placement together in the same burial was not the result of natural accretional processes typically seen in the formation of a cemetery population (e.g., Duering and Wahl 2014).

TABLE 3.1. Sex and Age-at-Death Estimates, Paquimé

Burial	*Sex*	*Age (Point Estimate)*	*Age Range*
44A	M	48.2	31.2–86.3
44B	F	27.6	12.0–68.7
44C	F	20.1	20.1–32.4
44D	F	43.7	17.0–96.8
44E	M	42.1	29.5–72.1
44F	F	21.5	15.1–64.1
44G	F	21.5	15.0–21.7
44H	F?		18.0–35.0*
44I		15.8	
44J		11.9	
44K		7.2	
44L		13.2	

* Age estimation for 44H derived from Di Peso, Rinaldo, and Fenner 1974.

SKELETAL PROCESSING AND TRAUMA

Although we were unable to assign postmortem processing to specific individuals in all cases because the majority of disarticulated remains were adolescents of a similar age, a distinct pattern of postmortem processing was apparent. We found evidence for postmortem processing on six of the identifiable skeletons, including all of the disarticulated individuals (44H–L), and on many of the commingled fragments from the top layer of the burial. The most common type of postmortem processing was cut marks, which were distributed throughout various regions of the skeleton, including on the cranium (frontal, mastoids, and parietals), vertebrae, ribs, clavicles, radii, ulnae, femora, and os coxae. On the long bones, cut marks were most often oriented perpendicular (~90° angle) to the long axis of the bone, primarily on proximal and distal ends (figures 3.3–3.5). A useful diagnostic criterion for dismemberment is the presence of cut marks at either 90° or oblique angles to the long axis of the bones, which are primarily found on the proximal and distal ends of long bones (Pérez 2006; Tiesler 2007). Meanwhile, cut marks located at muscle-attachment points along bone shafts are associated with defleshing (Tiesler 2007).

Another frequent observation was the extensive processing of clavicles recovered from the uppermost burial layer. Cut marks were generally on the inferior surface of the bone and appeared in high frequencies. One extraordinary individual, 44J, a 12–14-year-old adolescent, had at least 25 distinct cut marks on the

Figure 3.3. Cut marks on 44H-13 left radius.

Figure 3.4. Cut marks on 44L-13 right radius.

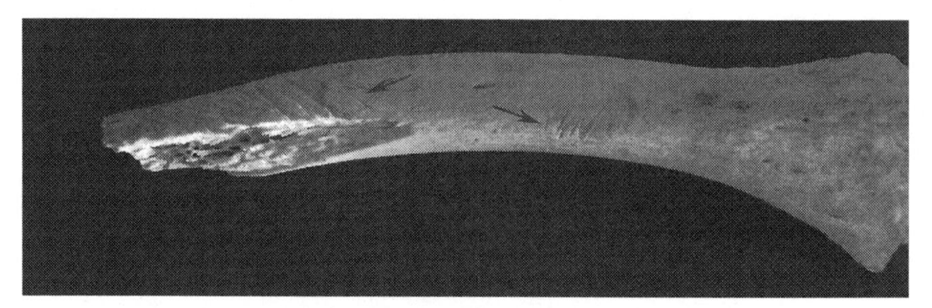

Figure 3.5. Cut marks on 44K-13 left ulna.

inferior aspect of the sternal end of the clavicle (figure 3.6). Other forms of postmortem processing observed among the disarticulated remains include burning, spiral fracturing, and potential "pot polish." Long bones from individual 44I, a 14–16-year-old possible female, exhibited spiral fracturing and pot polish, the latter of which is possibly indicative of cooking (Turner and Turner 1999; White 1992). The pot polish was found on a femoral fragment and was characterized by rounding of the fractured edge of the bone that exhibited a smooth and somewhat polished surface (figure 3.7). There is also evidence of burning on several of the fragmentary elements, including an acromion process (figure 3.8), and a femoral shaft fragment (figure 3.9).

This pattern is suggestive of defleshing or flaying, as the cut marks are on the portion of the clavicle that is adjacent to the surface of the skin (Medina Martín and Sánchez Vargas 2007; Tiesler 2007). Flaying is also likely due to the anteroinferior placement and 35–45° angle of the cut marks, which are consistent with the peeling away of skin from the upper chest region. Additionally, several individuals had deep cut marks on the inferior and posterior aspects of the mastoid process. The pattern of cut marks observed on the clavicles and mastoid processes corresponds to the origin and insertion points of the sternocleidomastoid muscle, which suggests that processing involved cutting through this particular muscle. Several researchers have noted similar patterns, suggesting that the sternocleidomastoid muscles may have been cut during processing (Medina Martín and Sánchez Vargas 2007; Ogilvie and Hilton 2000; Pérez 2006; Stodder et al. 2010).

DISCUSSION

There was no conclusive evidence of ante- or perimortem trauma among the disarticulated and fragmentary remains. However, it is possible that cut marks on bones from the thoracic region may be stab wounds or trauma resulting from evisceration. The atypical demographic profile of the subadults, their haphazard deposition atop the high-status burials, and their extensive processing, which included burning, defleshing, dismemberment, flaying, and pot polish, are consistent with Mesoamerican human sacrifices (Cucina and Tiesler 2006; Tiesler 2007). Thus, it is likely that these processed individuals were sacrificed, therefore reflecting a violent death, even though evidence of perimortem trauma is absent (see Waller et al. 2018 for further discussion of human sacrifice at Paquimé).

Rakita (2001) suggests that 44-13 is a charnel house, where a "charnel house" is a single structure employed for the cumulative disposal of the dead (O'Shea 1984, 37). The shelf at one end of the burial to allow ongoing access, and multiple depositional events of the articulated burials support this hypothesis. The form of the burial tomb appears broadly similar to West Mexican Aztatlan shaft-and-chamber tombs, in which vertical shafts were dug to various depths, terminating in a horizontal chamber in which multiple corpses and grave goods were laid over an extended period of time (Beekman 2000). Beekman notes that the West Mexican burial tombs were restricted, and likely reflect single elite lineages (Beekman 2000). However, the presence of individuals who have received postmortem processing is inconsistent with West Mexican shaft-and-chamber tombs.

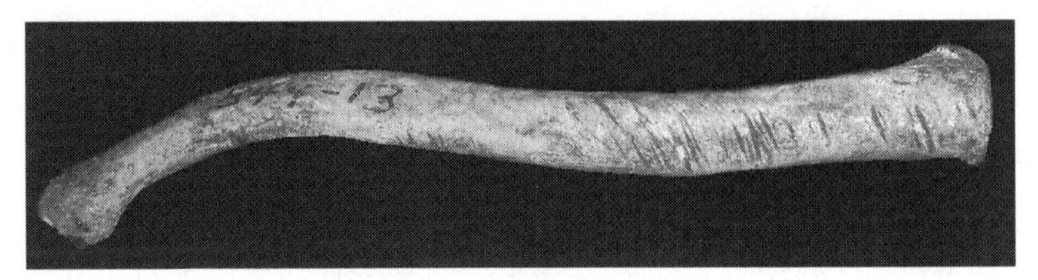

Figure 3.6. Cut marks on 44J-13 left clavicle.

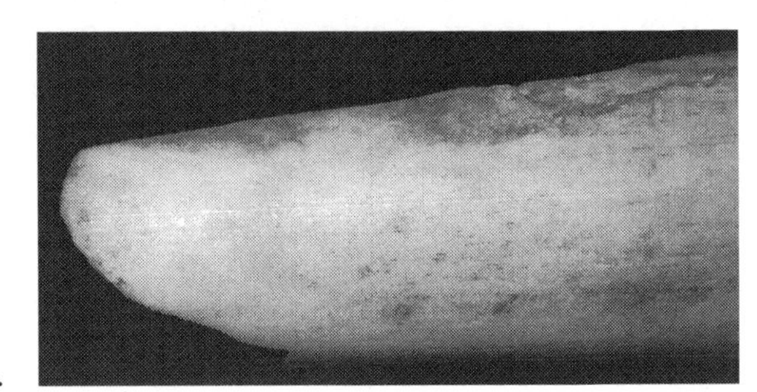

Figure 3.7. Pot polish on 44I-13 right femur.

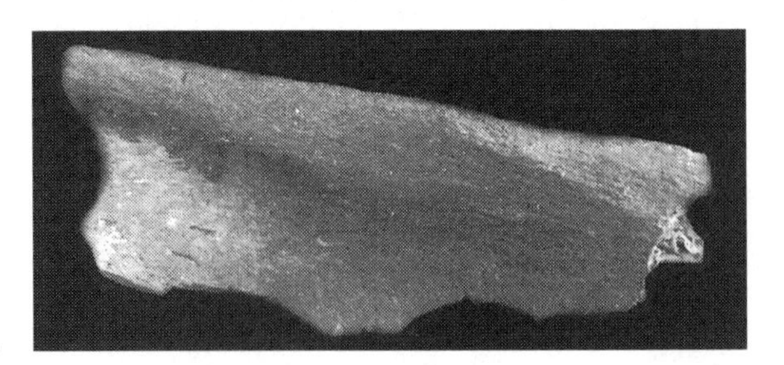

Figure 3.8. Burning on acromion process from adult individual in Burial 44-13.

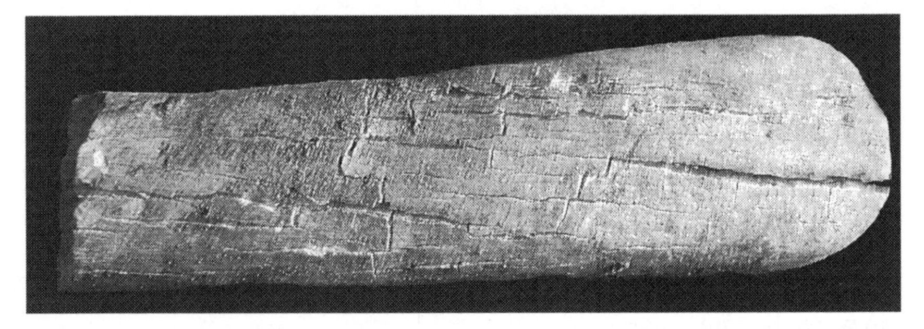

Figure 3.9. Burning on 44L-13 femur.

Thus, it appears that the 44-13 tomb reflects two distinct ritual processes, both related to status and negotiations of power. The first process is the elaborate mortuary rituals of at least two individuals: 44A and 44E, though two females (44F and 44G) were the first interred and had significant grave goods. These two individuals were the focus of a high-status, elaborate burial facility that echoes Aztatlan tomb-shaft burials. They were interred with the majority of the grave goods and were buried in unique positions. Burial 44E in particular was interred in a highly unusual position with his legs flexed to either side (figure 3.2); a burial position that only he, the burial atop of him, and one other individual at the site were afforded (Di Peso, Rinaldo, and Fenner 1974). The completeness of their remains, including the presence of phalanges, vertebrae, and other small skeletal elements, indicates that these are undisturbed primary interments. Thus, these individuals were not directly manipulated, like the high-status human skeletons in the urn burials discussed previously. Instead, the opening that allows ongoing access to the burial suggests that these high-status individuals are linked to the ancestor/political cult suggested by Rakita, whereby ritual practices related to ancestor veneration likely occurred. Furthermore, in addition to the overall wealth of the burial tomb, several of the grave goods in 44-13 were rare socioreligious objects, including a turkey sacrifice, smashed ceramic hand drums, and concretions (Di Peso, Rinaldo, and Fenner 1974; Rakita 2009; Ravesloot 1988). Thus, there appears to be an association between social status—as indicated by the fact that 44-13 was one of the richest burials discovered at the site (Di Peso, Rinaldo, and Fenner 1974; Rakita 2009; Ravesloot 1988)—and the ritual/religious realm at Paquimé. Indeed, Rakita has suggested that one of the ways in which aspiring elites obtained and legitimized power and authority during the Medio Period was by occupying priestly positions in the cult/religious organizations (Rakita 2009).

In contrast to the elaborate mortuary treatment of the articulated burials, the individuals in the uppermost burial layer were treated very differently in death. This likely represents a second and distinct mortuary process involving a series of rituals that included human sacrifice, defleshing, dismemberment, and possible anthropophagy of older subadult and young adult females. Unlike the articulated burials beneath them, these individuals (44H–L) do not appear to be of high status. First, bioarchaeological analyses of the recognizably high-status skeletons at Paquimé (e.g., Burial 44-13 and the urn burials) have not found evidence of dismemberment or defleshing. Second, the uppermost burial layer consisted of disarticulated, fragmentary, and disorderly skeletal remains, which suggests that these individuals were discarded or perhaps deposited as secondary offerings to the individuals below. Finally, when compared to both the high-status individuals below them and to the Paquimé population as a whole, these individuals experienced poor health, which may indicate that they had disproportionately poor access to resources during life (Waller et al. 2018).

VIOLENCE, POETICS, AND MEANING

Burial 44-13 is located in an internal room in the House of the Dead, where the deposition of the sacrificed individuals and associated rituals likely would not have been viewed by the general public. However, ethnohistorical and iconographic evidence indicate that in Mesoamerica, sacrifice was often performed in public spaces, like plazas, pyramids, and ballcourts (e.g., Vail and Hernández 2007). By analogy, the presence of public ritual architecture at Paquimé (e.g., platform mounds, ballcourts) suggests that sacrificial rituals were likely conducted in public, perhaps on top of one of the several large, highly visible platform mounds at the site.

When the contextual and osteological data from this unique mortuary context are considered in tandem, it is clear that mortuary rituals for elite Paquimeños included ritual violence. As Inomata (Inomata 2006, 833) notes, "mass spectacles become effective only through their connection and contrast with more intimate but equally political actions, including food production, craft production, gift exchange, and small scale meetings." Pilgrimages at Paquimé provided just such a setting, with public rituals, feasting, and competition on the ballcourts (e.g., VanPool and VanPool 2018).

The poetics model emphasizes contextualizing cultural conceptions of violence, and the associated signs and symbols of violence manipulated during performances of violence (Whitehead 2004, 2007). While violent death and associated imagery at Paquimé was infrequent (Casserino 2009; VanPool and O'Brien 2013), bones and bodies appear to have been an important component of exclusive rituals of power and social control at Paquimé. Beyond the 44-13 tomb, a number of bodies were manipulated, cut, and processed during mortuary rituals (Casserino 2009; Kohn 2008, 2011). Curated bones were likely manipulated as part of public and private rituals, while visitors to symbolic, spiritual locations, such as the walk-in well, literally stepped over human skulls and bones (VanPool and VanPool 2007). Thus, bodies and bones at Paquimé were an important medium for ritual messaging and status negotiations (Rakita 2009).

The ritual actions that led to violent death and that produced bodies to be manipulated, however, were exclusive. Taking place as part of events designed in part to highlight community cohesion and group membership, performing such violent actions likely would have further cemented both this exclusivity and the social control of the ritual actors. While community norms and group identities were celebrated during feasting and other rituals, the symbolic and overt threat communicated by viewing human sacrifices and subsequent processing would simultaneously deliver a message about the need for social conformity, and the potential consequences for departure from these norms (Osterholtz 2013). The deliberate juxtaposition between integrative rituals and the infliction of death and terror would have significantly amplified this message to witnesses, particularly those potentially traveling hundreds of kilometers to Paquimé.

The timing of such unique performance violence, during public rituals of cohesion and group identity, would have had two significant additional effects beyond communicating threats about conformity. First, integrating such unique violent actions into public performances replete with communal, interpretable symbols may have legitimized and normalized the actions of those performing the sacrifices. This legitimation may have further established elite authority and social hierarchy. Second, the impact of these events would not have been limited to witnesses who directly viewed the sacrifice and subsequent processing. Threats of future violence are just as effective a deterrent as actual direct violence (Ferguson 2008; Parsons 2007). Thus, the message of social control and conformity would not have been limited to individuals who personally viewed the sacrificial event.

The subsequent extensive dismemberment, defleshing, burning, and possible consumption of these sacrificed individuals, and their deposition in a restricted, high-status location in the site would have further amplified the message of social control, even if witnesses were unable to witness the processing themselves. Nelson and Martin (2015) cite ethnohistoric literature from the Mesoamerican frontier to document what they call "extended killing," in which disarticulation and postmortem processing are used to extend the mortuary ritual of enemy bodies. It is likely that the processing of the sacrificed individuals served a similar function at Paquimé, further amplifying the manipulated symbols and messages from the sacrifice ritual. The deposition of the sacrificed and processed individuals above the tomb shaft may have demonstrated the ritual actors' exclusive access to the high-status burials in the private burial tomb, similar to the manipulation of the bones in the urn burial.

CONCLUSIONS

Bioarchaeological analysis of 12 individuals in a burial tomb at Paquimé suggests that at least five individuals were publicly sacrificed. It is likely that these sacrifices occurred during large-scale ritual events bringing together people at Paquimé from across the Casas Grandes region. After they were sacrificed, these individuals were then heavily processed and deposited in a high-status burial with restricted access.

Applying the poetics model developed by Whitehead to these ritual performances allows inferences about the meaning of these sacrifice rituals (Whitehead 2004, 2007). This chapter suggests that ritual actors conducted human sacrifices to create a spectacle, in a display of social control and dominance. Conducting the sacrifice ritual in concert with other rituals that emphasized community and group ideology legitimized the sacrifices and further normalized social hierarchy and elite authority. The timing of the rituals served to significantly amplify the message of social control and the importance of maintaining the community norms celebrated during the integrative rituals, and would have been a potent reminder of the consequences of deviations from the proscribed norms.

ACKNOWLEDGMENTS

This chapter took an armada of support to come to fruition. First, we would like to thank Dr. Anna Osterholtz for her gracious invitation to participate in the volume, her patience as we promptly missed the chapter deadline, and her extremely helpful edits. Dr. Todd VanPool and three anonymous reviewers provided helpful edits that significantly strengthened and clarified our arguments. We would like to thank Dr. M. Anne Katzenberg, the late Dr. Jane Kelley, and Dr. Deb Martin for obtaining the INAH permit that allowed us to conduct the osteological analyses for this chapter. Further acknowledgements go to Dr. Katzenberg for obtaining the SSHRC grant that paid for the bulk of the research and expenses while in Mexico, as well as financial assistance from the University of Missouri Department of Anthropology W. Raymond Wood Fund, and from Dr. Mike Searcy of Brigham Young University. We would like to thank Andrew Krug for creating figure 3.1 for us, and Dr. Eric Kaldahl of the Amerind Foundation for providing his digitization of Alice Wesche's original line drawing, used for figure 3.2, and permission to use it. In Mexico we'd like to thank Dr. Eduardo Gamboa, Mauricio Selgido, and Luis Tena, as well as the rest of the Museo de las Culturas del Norte staff for their gracious assistance in facilitating access to the Paquimé human skeletal remains. Finally, we dedicate this chapter to Dr. Jane H. Kelley, who was the impetus for much of our research at Casas Grandes and a constant source of support and guidance.

REFERENCES

Anderson, Cheryl P. 2014. "Victims of Violence? A Methodological Case Study from Precolonial Northern Mexico." In *Bioarchaeological and Forensic Perspectives on Violence: How Violent Death is Interpreted From Skeletal Remains*, edited by Debra L. Martin and Cheryl P. Anderson, 83–100. Cambridge, UK: Cambridge University Press.

Anderson, Cheryl P., Debra L. Martin, and Jennifer L. Thompson. 2012. "Indigenous Violence in Northern Mexico on the Eve of Contact." *International Journal of Paleopathology* 2 (2): 93–101.

Beekman, Christopher S. 2000. "The Correspondence of Regional Patterns and Local Strategies in Formative to Classic Period West Mexico." *Journal of Anthropological Archaeology* 19 (4): 385–412.

Binford, Lewis. 1971. "Mortuary Practices: Their Study and Their Potential." *Memoirs of the Society for American Archaeology, Number 25*: 6–29.

Boldsen, Jesper L., George R. Milner, Lyle W. Konigsberg, and James W Wood. 2002. "Transition Analysis: A New Method for Estimating Age from Skeletons." In *Paleodemography: Age Distributions from Skeletal Samples*, edited by Robert D. Hoppa and James W. Vaupel, 73–106. Cambridge, UK: Cambridge University Press.

Bradley, Ronna J. 1999. "Shell Exchange within the Southwest: The Casas Grandes Interaction Sphere." In *The Casas Grandes World*, edited by Curtis F. Schaafsma and Carrol L. Riley, 213–228. Salt Lake City: University of Utah Press.

Brown, James. 1995. "On Mortuary Analysis—with Special Reference to the Saxe-Binford Research Program." In *Regional Approaches to Mortuary Analysis*, edited by Lane Anderson Beck, 3–25. New York: Plenum Press.

Buikstra, Jane, and D. H. Ubelaker, eds. 1994. *Standards for Data Collection from Human Skeletal Remains. Arkansas Archeological Survey* Research Series Number 44. Fayetteville, AR: Arkansas Archeological Survey.

Casserino, Christopher Michael. 2009. "Bioarchaeology of Violence and Site Abandonment at Casas Grandes, Chihuahua, Mexico." PhD, Anthropology, University of Oregon, Eugene, OR.

Chinchilla Mazariegos, Oswaldo, Vera Tiesler, Oswaldo Gomez, and T. Douglas Price. 2015. "Myth, Ritual and Human Sacrifice in Early Classic Mesoamerica: Interpreting a Cremated Double Burial from Tikal, Guatemala." *Cambridge Archaeological Journal* 25 (1): 187–210.

Cucina, Andrea, and Vera Tiesler. 2006. "The Companions of Janaab' Pakal and the 'Red Queen' from Palenque, Chiapas: Meanings of Human Companion Sacrifice in Classic Maya Society." In *Janaab' Pakal of Palenque: Reconstructing the Life and Death of a Maya Ruler*, edited by Vera Tiesler and Andrea Cucina, 102–125. Tucson: University of Arizona.

Darling, J. Andrew. 1998. "Mass Inhumation and the Execution of Witches in the American Southwest." *American Anthropologist* 100 (3): 732–752.

Di Peso, Charles Corradino. 1974. *Casas Grandes: A Fallen Trading Center of the Gran Chichimeca*. Volume 1: *Preceramic-Viejo Periods*. Dragoon, AZ: Amerind Foundation.

Di Peso, Charles C., John B. Rinaldo, and Gloria Fenner. 1974. *Casas Grandes: A Fallen Trading Center of the Grand Chichimeca*, Volume 8: *Bone, Economy, and Burials*. Dragoon, AZ: Amerind Foundation.

DiGangi, Elizabeth A., Jonathan D. Bethard, Erin H. Kimmerle, and Lyle W. Konigsberg. 2009. "A New Method for Estimating Age-at-Death from the First Rib." *American Journal of Physical Anthropology* 138 (2): 164–176. doi: 10.1002/ajpa.20916.

Duering, Andreas, and Joachim Wahl. 2014. "A Massacred Village Community? Agent-Based Modelling Sheds New Light on the Demography of the Neolithic Mass Grave of Talheim." *Anthropologischer Anzeiger* 71 (4): 447–468.

Ferguson, Brian. 2008. "Ten Points of War." *Social Analysis* 52 (2): 32–49.

Foster, Michael S. 1999. "The Aztatlán Tradition of West and Northwest Mexico and Casas Grandes: Speculations on the Medio Phase Florescence." In *The Casas Grandes World*, edited by Curtis F. Schaafsma and Carroll L. Riley, 149–163. Salt Lake City: University of Utah Press.

Inomata, Takeshi. 2006. "Plazas, Performers, and Spectators: Political Theaters of the Classic Maya." *Current Anthropology* 47 (5): 805–842.

Kantner, John. 1999. "Anasazi Mutilation and Cannibalism in the American Southwest." In *The Anthropology of Cannibalism*, edited by Laurence R. Goldman, 75–104. Westport, CT: Bergin and Garvey.

Kelley, J. Charles. 1986. "The Mobile Merchants of Molino." In *Ripples in the Chichimec Sea: New Considerations of Southwestern-Mesoamerican Interactions*, edited by Francis J Mathien and Randall H. McGuire, 81–104. Carbondale: Southern Illinois University Press.

Kelley, J. Charles. 2000. "The Aztatlan Mercantile System." In *Greater Mesoamerica: The Archaeology of West and Northwest Mexico*, edited by Michael S. Foster and Shirley Gorenstein, 137–154. Salt Lake City: University of Utah Press.

King, Daniel J., Michael T. Searcy, Chad L. Yost, and Kyle D. Waller. 2017. "Corn, Beer, and Marine Resources at Casas Grandes, Mexico: An Analysis of Prehistoric Diets Using Microfossils Recovered from Dental Calculus." *Journal of Archaeological Science: Reports* 16: 365–379.

Kohn, Sophie. 2008. "He's Not the Skeleton They Thought She Was: A Reanalysis of Skeletal Material from Paquimé, Chihuahua." Society for American Archaeology, Vancouver, BC, March 28, 2008.

Kohn, Sophie. 2011. "Mortuary Practices at Paquimé and in the Casas Grandes Region." Society for American Archaeology, Sacramento, April 1, 2011.

LeBlanc, Steven A. 1999. *Prehistoric Warfare in the American Southwest*. Salt Lake City: The University of Utah Press.

Lekson, Stephen H. 2002. "War in the Southwest, War in the World." *American Antiquity* 67 (4): 607–624.

Lekson, Stephen H. 2015. *The Chaco Meridian: One Thousand Years of Political and Religious Power in the Ancient Southwest*. 2nd ed. Lanham, MD: Rowman and Littlefield.

Martin, Debra L. 2016. "Hard Times in Dry Lands: Making Meaning of Violence in the Ancient Southwest." *Journal of Anthropological Research* 72 (1): 1–23.

McAnany, Patricia A. 2013. *Living with the Ancestors: Kinship and Kingship in Ancient Maya Society*. 2nd ed. New York: Cambridge University Press.

Medina Martín, Cecilia, and Mirna Sánchez Vargas. 2007. "Posthumous Body Treatments and Ritual Meaning in the Classic Period Northern Peten: A Taphonomic Approach."

In *New Perspectives on Human Sacrifice and Ritual Body Treatments in Ancient Maya Society*, edited by Vera Tiesler and Andrea Cucina, 102–119. New York: Springer.

Milner, George R, and Jesper L Boldsen. 2012. "Transition Analysis: A Validation Study with Known-Age Modern American Skeletons." *American Journal of Physical Anthropology* 148 (1): 98–110.

Moorrees, Coenraad F.A., Elizabeth A. Fanning, and Edward E. Hunt Jr. 1963. "Age Variation of Formation Stages for Ten Permanent Teeth." *Journal of Dental Research* 42 (6): 1490–1502.

Nelson, Ben A., J. Andrew Darling, and David A. Kice. 1992. "Mortuary Practices and the Social Order at La Quemada, Zacatecas, Mexico." *Latin American Antiquity* 3 (4): 298–315.

Nelson, Ben A., and Debra L Martin. 2015. "Symbolic Bones and Interethnic Violence in a Frontier Zone, Northwest Mexico, ca. 500–900 CE." *Proceedings of the National Academy of Sciences* 112 (30): 9196–9201.

O'Shea, J. M. 1984. *Mortuary Variability: An Archaeological Investigation*. New York: Academic Press.

Offenbecker, Adrianne. 2018. "Geographic Origins, Status, and Identity at Paquimé, Northwest Chihuahua, Mexico." PhD, Departmnt of Anthropology and Archaeology, University of Calgary, Alberta.

Ogilvie, Marsha D., and Charles E. Hilton. 2000. "Ritualized Violence in the Prehistoric American Southwest." *International Journal of Osteoarchaeology* 10: 27–48.

Osterholtz, Anna J. 2012. "The Social Role of Hobbling and Torture: Violence in the Prehistoric Southwest." *International Journal of Paleopathology* 2 (2–3): 148–155. doi: http://dx.doi.org/10.1016/j.ijpp.2012.09.011.

Osterholtz, Anna J. 2013. "Hobbling and Torture as Performative Violence: An Example from the Prehistoric Southwest." *Kiva* 78 (2): 123–144.

Parsons, Kenneth. 2007. "Structural Violence and Power." *Peace Review: A Journal of Social Justice* 19 (2): 173–181.

Pérez, Ventura R. 2006. "The Politicization of the Dead: An Analysis of Cutmark Morphology and Culturally Modified Human Remains from La Plata and Peñasco Blanco (AD 900–1300)." Unpublished PhD dissertation, Anthropology, University of Massachusetts Amherst.

Pérez, Ventura R., Ben A. Nelson, and Debra L. Martin. 2008. "A Study of Variations in Patterns of Human Bone Modification at La Quemada." In *Social Violence in the Prehispanic American Southwest*, edited by Deborah L. Nichols and Patricia Crown, 123–142. Tucson: University of Arizona Press.

Phenice, T. W. 1969. "A Newly Developed Visual Method of Sexing the Os Pubis." *American Journal of Physical Anthropology* 30 (2): 297–301.

Punzo, Jose Luis, and Elisa Villalpando. 2015. "Paquimé: A Revision of Its Relationships to the South and West." In *Ancient Paquimé and the Casas Grandes World*, edited by Paul E Minnis and Michael E Whalen, 172–191. Tucson: University of Arizona Press.

Rakita, Gordon F. M. 2001. "Social Complexity, Religious Organization, and Mortuary Ritual in the Casas Grandes Region of Chihuahua, Mexico." PhD, Anthropology, University of New Mexico, Albuquerque.

Rakita, Gordon F. M. 2008. "Mortuary and Non-Mortuary Ritual Practices at the Pre-Hispanic site of Paquimé (Casas Grandes), Chihuahua, Mexico." In *Reanalysis and Reinterpretation in Southwestern Bioarchaeology*, edited by Ann L. W. Stodder, 55–79. Tempe: Arizona State University Press.

Rakita, Gordon F. M. 2009. *Ancestors and Elites: Emergent Complexity and Ritual Practices in the Casas Grandes Polity*. Lanham, MD: AltaMira Press.

Ravesloot, John C. 1988. *Mortuary Practices and Social Differentiation of Casas Grandes, Chihuahua, Mexico*. Anthropological Papers of the University of Arizona, No. 49. Tucson: University of Arizona Press.

Ríos, Luis, Katy Weisensee, and Carme Rissech. 2008. "Sacral Fusion as an Aid in Age Estimation." *Forensic Science International* 180 (2–3): 111.e1–7.

Saxe, Arthur Alan. 1970. "Social Dimensions of Mortuary Practices." Doctor of Philosophy, Department of Anthropology, University of Michigan, Ann Arbor.

Shackelford, Laura L., Stinespring Harris, E. Ashley, and Lyle W. Konigsberg. 2012. "Estimating the Distribution of Probable Age-at-Death from Dental Remains of Immature Human Fossils." *American Journal of Physical Anthropology* 147 (2): 227–253.

Springer, Simon. 2011. "Violence Sits in Places? Cultural Practice, Neoliberal Rationalism, and Virulent Imaginative Geographies." *Political Geography* 30 (2): 90–98.

Stodder, Ann L.W., Anna J. Osterholtz, Kathy Mowrer, and Jason P. Chuipka. 2010. "Processed Human Remains from the Sacred Ridge Site: Context, Taphonomy, Interpretation." In *Animas–La Plata Project, Volume XV: Bioarchaeology*, edited by Elizabeth M. Perry, Ann L. W. Stodder, and Charles A. Bollong, 279–415. SWCA Anthropological Research Paper Number 10. Phoenix: University of Arizona Press.

Tiesler, Vera. 2007. "Funerary and Nonfunerary? New References in Identifying Ancient Maya Sacrificial and Postsacrifical Behaviors from Human Assemblages." In *New Perspectives on Human Sacrifice and Ritual Body Treatments in Ancient Maya Society*, edited by Vera Tiesler and Andrea Cucina, 14–45. New York: Springer.

Turner, Christy G., II, and Jacqueline A. Turner. 1999. *Man Corn: Cannibalism and Violence in the Prehistoric American Southwest*. Salt Lake City: University of Utah Press.

Vail, G., and C. Hernández. 2007. "Human Sacrifice in Late Postclassic Maya Iconography and Texts." In *New Perspectives on Human Sacrifice and Ritual Body Treatments in*

Ancient Maya Society, edited by Vera Tiesler and Andrea Cucina, 120–164. New York: Springer.

VanPool, Todd L., and Michael J. O'Brien. 2013. "Sociopolitical Complexity and the Bow and Arrow in the American Southwest." *Evolutionary Anthropology* 22 (3): 111–117.

VanPool, Christine S., and Todd L. VanPool. 2007. *Signs of the Casas Grandes Shamans*. Salt Lake City: University of Utah Press.

VanPool, Todd L., and Christine S. VanPool. 2018. "Visting the Horned Serpent's Home: A Relational Analysis of Paquimé as a Pilgrimmage Site in the North American Southwest." *Journal of Social Archaeology* 18 (3): 306–324.

Walker, William H. 1998. "Where Are the Witches of Prehistory?" *Journal of Archaeological Method and Theory* 5 (3): 245–308.

Waller, Kyle D. 2017. "Bioarchaeological Analyses of Paleodemography and Violence at Paquimé, Chihuahua, Mexico." PhD, Department of Anthropology, University of Missouri, Columbia.

Waller, Kyle D., Adrianne Offenbecker, Jane H. Kelley, and M. Anne Katzenberg. 2018. "Elites and Human Sacrifices at Paquimé: A Bioarchaeological Assessment." *KIVA* 84 (4): 403–423.

Watson, James T., and Danielle O. Phelps. 2016. "Violence and Perimortem Signaling among Irrigation Communities in the Sonoran Desert." *Current Anthropology* 57 (5): 586–609.

Whalen, Michael E. 2013. "Wealth, Status, Ritual, and Marine Shell at Casas Grandes, Chihuahua, Mexico." *American Antiquity* 78 (4): 624–639.

Whalen, Michael E., Art MacWilliams, and Todd Pitezel. 2010. "Reconsidering the Size and Structure of Casas Grandes, Chihuahua, Mexico." *American Antiquity* 75 (3): 527–550.

White, Tim D. 1992. *Prehistoric Cannibalism at Mancos 5MTUMR-2346*. Princeton, NJ: Princeton University Press.

Whitehead, Neil L. 2004. "On the Poetics of Violence." In *Violence*, edited by Neil L. Whitehead, 55–78. Santa Fe, NM: SAR Press.

Whitehead, Neil L. 2007. "Violence a the Cultural Order." *Daedalus* 136 (1): 40–50. doi: 10.2307/20028088.

4

Ritual Modification of Human Remains in the Context of Social Turmoil among Ancestral Pueblo Peoples of the Northern San Juan

KRISTIN A. KUCKELMAN

The bioarchaeological remains of many individuals worldwide who perished as a result of violence exhibit evidence of ritual modification and processing that indicates these bodies were used as social tools in a variety of performative violent actions. The bodies of these individuals who died violently were thus subjected to performative modification that constituted additional violent cultural expression: The remains of enemy victims were employed as mechanisms to communicate a variety of culturally constructed messages to multiple audiences.

Anthropologically, violence has been conceptualized as the means to specific ends (Whitehead 2004, 69) and a form of social control. Schröder and Schmidt (2001, 5–6) observe that violence without an audience is socially meaningless. Violence is thus a cultural performance in which perpetrators, victims, and observers form a "triangle of violence," and each of these groups possesses its own interpretive frameworks and agendas (Riches 1986). Accordingly, Schröder and Schmidt (2001, 17) correctly caution that violence "should be approached with careful attention to the sociocultural specificity of the historical context."

In this chapter, selected cases of ritual modification among the ancestral Pueblo residents of the US Southwest are examined to explore the poetics—that is, culturally structured actions and their meanings—of the modification of enemy bodies as performative violence. Evidence of ritual processing of enemy remains was found at multiple late-thirteenth-century sites in the Sand Canyon locality of the northern San Juan region (figure 4.1). This study also explores—to the extent possible from

DOI: 10.5876/9781646420612.c004

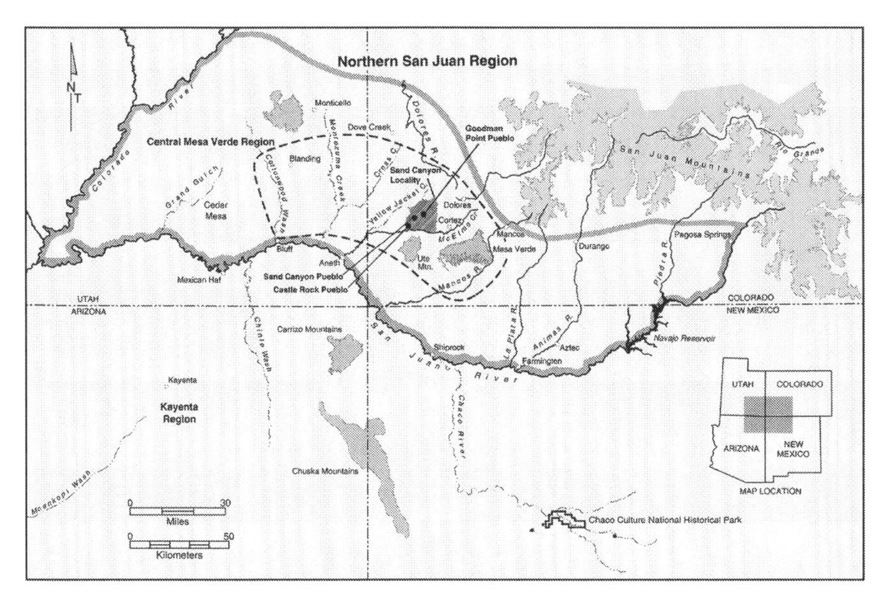

FIGURE 4.1. The northern San Juan region. (Courtesy Crow Canyon Archaeological Center.)

archaeological and bioarchaeological data, as opposed to ethnographic data—the performative aspects of the processing of enemy remains in the context of a natural environment turned hostile and the concurrent social turmoil that occurred throughout the region in the tumultuous years before the complete depopulation of the area by Pueblo peoples late in the thirteenth century.

HISTORICAL CONTEXT AND BACKGROUND

The sociopolitical and ritual order that structured Pueblo communities in the northern San Juan between AD 1250 and the regional depopulation about 1280 was stressed by significant challenges stemming from deteriorating environmental conditions and population packing beyond optimal levels. Data suggest that, although the population of the region had begun to decline during the first half of the thirteenth century (Kohler, Varien, and Wright 2010; Varien 2010), a midcentury shift in settlement patterning had resulted in a coalescence of the remaining populace on or near the most agriculturally productive soils. Many communities of dispersed farmsteads aggregated and constructed villages in the central Mesa Verde area, which resulted in an unprecedented density of population in the central portion of the region about AD 1250 (Glowacki 2010; Kohler et al. 2007; Varien et al. 2007). Many such pueblos were constructed near community water sources in defensible locations on canyon rims and in cliff alcoves.

The subsistence system was dependent on maize (*Zea mays*), a dietary staple (Decker and Tieszen 1989; Katzenberg 1992; Matson and Chisholm 1991), and on domesticated turkeys (*Meleagris gallopavo*), which were also fed maize (Bocinsky, Chisholm, and Kemp 2011; McCaffery et al. 2014; Munro 1994; Nott 2010; Rawlings and Driver 2010). By the mid-1200s, maize composed as much as 90 percent of the caloric intake of Pueblo peoples (Matson 2016). Other culturally and economically important resources such as mule deer (*Odocoileus hemionus)* had been depleted by this time (Driver 2002), which exerted additional pressures on Pueblo economic and social systems. Heightened intercommunity tensions were manifest by midcentury, and violent interactions, which were probably associated with resource competition, are evidenced in cranial fractures on human remains across the region (Cattanach 1980, 145–146; Kuckelman 2010; Lambert 1999; Street 2001, 198). During these decades, climatic volatility (Benson, Petersen, and Stein 2007; Larson et al. 1996; Van West and Dean 2000; Wright 2006, 2010) included disrupted patterns of precipitation (Van West and Dean 2000; Wright 2010), periodic drought conditions (Dean and Van West 2002), and growing seasons curtailed by cooler temperatures (Adams and Petersen 1999; Petersen 1988; Salzer 2000) that might have been associated with massive volcanic eruptions in other regions of the globe (Mann, Fuentes, and Rutherford 2012; Salzer 2000).

The catastrophic "great drought" descended on the region about AD 1276 and persisted for more than 20 years (Douglass 1929). The archaeological record reveals evidence of famine and intensified violence that coincided with the multifaceted environmental downturn (Kuckelman 2010; Kuckelman, Lightfoot, and Martin 2002). Archaeological data indicate that, with the advent of the "great drought," the limit of the sociocultural system to adjust to unusually negative conditions was reached; raiding that was probably interpueblo in scale (Kuckelman, Lightfoot, and Martin 2002; LeBlanc 1999, 52–54; Lipe 1995, 161–162) escalated into widespread attacks on settlements. As observed by Schröder and Schmidt (2001, 15), violence is "a strategy generated by competition over scarce resources."

Evidence of lethal violence late in the thirteenth century has been documented for numerous sites in the region, including multiple Mesa Verde cliff dwellings, such as Long House (Street 2001), Spruce Tree House (Fewkes 1909, 24), and Ruin 6 (Morris 1939, 42), and several sites in the nearby Montezuma Valley, such as Goodman Point Pueblo (Kuckelman 2017b), Sand Canyon Pueblo (Kuckelman 2010), and Castle Rock Pueblo (Kuckelman, Lightfoot, and Martin 2002). Thus, just before regional depopulation by Pueblo peoples about AD 1280, a final period of intensified violence in the northern San Juan ended the occupations of numerous villages in the region, and bioarchaeological data contain evidence of widespread violence and multiple forms of ritual modification of enemy remains.

The Crow Canyon Archaeological Center conducted excavations at the sites of Goodman Point, Sand Canyon, and Castle Rock pueblos, which were occupied from the 1250s until regional depopulation. From 2005 through 2008, about 1 percent of the 8.7-acre Goodman Point Pueblo (figures 4.2 and 4.3) was excavated (Kuckelman 2017b). Excavation of about 5 percent of the 5.42-acre Sand Canyon Pueblo (figure 4.4) occurred from 1984 through 1993 (Kuckelman 2007; Kuckelman et al. 2007). Field work at the 1.88-acre Castle Rock Pueblo (figure 4.5) was undertaken from 1990 through 1994, during which approximately 5 percent of the site was excavated (Kuckelman 2000). Excavations at these three sites were part of Crow Canyon's long-term research in the Sand Canyon locality, which focused on the causes of the complete and permanent depopulation of the northern San Juan region by Pueblo peoples.

Goodman Point and Sand Canyon pueblos were large, walled villages constructed around canyon-head springs, and Goodman Point Pueblo—the largest village in the region at the time—was home to an estimated 600–900 residents. Approximately 450–720 villagers resided at Sand Canyon Pueblo, which was second in size only to Goodman Point Pueblo. Castle Rock Pueblo was a medium-size village constructed in a defensive posture on and around the base of a butte; this settlement housed a population of 75–150 residents. The occupations of each of these pueblos ended as the result of an attack that was probably interpueblo in scale and cultural affiliation (Kuckelman, Lightfoot, and Martin 2002; LeBlanc 1999, 52–54; Lipe 1995, 161–162).

PERFORMATIVE VIOLENCE

Whitehead (2004, 74) states that "specific forms of violence are . . . cultural performances whose poetics derive from the history and sociocultural relationships of the locale." This concept is exemplified in evidence of pervasive, late-thirteenth-century violence in the northern San Juan, which is preserved in the form of antemortem as well as lethal-level perimortem trauma on the remains of men, women, and children left in abandonment contexts; most of these remains were found on structure floors and roofs (Kuckelman 2010, 2017c; Kuckelman, Lightfoot, and Martin 2002). "Abandonment context" is defined as a context for which there is no evidence of later cultural activity. For example, the floor of a kiva is considered to be an abandonment context if the kiva fill contains no culturally deposited materials.

FIGURE 4.2. Three-dimensional reconstruction of Goodman Point Pueblo superimposed on a photograph of the landscape. (Reconstruction by Dennis R. Holloway, architect; aerial photograph by Adriel Heisey.)

FIGURE 4.3. Map of Goodman Point Pueblo. (Courtesy Crow Canyon Archaeological Center.)

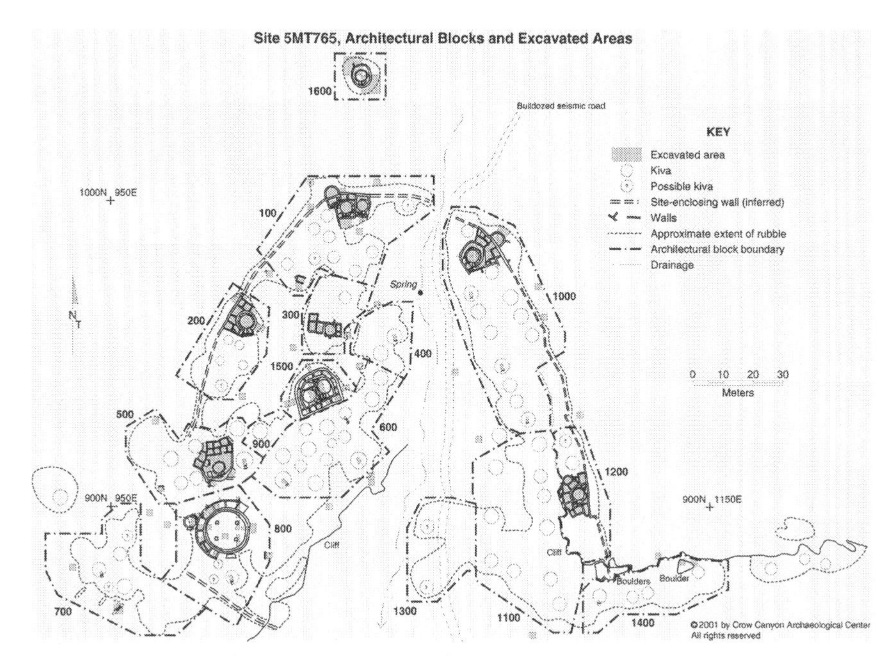

FIGURE 4.4. Map of Sand Canyon Pueblo. (Courtesy Crow Canyon Archaeological Center.)

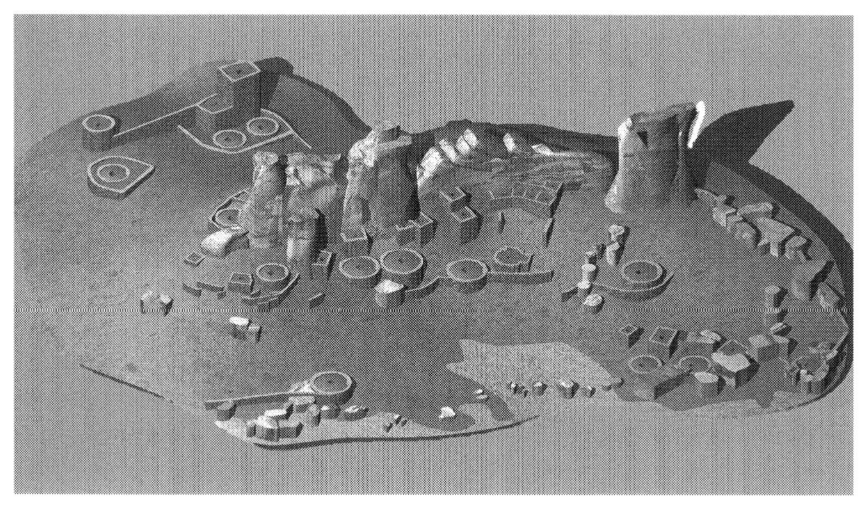

FIGURE 4.5. Reconstruction of Castle Rock Pueblo. (Computer model by Dennis R. Holloway. Courtesy Crow Canyon Archaeological Center.)

Keeping in mind that "the performative felicity of a given violent act is itself part of the wider meaning of violent acts" (Whitehead 2004, 63), I focus this study on perimortem modification suggestive of processing associated with trophy-taking and other performative violence that might have included anthropophagy (the consumption of human flesh).

Trophy-Taking

In late-thirteenth-century warfare in the northern San Juan, large-scale assaults were perpetrated on settlements with the intent to end the lives of the residents. A full record of the performative dimension of the execution of violent assaults on victim groups has been preserved neither archaeologically nor bioarchaeologically. However, ritual modification in the form of trophy-taking, one of the most observable of violent performative acts in the bioarchaeological record, was associated with lethal attacks during this time. Evidence of multiple forms of trophy-taking has been documented on human remains found in abandonment contexts at Castle Rock Pueblo (Kuckelman, Lightfoot, and Martin 2002) and Sand Canyon Pueblo (Kuckelman 2010).

Trophies such as scalps, taken in warfare, have been used for many centuries cross-culturally as portable, enduring, recognized, and acknowledged symbols of victory, courage, military superiority, power, and even cosmological favor over victim groups. Scalps also traditionally garner significant intra- and intergroup prestige and privilege for those who obtain them.

Evidence of the taking of scalps has been documented on the remains of Pueblo peoples from Basketmaker II times, about 500 BC–AD 500 (Hurst and Turner 1993, 169), through the remainder of the Pueblo occupation of the northern Southwest (Baker 1994; France 1988; Kuckelman, Lightfoot, and Martin 2002; Lambert 1999; Malville 1989; Stodder et al. 2010; Turner and Turner 1999; White 1992), and the practice continued into historic times (Ellis 1951; Parsons 1939; 1974, 139; Stephen 1969, 99–100; Titiev 1992).

Historically, "scalp societies" figured prominently in the ritual, ceremonial, sociopolitical, and even medicinal spheres of Pueblo life (Parsons 1939; Stevenson 1904, 576–608). Membership to these societies was typically restricted to those who had taken a scalp in warfare (Eggan 1983, 725; Keeley 1996, 101). Scalps were imbued with powerful symbolism. They were initially abused in order to take power away from the enemy and then were carefully stored in designated locations within the village when not displayed during various elaborate rituals (Stevenson 1904, 576–608) and other societal functions for years thereafter. Pueblo war societies in general were associated with weather control (Parsons 1939, 126), and some groups believed that enemy scalps promoted rainfall (Ellis 1979, 444–445; Parsons 1939, 31; Stevenson 1904, 578) or generally brought "good" to the pueblo (Strong 1979, 401). War trophies thus symbolized important aspects of relationships and interactions between victors and victims, and scalps in particular possessed the power to intercede with spiritual beings on behalf of those who had procured them.

The presence of bioarchaeological evidence of the taking of scalps on the remains of individuals left in abandonment contexts at late-thirteenth-century Pueblo sites supports an interpretation of violent death for those individuals as well as for other individuals represented by remains left in similar contexts at those sites but for which no evidence of trophy-taking was detected. In addition, the bioarchaeological evidence of the taking of scalps prehistorically and the documented presence of scalp-taking among historic-era Pueblo groups demonstrate the deep history and continuity of this activity as an important form of performative violence among Pueblo peoples.

Other Processing

Evidence of more-extensive processing has also been documented for this late-thirteenth-century period of subsistence stress and escalated violence. Modification suggestive of anthropophagy is especially compelling for Castle Rock Pueblo and, to a lesser degree, Sand Canyon Pueblo; these findings have been reported elsewhere (Kuckelman 2010; Kuckelman, Lightfoot, and Martin 2002). The remains of numerous additional possibly anthropophagous events are contained in the bioarchaeological record of the region for this period (Kuckelman 2010; Turner and Turner 1999). The documented cases of anthropophagy of the late thirteenth century in the northern San Juan are associated with warfare and are likely to have been at least partly motivated by acute food shortages.

Among the bioarchaeological remains documented at Castle Rock and Sand Canyon pueblos, those that exhibit the most compelling evidence of being subjected to anthropophagy had been left in residential areas on kiva floors or roofs. Acute subsistence stress during this period could have resulted in starvation anthropophagy in which the processing and consumption of enemy remains was pragmatic or mostly pragmatic in nature. Malotki and Gary have documented traditional accounts of starvation cannibalism among the Hopi during famine in historic times, and Hopi oral traditions contain vocabulary that "prove unequivocally that the topic of cannibalism was once fully part of Hopi linguistic and cultural reality" (Malotki and Gary 1999, 12). Alternatively, some anthropophagous events in the northern San Juan might have been performative in nature or at least included a performative dimension. Among some Pueblo groups historically, anthropophagous actions were designed to promote bravery (Malotki and Gary 1999) or guard against disaster caused by the victim (Parsons 1939, 625) and were thus mostly performative and ritual in nature.

Processed remains found at the sites of villages such as Castle Rock Pueblo were found in abandonment contexts and were associated with residential kivas and possibly the hearths therein. Those remains are probably those of residents who perished in the final attack on the village, and these remains were then processed on site by attackers. The bioarchaeological data for Goodman Point Pueblo, however, contain evidence not only of violence that ended the occupation of the village but also of violent activity that preceded the final attack. That is, some remains that were found at this site had been subjected to violence and to modification such as thermal alteration and reduction by fracturing while occupation of the settlement was ongoing. These actions were presumably perpetrated by the residents of Goodman Point Pueblo on the remains of enemies. The thermally altered and reduced, commingled remains at this site were not found in abandonment contexts; rather, these remains had been deposited in multiple established midden areas sometime before village depopulation.

For example, thermally altered adult cranial fragments were found in refuse just outside a doorway into the D-shaped biwall complex in Block 700, which was, in all likelihood, a special-use structure (Kuckelman 2017a). Numerous additional thermally altered remains were found in two separate midden deposits in the vicinity of Great Kiva 1213. One of these deposits, east of the great kiva, yielded a charred adult frontal fragment with a perimortem fracture. Thermally altered infant cranial fragments and a fragment of an adult diaphysis were found in a midden south of the great kiva and the same stratum yielded additional, unburned, fragmentary elements that represented at least one child, one young adult, one middle adult, and one subadult. The remains that were not thermally altered were fragmentary, commingled, and in the same deposit as thermally altered remains, which suggests a similar, though not identical, taphonomy for the entire group of fragmentary remains in this location. Most likely, then, these remains in proximity to Great Kiva 1213 were deposited in an inconsiderate manner by residents of the village during the occupation of the settlement, were not the remains of village residents, and were associated with rituals of performative violence that had been conducted in the great kiva by village residents.

Charred cranial fragments were also discovered in an expedient firepit at the edge of a plaza area along the north wall of the D-shaped biwall structure in Block 700. The timing of the actions that resulted in this deposit is more ambiguous than that of the remains in middens. That is, the presence of these fragments in primary refuse *in situ* within an extramural thermal feature leaves open the possibility that these remains resulted from actions, anthropophagous or otherwise, of attackers after the settlement had been defeated and overrun.

The described remains that were deposited in refuse associated with ritual and sacred space suggest a ritual dimension of purpose and meaning in the processing of enemy remains in the northern San Juan during the late AD 1200s. In large, late Pueblo III villages such as Goodman Point and Sand Canyon pueblos, ritual structures and sacred spaces had proliferated and were more diverse and elaborate than ever before in this region. For example, in each of these two villages, residents constructed not only a traditional great kiva, but also an unusual, massive, D-shaped biwall structure. Large, enclosed plaza spaces were also created. In addition, the residents of Goodman Point Pueblo constructed a four-kiva biwall complex and multiple additional biwall structures. When considered in concert with the simultaneous population aggregation around the community domestic water source and the considerable labor expended on defensive constructions, these measures could be interpreted as an explosion of effort by a community to protect itself against enemy onslaught and to curry favor with supernaturals that influenced or controlled the natural world.

The performative aspects of the proposed processing at Goodman Point Pueblo are perhaps underscored by the separation of space for the living, space for the formally interred dead, and space for the processed remains of enemy victims. Daily activities and formal interments were centered in residential areas in the village. No processed (that is, thermally altered, fractured) remains were discovered in those areas. The burned and fractured remains at this site, which were deposited in special-use areas rather than in residential space, suggest ritual and symbolic significance that might or might not have included anthropophagy, but probably did involve the procuring of captives or enemy remains from other communities for purposes that included ritualized performative violence. The disposal of the processed remains of enemy victims in sacred space would have bestowed a sacred, ritual endorsement on the lethal actions of the perpetrators. It would have legitimized and enhanced residents' actions and power over the victims, and perhaps over the surviving members of the enemy sociopolitical group.

It is not impossible that the processed remains were those of residents of Goodman Point Pueblo who died of disease, starvation, or violence in the months before the village was defeated. However, the discard of processed, commingled remains into middens suggests otherwise. As well, fragmentary and thermally altered remains appear to be neither numerous enough nor widespread enough to reflect an anthropophagous strategy to relieve starvation for hundreds of residents late in the occupation of the pueblo. Thus, these processed remains appear to be those of enemies whose bodies were employed in rituals of performative violence conducted by the residents of Goodman Point Pueblo. These remains constitute the only documented evidence to date of militarily offensive actions by the residents of a settlement in this region in the late AD 1200s and are also thus the first evidence of an identity for at least some of the violent aggressors in the warfare perpetrated just before regional depopulation. Evidence of processing by residents qualifies Goodman Point Pueblo as a "perpetrator" settlement before the final attack; it became a "victim" settlement during the final attack (*sensu* Billman, Lambert, and Leonard 2000, 173; Kuckelman, Lightfoot, and Martin 2002, 506). Although Sand Canyon and Castle Rock pueblos were both victim settlements, no bioarchaeological data available to date support an inference of a perpetrator role for the residents of those villages.

DISCUSSION

During the pronounced environmental downturn of the late Pueblo III period in the northern San Juan, drastic adaptations were required to preserve and reinforce the existing sociocultural system. This period was a time of strengthening corporate, community identities and continuing earlier forms of ritual architecture, such as the great kiva. It was also a time of intensification of the ritual system, as evidenced by new forms of sacred architecture and a substantial investment in the design, construction, and maintenance of extra-domestic buildings such as D-shaped biwall structures and the four-kiva complex at Goodman Point Pueblo. Thus, communities were using traditional, established ritual strategies while also creating new ritual forms and expression to cope with sociocultural and economic stresses arising from aggregation, environmental volatility, regional population packing, subsistence stress, and increasing sociopolitical instability that was erupting into violent intercommunity interactions.

Trophies served as valued and powerful social tools and palpable symbols of the strength, domination, and victory of attacker groups over victim groups. In trophy-taking, the perpetrator further conquered the victim by taking possession of a portion of the body as a portable and enduring physical symbol of the vanquished individual and, by extension, his or her wider sociopolitical group. Pueblo groups had engaged in trophy-taking such as the taking of scalps as early as Basketmaker II times (Hurst and Turner 1993; Turner and Turner 1999, 59–65); thus, the practice had been known for a minimum of 770 years before the heightened violence of the late thirteenth century. It is likely, therefore, that by the late AD 1200s, the taking of scalps, the symbolism of the scalps themselves, and rituals of performative violence associated with procured scalps had already become entrenched in the praxis of warfare. Scalps provided highly visible and enduring symbols of warrior prowess and served to strengthen internal community cohesion. Prehistorically, as in historic times, scalps might have been used as tools of supplication that interceded with spiritual beings on behalf of mortals to end droughty conditions. Scalping could thus have enjoyed societal sanction for the possible regionwide benefit of increased precipitation, other improvement in environmental conditions, and a general increase in community well-being.

Physical aggregation into villages in late Pueblo III times served to enhance social cohesion and community integration and added a new facet to social identity, especially for those who witnessed rituals of community-level performative violence. The more-robust audiences created by aggregation also increased the effectiveness of these events. However, aggregation also gave rise to challenges of social control, and acts of performative violence might have proliferated as a result, as tools of social control (Osterholtz 2013). In addition to providing anthropophagous sustenance during times of subsistence stress, ritual processing of enemy remains thus might have been stimulated by a need for the intimidation of Others for the purpose of social control. It might also have served to further integrate community members, or it could have been an attempt to gain favor with supernaturals. The Other, or outsider, is integral to the reproduction of social identity (Whitehead 2004, 69).

Hints of the perpetrator, victim, and observer perspectives of the violence at Goodman Point Pueblo are contained in the physical remains and their treatment, condition, and locations at the site. The community was heavily invested in creating and maintaining constructed ritual space and in performing increasingly elaborate rituals. Data suggest that the great kivas at Goodman Point and Sand Canyon pueblos were not roofed (Kuckelman 2017a; Kuckelman et al. 2007, par. 111). This has been interpreted as evidence that the activities associated with these structures were socially inclusive. In contrast, the closed, access-restrictive design of D-shaped structures suggests exclusive use by a privileged few (Ortman and Bradley 2002). Thus, processed remains associated with the D-shaped structure might have been associated with restricted and exclusive ritual activities, whereas the remains associated with Great Kiva 1213 could have been used in community-level ritual that was inclusive in nature, scope, and purpose. Both types of ritual processing occurred shortly before the attack on the village and regional depopulation. These acts of performative violence at least reflect aspects of the sociocultural milieu late in the occupation of the region, and could even have played a material role in the sequence of events that led to the depopulation of the region.

CONCLUSIONS

Whitehead (2004) observes that violence is structured by society, culture, and history, and that the social realization of violence takes many forms. Further, according to Riches (1986, 11), the violent act is an efficient way of "staging an ideological message before a public audience." In late-thirteenth-century pueblos of the northern San Juan, violence was manifest in somewhat predictable large-scale attacks on settlements of Others. The power display inherent in bringing about the demise of Others or an entire Other group served to legitimize the authority and continued existence of the victors and their allies. These violent actions could have been effective means to proclaim, communicate, and legitimize aggressor-victim relationships. As Osterholtz (2013) points out, social identity is reinforced through violent, performative, processing actions, and violence increases social cohesion for the aggressor group, victim group, and observer group.

The widespread lethal violence of the northern San Juan region included trophy-taking and also appears to have involved additional performative actions such as the ritual modification of enemy remains back in the home settlement. It exemplifies a proliferation of strategies to survive largely uncontrollable conditions that created an untenable and unsustainable reality for the ancestral Pueblo residents of the region. With performative violence and the modification and processing of enemy remains, perpetrators attempted to gain control over their circumstances in part by dominating the corporeal beings of their enemies in ways that were observable to large and multiple audiences.

In sum, when an elaboration of ritual architecture, and presumably, of ritual itself, in the mid-to-late thirteenth century failed to provide relief from deleterious conditions in the natural realm, perpetrator groups acted to gain some dominion over the survival, destiny, and future of themselves and their communities by constructing a reality in which they controlled the lives, deaths, and remains of their adversaries. The act of ritually processing enemy remains communicated and underscored to perpetrators, victims, and witnesses a relationship of possession and control of the aggressors over their victims. Additional benefit to the processors was obtained through the deconstruction of the physical bodies, actions that also deconstructed the physical, sociopolitical, and ritual identities of the victims. Further, the power of discretionary disposal of enemy remains served to legitimize the authority of the perpetrators over the victims and their sociopolitical groups, as well as other potential victim groups in the region. Processing also replicated and perpetuated the deaths themselves, thus magnifying and multiplying the power and perceived benefit to the aggressors. Perpetrators used the ritual processing of the physical remains of enemies to ply supernaturals with potent inducement to relieve disastrous natural conditions. With these actions, the aggressors also took proactive measures to reimagine and refashion the world as a place where they themselves exerted influence over competing sociopolitical groups and, indirectly, over the resources of the natural world.

It is likely that community-instigated violence in the context of ancestral Pueblo society in the northern San Juan region in the late AD 1200s was socially legitimated in ways that individual violence was not. That is, in prestate contexts, the largest identifiable, integrated social group—the community, in this case—typically holds the exclusive and legitimate right to exercise violent force. Thus, in all likelihood, the residents of the northern San Juan region held community-level violence and established rituals of performative violence to be legitimate actions within that specific cultural and historical context. Performative violence and the associated ritual actions utilizing the remains of enemies were therefore part of an internal cultural logic that was anchored temporally and spatially, and such events undoubtedly became woven into the collective social memory, oral traditions, and intergroup relationships for generations thereafter.

REFERENCES

Adams, Karen A., and Kenneth L. Petersen. 1999. "Environment." In *Colorado Prehistory: A Context Document for the Southern Colorado River Basin*, edited by William D. Lipe, Mark D. Varien and Richard H. Wilshusen, 14–50. Denver: Colorado Council of Professional Archaeologists.

Baker, Shane A. 1994. "The Question of Cannibalism and Violence in the Anasazi Culture: A Case Study from San Juan County, Utah." *Blue Mountain Shadows* 13: 30–41.

Benson, Larry, Kenneth Petersen, and John Stein. 2007. "Anasazi (Pre-Columbian Native-American) Migrations During the Middle-12th and Late-13th Centuries—Were they Drought Induced?" *Climatic Change* 83: 187–213.

Billman, Brian R., Patricia M. Lambert, and Banks L. Leonard. 2000. "Cannibalism, Warfare, and Drought in the Mesa Verde Region During the Twelfth Century AD." *American Antiquity* 65 (1): 145–178.

Bocinsky, R. Kyle, Brian S. Chisholm, and Brian M. Kemp. 2011. "Basketmaker III Turkey Use: Multiple Lines of Evidence." 76th Annual Meeting of the Society for American Archaeology, Sacramento, CA.

Cattanach, George S., Jr. 1980. *Long House: Mesa Verde National Park, Colorado*. Publications in Archeology, No. 7H. Washington, DC: National Park Service.

Dean, Jeffrey S., and Carla R. Van West. 2002. "Environment-Behavior Relationships in Southwestern Colorado." In *Seeking the Center Place: Archaeology and Ancient Communities in the Mesa Verde Region*, edited by Mark D. Varien and Richard H. Wilshusen, 81–99. Salt Lake City: University of Utah Press.

Decker, Kenneth W., and Larry L. Tieszen. 1989. "Isotopic Reconstruction of Mesa Verde Diet from Basketmaker III to Pueblo III." *Kiva* 55: 33–47.

Douglass, A. E. 1929. "The Secret of the Southwest Solved by Talkative Tree Rings." *National Geographic Magazine* 56: 736–770.

Driver, Jonathan C. 2002. "Faunal Variation and Change in the Northern San Juan Region." In *Seeking the Center Place: Archaeology and Ancient Communities in the Mesa Verde Region*, edited by Mark D. Varien and Richard H. Wilshusen, 143–160. Salt Lake City: University of Utah Press.

Eggan, Fred. 1983. "Comparative Social Organization." In *Southwest*, edited by Alfonso Ortiz, 723–742. Handbook of North American Indians, volume 10. W. C. Sturtevant, general editor. Washington, DC: Smithsonian Institution.

Ellis, Florence Hawley. 1951. "Patterns of Aggression and the War Cult in Southwestern Pueblos." *Southwestern Journal of Anthropology* 7: 177–201.

Ellis, Florence Hawley. 1979. "Laguna Pueblo." In *Southwest*, edited by Alfonso Ortiz, 438–449. Handbook of North American Indians, volume 9. W. C. Sturtevant, general editor. Washington, DC: Smithsonian Institution.

Fewkes, Jesse Walter. 1909. "Antiquities of the Mesa Verde National Park: Spruce-Tree House." *Bureau of American Ethnology Bulletin* 41: 1–57. Washington, DC: Government Printing Office.

France, Diane L. 1988. *A Human Burial from Dolores County, Colorado*. Cultural Resource Series, Number 24. Denver, CO: Bureau of Land Management.

Glowacki, Donna M. 2010. "The Social and Cultural Contexts of the Central Mesa Verde Region during the Thirteenth-Century Migrations." In *Leaving Mesa Verde: Peril and Change in the Thirteenth-Century Southwest*, edited by Timothy A. Kohler, Mark D. Varien, and Aaron M. Wright, 200–221. Tucson: University of Arizona Press.

Hurst, Winston B., and Christy G. Turner II. 1993. "Rediscovering the 'Great Discovery': Wetherill's First Cave 7 and Its Record of Basketmaker Violence." In *Anasazi Basketmaker: Papers from the 1990 Wetherill-Grand Gulch Symposium*, edited by Victoria M. Atkins, 142–191. Salt Lake City, Utah: Bureau of Land Management.

Katzenberg, M. Anne. 1992. *Human Skeletal Remains from Sand Canyon Pueblo Excavated from 1988–1991*. Cortez, CO: Crow Canyon Archaeological Center.

Keeley, Lawrence. 1996. *War Before Civilization: The Myth of the Peaceful Savage*. New York: Oxford University Press.

Kohler, Timothy A., C. D. Johnson, Mark D. Varien, Scott G. Ortman, Robert G. Reynolds, Z. Kobti, J. Cowan, K. Kolm, S. Smith, and L. Yap. 2007. "Settlement Ecodynamics in the Prehispanic Central Mesa Verde Region." In *The Model-Based Archaeology of Socionatural Systems*, edited by Timothy A. Kohler and S. van der Leeuw, 61–104. Santa Fe, NM: SAR Press.

Kohler, Timothy A., Mark D. Varien, and Aaron M. Wright, eds. 2010. *Leaving Mesa Verde: Peril and Change in the Thirteenth-Century Southwest*. Tucson: University of Arizona Press.

Kuckelman, Kristin A., ed. 2000. *The Archaeology of Castle Rock Pueblo: A Late-Thirteenth-Century Village in Southwestern Colorado*. Cortez, CO: Crow Canyon Archaeological Center, http://www.crowcanyon.org/castlerock.

Kuckelman, Kristin A., ed. 2007. *The Archaeology of Sand Canyon Pueblo: Intensive Excavations at a Late-Thirteenth-Century Village in Southwestern Colorado*. Cortez, CO: Crow Canyon Archaeological Center, http://www.crowcanyon.org/sandcanyon.

Kuckelman, Kristin A. 2010. "The Depopulation of Sand Canyon Pueblo, A Large Ancestral Pueblo Village in Southwestern Colorado." *American Antiquity* 75 (3): 497–525.

Kuckelman, Kristin A. 2017a. "Architecture and Village Layout." In *The Goodman Point Archaeological Project: Goodman Point Pueblo Excavations*, edited by Kristin A. Kuckelman. https://core.tdar.org/document/446779/the-goodman-point-archaeological-project-goodman-point-pueblo-excavations.

Kuckelman, Kristin A., ed. 2017b. *The Goodman Point Archaeological Project: Goodman Point Pueblo Excavations*. https://core.tdar.org/document/446779/the-goodman-point-archaeological-project-goodman-point-pueblo-excavations.

Kuckelman, Kristin A. 2017c. Village Depopulation. In *The Goodman Point Archaeological Project: Goodman Point Pueblo Excavations*, edited by Kristin A. Kuckelman. https://core.tdar.org/document/446779/the-goodman-point-archaeological-project-goodman-point-pueblo-excavations.

Kuckelman, Kristin A., Bruce A. Bradley, Melissa J. Churchill, and James H. Kleidon. 2007. "A Descriptive and Interpretive Summary of Excavations, by Architectural Block." In *The Archaeology of Sand Canyon Pueblo: Intensive Excavations at a Late-Thirteenth-Century Village in Southwestern Colorado*, edited by Kristin A. Kuckelman. Cortez, CO: Crow Canyon Archaeological Center, http://www.crowcanyon.org/sandcanyon.

Kuckelman, Kristin A., Ricky R. Lightfoot, and Debra L. Martin. 2002. "The Bioarchaeology and Taphonomy of Violence at Castle Rock and Sand Canyon Pueblos, Southwestern Colorado." *American Antiquity* 67: 486–513.

Lambert, Patricia M. 1999. "Human Skeletal Remains Recovered during the 1995–1996 Seasons." In *The Puebloan Occupation of the Ute Mountain Piedmont, Volume 5: Environmental and Bioarchaeological Studies*, edited by Brian R. Billman, 203–236. Phoenix, AZ: Soil Systems Publications in Archaeology.

Larson, Daniel O., Hector Neff, Donald A. Graybill, Joel Michaelson, and Elizabeth Ambos. 1996. "Risk, Climatic Variability, and the Study of Southwestern Prehistory: An Evolutionary Perspective." *American Antiquity* 6 (2): 217–241.

LeBlanc, Steven A. 1999. *Prehistoric Warfare in the American Southwest*. Salt Lake City: University of Utah Press.

Lipe, William D. 1995. "The Depopulation of the Northern San Juan: Conditions in the Turbulent 1200s." *Journal of Anthropological Archaeology* 14: 143–169.

Malotki, Ekkehart, and Ken Gary. 1999. "Hopisosont—'Human Cravers': Echoes of Anthropophagy in Hopi Oral Traditions." *European Review of Native American Studies* 13 (1): 9–15.

Malville, Nancy. 1989. "Two Fragmented Human Bone Assemblages from Yellow Jacket, Southwestern Colorado." *Kiva* 55: 3–22.

Mann, Michael E., Jose D. Fuentes, and Scott Rutherford. 2012. "Underestimation of Volcanic Cooling in Tree-Ring Based Reconstructions of Hemispheric Temperatures." *Natural Geoscience* 5: 202–205.

Matson, R. G. 2016. "The Nutritional Context of the Pueblo III Depopulation of the Northern San Juan: Too Much Maize?" *Journal of Archaeological Science: Reports* 5 (2016): 622–641.

Matson, R. G., and Brian S. Chisholm. 1991. "Basketmaker II Subsistence: Carbon Isotopes and Other Dietary Indicators from Cedar Mesa, Utah." *American Antiquity* 56: 444–459.

McCaffery, Harlan, Robert H. Tykot, Kathy D. Gore, and Beau R. DeBoer. 2014. "Stable Isotope Analysis of Turkey (*Meleagris gallopavo*) Diet from Pueblo II and Pueblo III Sites, Middle San Juan Region, Northwest New Mexico." *American Antiquity* 79 (2): 337–352.

Morris, Earl H. 1939. *Archaeological Studies in the La Plata District, Southwestern Colorado and Northwestern New Mexico*. Washington, DC: Carnegie Institution of Washington, Pub. 519.

Munro, Natalie D. 1994. "An Investigation of Anasazi Turkey Production in Southwestern Colorado." MA, Department of Archaeology, Simon Fraser University, Burnaby, British Columbia.

Nott, Breanne M. 2010. "Documenting Domestication: Molecular and Palynological Analysis of Ancient Turkey Coprolites from the American Southwest." MS, School of Biological Sciences, Washington State University, Pullman.

Ortman, Scott G., and Bruce A. Bradley. 2002. "Sand Canyon Pueblo: The Container in the Center." In *Seeking the Center Place: Archaeology and Ancient Communities in the Mesa Verde Region*, edited by Mark D. Varien and Richard H. Wilshusen, 41–78. Salt Lake City: University of Utah Press.

Osterholtz, Anna J. 2013. "Hobbling and Torture as Performative Violence: An Example from the Prehistoric Southwest." *Kiva* 78 (2): 123–144.

Parsons, Elsie Clews. 1939. *Pueblo Indian Religion*. Volumes 1 and 2. Chicago, IL: University of Chicago.

Parsons, Elsie Clews. 1974. "Some Aztec and Pueblo Parallels." In *The Mesoamerican Southwest: Readings in Archaeology, Ethnohistory, and Ethnology*, edited by Basil C. Hedrick, J. Charles Kelley, and Carroll L. Riley, 131–172. Carbondale: Southern Illinois University Press.

Petersen, Kenneth L. 1988. *Climate and the Dolores River Anasazi: A Paleoenvironmental Reconstruction from a 10,000 Year Pollen Record, La Plata Mountains, Southwestern Colorado*. Salt Lake City: University of Utah Press.

Rawlings, Tiffany A., and Jonathan C. Driver. 2010. "Paleodiet of Domestic Turkey, Shields Pueblo (5MT2307), Colorado: Isotopic Analysis and Its Implications for Care of a Household Domesticate." *Journal of Archaeological Science* 37 (10): 2433–2441.

Riches, David. 1986. "The Phenomenon of Violence." In *The Anthropology of Violence*, edited by David Riches, 1–27. New York: Blackwell.

Salzer, Matthew W. 2000. "Temperature Variabilty and the Northern Anasazi: Possible Implications for Regional Abandonment." *Kiva* 65 (4): 295–318.

Schröder, Ingo W., and Bettina E. Schmidt. 2001. "Introduction: Violent Imaginaries and Violent Practices." In *Anthropology of Violence and Conflict*, edited by Bettina E. Schmidt and Ingo W. Schröder, 1–24. London, New York: Routledge.

Stephen, Alexander M., ed. 1969 [1936]. *Hopi Journal of Alexander M. Stephen*, 2 volumes, edited by Elsie Clews Parsons. Contributions to Anthropology, Number 23. New York: Columbia University Press.

Stevenson, M.C. 1904. *The Zuni Indians: Their Mythology, Esoteric Fraternities and Ceremonies*. Bureau of American Ethnology, Bulletin Number 23. Washington, DC: Smithsonian Institution Press.

Stodder, Ann L.W., Anna J. Osterholtz, Kathy Mowrer, and Jason P. Chuipka. 2010. "Processed Human Remains from the Sacred Ridge Site: Context, Taphonomy, Interpretation." In *Animas-La Plata Project, Volume XV: Bioarchaeology*, edited by Elizabeth M. Perry, Ann L.W. Stodder and Charles A. Bollong, 279–415. SWCA Anthropological Research Paper No. 10. Phoenix, AZ: SWCA Environmental Consultants.

Street, David J. 2001. "The Dendrochronology of Long House, an Anasazi Cliff Dwelling in the Mesa Verde National Park, Colorado, USA." PhD Dissertation, University of Sheffield.

Strong, Pauline T. 1979. "Santa Ana Pueblo." In *Southwest*, edited by Alfonso Ortiz, 398–406. Handbook of North American Indians, volume 10. W.C. Sturtevant, general editor. Washington, DC: Smithsonian Institution.

Titiev, Mischa. 1992 [1944]. *Old Oraibi: A Study of the Hopi Indians of Third Mesa*. Santa Fe: University of New Mexico Press. (Reprint of Papers of the Peabody Museum of American Archaeology and Ethnology, Volume 22, Number 1. Cambridge, MA: Museum, Harvard University.)

Turner, Christy G., II, and Jacqueline A. Turner. 1999. *Man Corn: Cannibalism and Violence in the Prehistoric American Southwest*. Salt Lake City: University of Utah Press.

Van West, Carla R., and Jeffrey S. Dean. 2000. "Environmental Characteristics of the AD 900–1300 Period in the Central Mesa Verde Region." *Kiva* 66: 19–44.

Varien, Mark D. 2010. "Depopulation of the Northern San Juan Region." In *Leaving Mesa Verde: Peril and Change in the Thirteenth-Century Southwest*, edited by Timothy A. Kohler, Mark D. Varien and Richard H. Wilshusen, 1–33. Tucson: University of Arizona Press.

Varien, Mark D., Scott G. Ortman, Timothy A. Kohler, Donna M. Glowacki, and C. David Johnson. 2007. "Historical Ecology in the Mesa Verde Region: Results from the Village Ecodynamics Project." *American Antiquity* 72 (2): 273–299.

White, Tim D. 1992. *Prehistoric Cannibalism at Mancos 5MTUMR-2346*. Princeton, NJ: Princeton University Press.

Whitehead, Neil L. 2004. "On the Poetics of Violence." In *Violence*, edited by Neil L. Whitehead, 55–78. Santa Fe, NM: SAR Press.

Wright, Aaron M. 2006. "A Low-Frequency Paleoclimatic Reconstruction from the La Plata Mountains, Colorado, and Its Implications for Agricultural Paleoproductivity in the Mesa Verde Region." Unpublished MA thesis, Anthropology, Washington State University, Pullman.

Wright, Aaron M. 2010. "The Climate of the Depopulation of the Northern Southwest." In *Leaving Mesa Verde: Peril and Change in the Thirteenth-Century Southwest*, edited by Timothy A. Kohler, Mark D. Varien and Aaron M. Wright, 75–101. Tucson: University of Arizona Press.

5

The Poetics of Corpse Fragmentation and Processing in the Ancient Southwest

DEBRA L. MARTIN AND ANNA J. OSTERHOLTZ

This chapter builds on the previous chapter by Kristin Kuckelman (chapter 4, this volume) that describes what she suggests is ritualized modification of corpses that occurred in the San Juan region in the late thirteenth century. She links commingled, fragmentary, and partially burned deposits of human bone with particular locations within sites known to be ritual and sacred spaces. This linking of bone processing with ritual and symbolism has many implications for how corpse fragmentation can be better understood. While Kuckelman's study provides an in-depth analysis of temporally and spatially distinctive assemblages in the ancient Southwest, this study takes a broader view, looking at context, treatment, and disposition of human remains across multiple time periods for the whole region (figure 5.1).

Although the archaeological and bioarchaeological literature on human remains from the Southwest show a wide range of both similarities and differences, the evidence is routinely reduced to several variables, such as presence and absence of cut marks and the presence of burning and breakage (Turner and Turner 1999). However, the site- and context-specific bioarchaeological data manifest dimensional aspects of intentionality, motivation, symbolism, communication, and performance (Martin 2016). These assemblages are composed of human bones that have been culturally modified using stone tools to disarticulate and dismember corpses as well as to create some combination of fractures, splintering, burning, cut marks, and other signs of human effort (Ogilvie and Hilton 2000). While most agree that this demonstrates manipulation of the corpses by human agents around

DOI: 10.5876/9781646420612.c005

FIGURE 5.1. The Four Corners region, showing archaeological sites discussed.

the time of death, what to call these assemblages and how to understand their relationship to the rest of the communities that they belong is not well understood and continues to be debated in the literature (Martin 2016).

Many studies using disarticulated assemblages assign them all to one category, and one might question why there is such a strong tendency to focus on the common denominator (i.e., disarticulation and fragmentation) and not the variability (i.e., in types of processing, reduction of the body, number and placement of cut marks, morphology of cut marks by kerf walls, bones over- or underrepresented, bones missing, and the demography of the victims) (Kohler et al. 2014). The variability is culturally significant and implies that specialists or group members processing the corpses may have been guided by complex rules or mandates about when, why, and how to process the bones (Osterholtz 2014a).

Context and nuance are both important in the interpretation of violence but reducing all of these assemblages to a single category obscures context and nuance. Ignoring variability in the assemblages creates the false notion that violence (killing the victims, processing the corpses) is a monolithic activity that can be understood by the presence or absence of a single category of data, such as the presence of processing (Martin, Akins, and Toll 2014). Homogenizing the bone data in this way and refusing to acknowledge and analyze variability means that the studies end up saying very little about the nature of violence carried out by early nonstate and non-Western peoples (Pérez 2006). That is why understanding context and variability is so important.

CORPSE FRAGMENTATION, WARFARE, AND VIOLENCE IN PUEBLO GROUPS

Several often-cited studies by archaeologists interpret the majority of the disarticulated assemblages as behaviors having something to do with violence, either controlling social order through violence (Lekson 2002), keeping the peace though violence (Turner and Turner 1999), or violent actions related to stressful conditions that promoted warfare and other forms of violence (LeBlanc 1999). This linkage of disarticulated assemblages with ideas about the general role of violence as a response to stressful conditions (such as droughts, environmental degradation, and decreasing resources) essentially masks the possible meanings of body-processing within the broader cultural milieu. This is akin to reducing something like magic and sorcery to forms of violence. While magic may have aspects of violence, it is also a category of social behavior that regulates codes of conduct and that is deeply embedded within the cultural memory of the community. Direct violence is something physical and painful but equally important is indirect violence whereby enemies may be killed from a distance through sorcery or symbolically destroyed through corpse fragmentation (Whitehead and Finnström 2013). Thus, because anthropologists do not reduce magic and sorcery to a monolithic category (in this case, violence), corpse fragmentation should also be viewed as behaviors that are important parts of the fabric of the culture.

Briefly, the Pueblo I period (PI, AD 700–950) has been considered to be fraught with hand-to-hand combat and skirmishes defined by raiding and light warfare. Following several hundred years of forced "peace" in the Pueblo II period (PII, AD 900–1150), a more aggressive form of warfare flourished in the Pueblo III period (PIII, AD 1150–1300) (Kohler et al. 2014; LeBlanc 1999). The "peaceful" period in the middle is where many of the disarticulated bone assemblages show forms of bone processing and manipulation variously dubbed as "cannibalism" (Turner and Turner 1999) or "extreme processing" (EP) events (Kuckelman, Lightfoot, and Martin 2002). Although a number of interpretations have been advanced, in general EP events are considered to be evidence of violent outbursts of killing followed by postmortem processing that left the victims badly dismembered and possibly eaten (Billman, Lambert, and Leonard 2000; Kuckelman, Lightfoot, and Martin 2002).

This strategy of conflating corpse fragmentation with broader notions of warfare and violence has limited the potential for understanding the underlying poetics of violence and processing (Whitehead 2004). Warfare has been the focus of many prior interpretations of corpse fragmentation. But warfare is not simply an aggregation of violence and killing; rather, warfare is integrated within a political agenda that "engages allies, enemies, civilians and soldiers in a moment of violent interaction" and there is never a clear distinction between combatants and noncombatants, or between direct and indirect violence (Whitehead and Finnström 2013, 7–8). If warfare in the past is viewed with this messier and complex notion of what it entails, it permits something like corpse fragmentation to be analyzed with more than the victims in mind. Furthermore, the visual and perceptual aspects of warfare make it an extremely good tool for the perpetrators or actors to establish power and control. Thus, corpse fragmentation may be one of several ways warfare does its job of establishing power and control, but without examining this specific behavior on its own, the poetics of this form of violence (processing corpses) will remain elusive.

As envisioned by Whitehead, a poetics approach provides a way to link something like corpse mutilation with other forms of social interactions and social relations versus simply assuming it to be a form of violence that can be subsumed under warfare (Whitehead 2004). Poetics is a shorthand term for extracting meaning from a behavior or an entity that relies on linked theories about how things might work under certain circumstances. For example, Whitehead (2004) uses the phrase "poetics of violence" to invoke a reconception or reimagining of culturally sanctioned social violence as meaningful within historically situated contexts. While some theories of violence focus on the destructive and chaotic meaninglessness of violent acts, a poetics of violence would acknowledge those aspects but also frame violent behaviors as part of a choreography or performance, something staged and therefore fraught with meaning for the perpetrators, the victims, and any witnesses. If violence is reconceived as a cultural performance, it can be interrogated as a symbolic act that contains and conveys cultural meaning (Whitehead 2004). But this approach requires a rich contextualization of violence that connects it more directly with other cultural formations such as politics, religion, cosmology, ideology, and symbolism. Thus, all forms of violence against the living and the dead are both literal as well as symbolic and a poetics approach integrates thinking simultaneously about both.

Most archaeological explanations of violence in the ancient Southwest use a positivist-scientific approach and view violence as one of many ways to respond to conflict and stress (Billman, Lambert, and Leonard 2000; Kohler et al. 2014; Schachner 2015). However, a poetics approach relies on a phenomenological-interpretive approach and it places violence as a form of political practice, social discourse, and symbolic representation. The former approach relies on the binary that there is warfare and there is peace, and the empirical correlates of each of these conditions can be scientifically explained. A poetics approach lies in the gray areas between war and peace because it examines violence as a fundamental part of everyday life that is entwined with memories, histories, and identities. This more interpretive approach also suggests that violence is fundamentally built into the scaffolding that produces and maintains social structures that often favor the wealthy and punish the poor. Identifying inequality and differential access to resources becomes a fundamental way of unpacking violence in order to see how it works and when it is called upon to communicate prevailing codes of conduct and values (Scheper-Hughes and Bourgois 2004).

It also follows that violent acts, because they are staged and choreographed, are often highly ritualized, performative, and communicative (see Kuckelman, chapter 4, this volume). Violence and fear of violence need witnesses who understand the symbolism behind various acts and performances of violence; this shared understanding gives violence tremendous power and meaning within specific cultural contexts and specific historical moments. It is also why violence is so difficult to define in a universal way—what is considered violence in one culture may not be so in another. Additionally, it is why violent acts and behaviors are so cross-culturally diverse. Distinctive cultural notions of what kind of symbolism is appropriate for which acts of violence, and how that fits into larger foundational aspects of the culture, are important. For example, Fontein provides a contemporary case study of the multilayered meaning of the bones of the dead in Zimbabwe. He states that bones "animate a myriad of personal, kin, clan, class and political loyalties and struggles" and that these entanglements are powerful historically situated symbols that have both an "effective presence and emotive materiality" (Fontein 2010, 423). Why would we think that ancestral Pueblo corpse reduction and mutilation would not also animate symbolic and political actions?

This study utilizes the theoretical framework of poetics to reconceive ancestral Pueblo bone-processing as a culturally meaningful form of sociality, communication, and symbolism related to cosmology and ideology. Seen this way, the performance of corpse fragmentation represents the *embodiment of social norms* through its ritualized performance. Corpse fragmentation also becomes part of memory-making for the group, and this is alleged based on the fact that this form of violence spans the entire occupation of the region in precolonial times all the way to the postcolonial era (circa AD 800 to 1700).

As has been discussed by us in other venues (Martin 2016; Martin, Harrod, and Pérez 2013; Osterholtz 2013, 2016), corpse-processing was likely tied to deeply held cosmological beliefs in addition to political, economic, and cultural practices that endured over time but also likely differed temporally and spatially across the Southwest. Most scholars generally agree that the arid environment, and particularly the increasingly impoverished environmental conditions in the twelfth and thirteenth centuries, served as a stimulus for a range of behaviors. These included not only use of violence but migration, increased trade, and innovation in water retention (Spielmann et al. 2016). There is also archaeological evidence for fortified sites, palisades, defensive architecture, aggregation of communities, and structures interpreted as watchtowers (Haas and Creamer 1997; LeBlanc 1999; Wilcox and Haas 1994). Warfare (which in the ancestral Pueblo literature is described as raiding, ambush, intercommunity violence, and intra-ethnic or tribal clashes) and fear of attack are provided as the most likely reasons for the defensive architecture used in the period leading up to the tenth century (LeBlanc 1999, 119). However, osteological indications of warfare are mostly absent, and collections in general show little evidence of lethal injuries (Martin 2000, 284).

Symbolism in Ritual Massacres and Corpse Fragmentation

Among the 75 disarticulated assemblages reviewed in Turner and Turner (1999) as well as an additional 20 sites from the literature (Kohler et al. 2014), almost all exhibit signs of being the product of a massacre, in our opinion. Using a poetics framework, massacres can be seen as social projects often used to provide a regeneration or renewal of group identity or group power over others. Whitehead and Finnström have described massacres as being essentially "spectacides"—attacks waged not only to eliminate and kill a group but more as performative acts in front of witnesses in order to promote and perpetuate particular memories (Whitehead and Finnström 2013, 22). While there are many references to cannibalism as the major reason for the corpse fragmentation, we argue here that the primary motive was the spectacide of mass killings combined with other symbolic acts that likely included destruction of the bodies, anthropophagy, and trophy-taking.

One of the earliest disarticulated assemblages to be documented is from the archaeological site of Sacred Ridge (~AD 800) (Osterholtz 2014b; Potter and Chuipka 2010), where at least 33 individuals were systematically tortured by beating the bottoms and tops of the feet and cutting the ligaments of the foot (Osterholtz 2013) prior to being executed in a highly ritualized and ordered fashion. This meant that victims were kept alive but could not escape; subsequently they were lethally struck on the side of the head creating a deadly blunt-force trauma, likely with a large club. The bodies were defleshed, dismembered, and processed into small fragments. Cut-mark analysis suggests that ears, lips, and other body parts may have been taken as trophies. Blood residue was found in vessels and on implements.

As discussed in Kuckelman (chapter 4, this volume), later in time (AD 1280), a small Pueblo farming community perched high on a fairly isolated mesa was ambushed and at least 41 individuals were killed, including infants, children, teenagers, and adult males and females (Kuckelman, Lightfoot, and Martin 2002). Although only a small percentage of Castle Rock Pueblo has been excavated, the amount of human bone that was retrieved was clearly the end result of a massacre. Taphonomic analysis of the human remains revealed that individuals left on the ground may have been torn apart by scavengers. Other remains seem to represent secondary burials that occurred days after the massacre, possibly by returning family members. A small portion of the human remains found in a kiva showed cut marks and dismemberment that indicated trophy-taking or anthropophagy. Thus, although this episode surely obliterated many of the local villagers, other symbolic activities seemed to be going on as well, such as trophy-taking and body-processing and reduction.

A third example occurred in the fall of 1700. Malotki (1993) and Brooks (2016) present accounts of the destruction of Hopi villages by other Hopi. The best-known is the demise of Awat'ovi. The general theme of stories about the destruction of Awat'ovi and the other villages is that the inhabitants of the villages strayed from traditional practices and beliefs, an extremely serious transgression for the Hopi. The other Hopi initially refused to consider destroying Awat'ovi on the grounds that they were fellow Hopi. Eventually, however, Awat'ovi was destroyed because they had strayed from Hopi ideals and so it was deemed that the entire community was consumed by witchcraft (Malotki 1993, 275–295). In a sense, the accused *villages* were ritually killed, not just the families and clans living there. The mass grave in Polacca Wash resulting from the Awat'ovi executions is one of the assemblages of disarticulated human remains that has been claimed to be the product of cannibalism (Turner and Turner 1999, 56). But in this example, the claim of cannibalism is inconsistent with the ethnohistoric data. The processed human remains, based on the evidence cited above, are most likely the result of a longstanding Puebloan belief in witchcraft, and the subsequent execution of transgressive nonconformists (Brooks 2016, 393).

Klusemann has studied the nature of massacres as a historical process (versus a discrete event) and he suggests that all massacres are preceded by political-economic and cultural events that shape the ideas of the perpetrators that a massacre would solve a perceived problem (Klusemann 2012). Local dynamics shape the how, why, when, and where of any given massacre, so context and history are crucial to examine when trying to understand the broader implications and effects of mass killing. Klusemann has also shown that the "sequential unfolding of micro-interactions and emotional dynamics" is important for understanding the symbolic meanings attached to massacres by the perpetrators, survivors, and witnesses, as well as distant audiences who hear about the event (Klusemann 2010, 272). This is why each massacre has different mortality rates and demographic profiles, and why some include corpse fragmentation, where the violence extends beyond killing people to desecrating the bodies as well (Nahoum-Grappe 2002).

The distinctive characteristics of these three massacre sites that are reflected in many of the other disarticulated and processed assemblages include a demographic pattern that reflects whole families, extended families, or communities/clans. They contain adult males and females, children, and infants. The remains are not formally buried and most of the bones show signs of perimortem trauma and processing. This includes blunt-force trauma to all parts of the body, cut marks, scrape marks, percussive pitting, fractures, burning, commingling, dental fractures, and broken noses. These have been interpreted to suggest processing of the corpse that includes trophy-taking (largely soft-tissue parts), defleshing, dismembering, and breakage of almost all possible bone elements (Osterholtz 2013; Potter and Chuipka 2010; White 1992). This generalized pattern is unique to massacres in the Southwest and suggests strong regional codes of conduct about how corpse fragmentation should be carried out (Ogilvie and Hilton 2000). These data suggest there may have been culturally appropriate ways in which extreme processing occurred and this basic pattern changed little through time, at least in the regions where this is found (i.e., the Colorado Plateau).

Based on data culled from Turner and Turner (1999) and Kohler and colleagues (2014), the current known distribution of disarticulated and fragmentary assemblages are spread throughout the Pueblo occupation. Much has been made by these researchers that this is a phenomenon seen in high frequencies in the Pueblo III phase. A perusal of all of the publications on processed bone across time reveals that these assemblages also occur in the earliest Pueblo I and subsequent Pueblo II periods, although in lower frequencies (Martin 2016). We have argued that these lower frequencies are more likely a function of fewer archaeological sites in general, and fewer that were fully excavated, rather than that processing was not part of the culture at those times.

The longevity of extreme processing through multiple social transitions, including increasing reliance on agriculture, increasing population size, and religious changes, is suggestive of its overall significance. The similarities in processing methodologies have been demonstrated for Sacred Ridge and Mancos (Osterholtz 2014a); there is a large degree of continuity between the two sites despite their being separated by hundreds of years. While much of this is likely due to biology (i.e., the structure of the hip necessitates similar procedures for dismemberment), there are differences that suggest either personal preference on the part of the practitioners or small changes in acceptable processing procedures through time (or a combination of both).

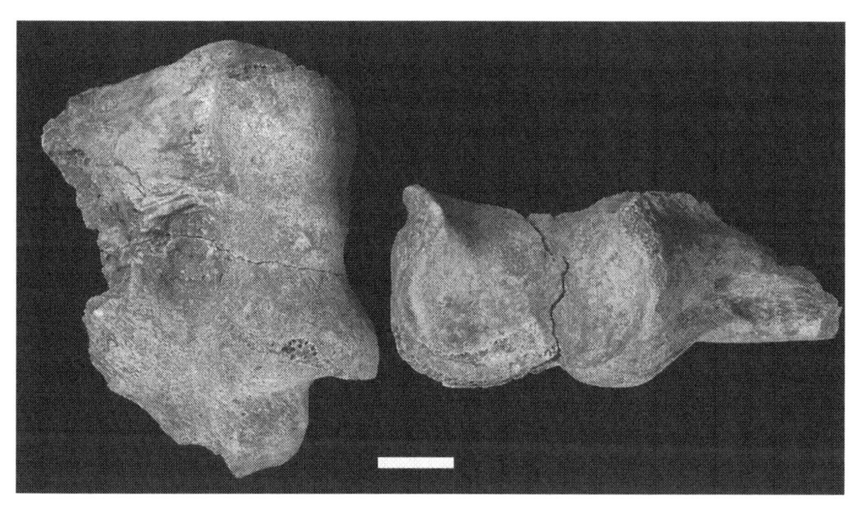

FIGURE 5.2. Articulated elbow from Sacred Ridge.

Processing of bodies along the lines of extreme processing (Kuckelman, Lightfoot, and Martin 2000) should be viewed as a complete deconstruction of the human body. The bodies at Sacred Ridge were systematically disassembled. In only one instance was an articulated joint recovered: an elbow consisting of an articulated olecranon process of the ulna and olecranon fossa of the humerus (figure 5.2). Only in rare cases could facial bone be associated with cranial vaults or mandibles. Disassembly of the body was complete, with the long bones being broken into fragments rarely longer than 5 mm in length. Signs of processing are evident from the top of the head to the toes of the feet and everywhere in between. For a thorough discussion of typical postmortem processing, see discussions by Stodder and colleagues (2010), Osterholtz (2013, 2014a, 2016), and White (1992), all of which describe element-by-element patterns of postmortem destruction of the body.

The fragments of different individuals were mixed together and it would have been impossible to identify specific individuals once processing began. In the case of Sacred Ridge, the assemblage also contained the remains of at least six dogs that were also heavily processed. In essence, the individuals subjected to processing were deprived of their humanity as well as their individuality. They would not only have been unrecognizable as individuals but also as human (Osterholtz 2013). The intermixing of the individuals, regardless of age at death or sex, with each other and with their dogs, and their placement outside the normal burial program, would have removed them from a normal cosmological place. The inability to mourn them along culturally appropriate lines further removes them from normal society (Pérez

2012). This separation continued through time, and this assemblage was repatriated separately from those who had been buried along "normal" lines. They were seen as separate and different, and were reburied in a commingled state, separated from the rest of the community.

Violent Identity Politics

Ancestral Puebloan people sustained their social identities and their communities not only through many layers of cosmology and beliefs, but also through the use of violence that was both mundane and extraordinary for its endurance across many generations and its creation of powerful memories that reinforced Pueblo values (Whiteley 2008). Oral tradition as analyzed by ethnographers suggest that the Pueblo people lived in societies where cycles of ritual acts of purification were deeply engrained (Malotki 1993). Effort to return communities who have experienced cultural rupture to a state of harmony and balance are carried out not through gentle reform, but rather through overwhelming supernatural force and intense annihilation of suspects (Brooks 2016). While massacres were an extreme expression of this, other forms of violence that facilitated social projects also existed alongside of massacres. For example, raiding and captivity that has been documented ethnohistorically could have linked communities and motivated trade, diffusion, and possibly marriages (Martin et al. 2008).

Massacres may have been somewhat synonymous with witch executions and ritual dismemberment because these combined actions communicated across both natural and supernatural spheres of influence while emphasizing ancestral ties and delegating spiritual power to elites. Body parts placed in sacred places such as kivas likely had memory-making components (Kuckelman, chapter 4, this volume). The endurance of distinctly Puebloan forms of violence over many generations and across many cultural upheavals and environmental catastrophies (AD 800–1700) suggest that it was part of the toolkit for negotiating social change and navigating environmental uncertainties. The complexity and symbolic force of violence speaks to its importance on an everyday level. Therefore, the events that archaeologists think of as discrete historical moments are better realized as long-term processual events with a persistent internal cultural logic that gets reinforced with each spectacide (Whitehead and Finnström 2013, 22).

Another useful way to reconceptualize some of the motivations and social projects behind the use of things such as body-processing is by considering these acts as politically motivated. Pérez developed a model based on theories about the ways that violence is culturally incorporated or avoided during times of increasing uncertainty (Pérez 2012, 16). As he points out, violence can have differential effects, depending on what scale is being examined: for example, it can be looked at on the four levels of the individual, the household, the community, and the intergroup. Drawing on the theoretical approach of Robben (2000), Pérez developed a framework for the ancient Southwest that demonstrated that violence and processing of the bodies make the most sense if viewed as political acts. His concept of the "politicization of the dead" is based on the idea that the corpse is a transitional object for both the perpetrators and the victims, centering on the passage from life to death (Robben 2000, 85). A form of physical and psychological violence is waged via both political and sociocultural violence. The political violence is manifested by the "annihilation" of the dead. The complete destruction of the human remains symbolizes the power over those who were deemed to be causing problems. The disarticulation and mutilation of the bodies symbolizes the political dismemberment of the vanquished and emphasizes their total subjugation while reinforcing the power and dominant ideology of the victors (Pérez 2012). The absence/annihilation of the corpse creates the inability to perform burial rites, and this can produce anxiety and impair mourning.

This politicization of the dead, through the use of violence, may explain why the disarticulated assemblages show variability in number of individuals as well as in age and sex. Perhaps these differences reflect variations in the kinds of political messages being delivered, and in the general relationship between the dead and the living. Some fragmentary assemblages may represent the execution of witches, but others may have been designed to create a "spectacle" or make a statement. Through the "display" of the remains, the victors can demonstrate their power and strength. By killing the young and old alike, and reducing them to an unrecognizable mass, the perpetrators create a substantial psychological impact on the regional interaction sphere in which they were operating.

This model facilitates integrating the bioarchaeological and ethnohistoric data on ancestral Puebloan cosmology and ideology. Kluckhohn and Strodtbeck (1961, 298) state that "Pueblo culture and society are integrated to an unusual degree, all sectors being bound together by a consistent, harmonious set of values, which pervade and homogenize the categories of world view, ritual, art, social organization, economic activity and social control." This integration makes it difficult to isolate any single aspect of Pueblo culture, including violence. The fact that Pueblo people live in extremely close proximity to each other explains the need to adhere strictly to community norms (Hawley 1950, 153). Pueblo children are taught at an early age to conform to Puebloan beliefs (Kluckhohn and Strodtbeck 1961, 298). Although there is individual autonomy, "the great emphasis on freedom of behavior is checked by a fear of non-conformity" (Titiev 1968, 65). Any individual who strays from the norms or who "thirsts for power" is subject to accusations of being a witch (Kluckhohn and Strodtbeck 1961, 297), the ramifications of which already have been discussed.

The sense of community goes beyond the individual village to the entire cluster of villages. Although not engaging in warfare in the modern sense of standing armies, the ancient Pueblos clearly engaged in warlike behaviors that resulted in the decimation of entire villages. The definition of warfare used here is that of "organized, purposeful group action, directed against another group involving the actual or potential application of lethal force" (Ferguson 1984, 5). Warfare and other forms of violence, integrated with the rest of Puebloan life, had economic, ritual, and political ramifications. An offensive against a village would need to be quite large, but ethnographic accounts suggest that 400 warriors from allied villages could be amassed for an attack (Hill and Lange 1982, 69).

It is possible that the full explanation for these complex processed assemblages may never be known, but it is important not to reduce them to analytical and imprecise categories such as cannibalism or violence. This kind of reductionist analysis of the data and interpretation leaves out all of the rich variability that is known to exist, and also plays into reinforcing stereotypes about indigenous people as excessively violent. Bringing a poetics framework into play permits thinking about the diverse data coming from the bones along with oral tradition, ethnography, and archaeology in ways that address the variability instead of factoring it out of the equation entirely. The motivations behind corpse mutilation and reduction were complex but were also deeply embedded within both the broad cosmological belief system as well as the everyday cultural ideologies that people lived by. To see any form of violence or processing of bodies as being outside of the cultural belief system is not productive. The approach taken here (and in other chapters in this volume) aims to open up how violence and corpse-handling is interpreted.

CONCLUSION

The agency of the dead in consort with the living is ever present. All human groups are guided and structured by interactions with the dead and as the ancestral Pueblo data suggest, the manipulation of the dead ensures the functioning of economies, political actions, cosmologies, and communities. For these reasons, the study of violence in bioarchaeological contexts must go beyond the proximate causes of violence and seek the underlying and historical precedents that create the need for violent actions. To do so requires the use of a theoretical framework that is responsive to locally constructed, historically contingent, and culturally sanctioned behaviors that produce and reproduce violence over many generations.

For the Pueblo people, violence is deeply symbolic, it is performed through ritual, and it is passed on in codes of conduct. Culturally sanctioned violence has multiple actors: perpetrators, witnesses, and victims. Violence is necessarily relational and dynamic. Destroying a particular demographic or a sacred place becomes all the more powerful because its symbolic nature is understood by the target audience. The violence becomes part of a larger cosmological narrative, tying the past, present, and future together as well as illuminating relationships between the living and the dead. Some locations were permanently changed by the inclusion of processed human remains. At Sacred Ridge, there are no signs of habitation throughout the Ridges Basin postdating the massacre. Other places, such as Mancos, show occupation of the space after the inclusion of the assemblages. Indeed, the rooms with human remains show occupation in later periods. Could this indicate the arrival of a new social or corporate group (such as a new moiety or clan) to the site? Or has the meaning behind extreme processing changed between the time of Sacred Ridge and Mancos? Study of the ancestral Puebloan groups during dynamic and tumultuous periods (circa AD 700 to European contact) offers important insights into how humans knit together strategic responses to threats and problems encroaching on their ability to survive.

REFERENCES

Billman, Brian R., Patricia M. Lambert, and Banks L. Leonard. 2000. "Cannibalism, Warfare, and Drought in the Mesa Verde Region During the Twelfth Century AD." *American Antiquity* 65 (1): 145–178.

Brooks, James F. 2016. *Mesa of Sorrows: A History of the Awat'ovi Massacre*. New York: W.W. Norton.

Ferguson, Brian. 1984. "Introduction: Studying War." In *Warfare, Culture, and Environment*, edited by Brian Ferguson, 1–81. Orlando: Academic Press.

Fontein, Joost. 2010. "Between Tortured Bodies and Resurfacing Bones: The Politics of the Dead in Zimbabwe." *Journal of Material Culture* 15 (4): 423–448.

Haas, Jonathan, and Winifred Creamer. 1997. "Warfare among the Pueblos: Myth, History, and Ethnology." *Ethnohistory* 44 (2): 235–261.

Hawley, Florence M. 1950. "The Mechanics of Perpetuation in Pueblo Witchcraft." In *For the Dean*, edited by E. K. Reed and D. S. King, 143–158. Tucson, AZ: Hohokam Museums Association and Southwestern Monuments Association.

Hill, W. W., and C. H. Lange. 1982. *An Ethnology of Santa Clara Pueblo*. Albuquerque: University of New Mexico Press.

Kluckhohn, F. R., and F. L. Strodtbeck. 1961. *Variations in Value Orientations*. Westport, CT: Greenwood Press.

Klusemann, Stephan. 2010. "Micro-Situational Antecedents of Violent Atrocity." *Sociological Forum* 25 (2): 272–295.

Klusemann, Stephan. 2012. "Massacres as Process: A Micro-Sociological Theory of Internal Patterns of Mass Atrocities." *European Journal of Criminology* 9 (5): 468–480.

Kohler, Timothy A., Scott G. Ortman, C. M. Grundtisch, S. M. Fitzpatrick, and S. M. Cole. 2014. "The Better Angels of Their Nature: Declining Violence through Time among Prehispanic Farmers of the Pueblo Southwest." *American Antiquity* 79 (3): 444–464.

Kuckelman, Kristin A., Ricky R. Lightfoot, and Debra L. Martin. 2000. "Changing Patterns of Violence in the Northern San Juan Region." *Kiva* 66 (1): 147–165.

Kuckelman, Kristin A., Ricky R. Lightfoot, and Debra L. Martin. 2002. "The Bioarchaeology and Taphonomy of Violence at Castle Rock and Sand Canyon Pueblos, Southwestern Colorado." *American Antiquity* 67: 486–513.

LeBlanc, Steven A. 1999. *Prehistoric Warfare in the American Southwest*. Salt Lake City: The University of Utah Press.

Lekson, Stephen H. 2002. "War in the Southwest, War in the World." *American Antiquity* 67 (4): 607–624.

Malotki, Ekkehart, ed. 1993. *Hopi Ruin Legends: Kiqotutuwutsi*. Narrated by M. Lomatuway'ma, L. Lomatuway'ma, and S. Namingha. Lincoln: University of Nebraska Press.

Martin, Debra L. 2000. "Bodies and Lives: Biological Indicators of Health Differentials and Division of Labor by Sex." In *Women and Men in the Prehispanic Southwest: Labor, Power and Prestige*, edited by P. L. Crown, 267–300. Sante Fe, NM: SAR Press.

Martin, Debra L. 2016. "Hard Times in Dry Lands: Making Meaning of Violence in the Ancient Southwest." *Journal of Anthropological Research* 72 (1): 1–23.

Martin, Debra L., Nancy J. Akins, Bradley J. Crenshaw, and Pamela K. Stone. 2008. "Inscribed on the Body, Written in the Bones: The Consequences of Social Violence at La Plata." In *Social Violence in the Prehispanic American Southwest*, edited by D. L. Nichols and P. L. Crown, 98–122. Tucson: University of Arizona Press.

Martin, Debra L., Nancy J. Akins, and H. Wolcott Toll. 2014. "Disarticulated and Disturbed, Processed and Eaten? Cautionary Notes from the La Plata Assemblage (AD 1000–1150)." In *Commingled and Disarticulated Human Remains*, edited by Anna J. Osterholtz, Kathryn M. Baustian, and Debra L. Martin, 129–147. New York: Springer.

Martin, Debra L., Ryan P. Harrod, and Ventura R. Pérez. 2013. *Bioarchaeology: An Integrated Approach to Working with Human Remains*. New York: Springer.

Nahoum-Grappe, Véronique. 2002. "The Anthropology of Extreme Violence: The Crime of Desecration." *International Social Science Journal* 54 (174): 549–557.

Ogilvie, Marsha D., and Charles E. Hilton. 2000. "Ritualized Violence in the Prehistoric American Southwest." *International Journal of Osteoarchaeology* 10: 27–48.

Osterholtz, Anna J. 2013. "Hobbling and Torture as Performative Violence: An Example from the Prehistoric Southwest." *Kiva* 78 (2): 123–144.

Osterholtz, Anna J. 2014a. "Extreme Processing at Mancos and Sacred Ridge: The Value of Comparative Studies." In *Commingled and Disarticulated Human Remains: Working Toward Improved, Theory, Method, and Data*, edited by Anna J. Osterholtz, Kathryn M. Baustian, and Debra L. Martin, 105–128. New York: Springer.

Osterholtz, Anna J. 2014b. "Patterned Processing as Performative Violence at Sacred Ridge." 79th Annual Meeting of the Society for American Archaeology, Austin, TX.

Osterholtz, Anna J. 2016. "Each One the Same: Performance, Demography, and Violence at Sacred Ridge." 2016 Meeting of the American Association of Physical Anthropologists, Atlanta, GA.

Pérez, Ventura R. 2006. "The Politicization of the Dead: An Analysis of Cutmark Morphology and Culturally Modified Human Remains from La Plata and Peñasco Blanco (AD 900–1300)." Unpublished PhD dissertation, Anthropology, University of Massachusetts, Amherst.

Pérez, Ventura R. 2012. "The Politicization of the Dead: Violence as Performance, Politics as Usual." In *The Bioarchaeology of Violence*, edited by Debra L. Martin, Ryan P. Harrod, and Ventura Pérez, 13–28. Gainesville: University Press of Florida.

Potter, James, and Jason P. Chuipka. 2010. "Perimortem Mutilation of Human Remains in an Early Village in the American Southwest: A Case for Ethnic Violence." *Journal of Anthropological Archaeology* 29 (4): 507–523.

Robben, A.C.G.M. 2000. "The Assault of Basic Trust: Disappearances, Protest, and Reburial in Argentina." In *Cultures Under Siege: Collective Violence and Trauma*, edited by A.C.G.M. Robben and M.M. Suárez-Orozco, 70–101. Cambridge, UK: Cambridge University Press.

Schachner, Gregson. 2015. "Ancestral Pueblo Archaeology: The Value of Synthesis." *Journal of Archaeological Research* 23: 49–113.

Scheper-Hughes, Nancy, and Philippe Bourgois. 2004. "Introduction: Making Sense of Violence." In *Violence in War and Peace: An Anthology*, edited by Nancy Scheper-Hughes and Philippe Bourgois, 1–32. Malden, MA: Blackwell Publishing.

Spielmann, Katherine A, Matthew A. Peeples, D.M. Glowacki, and A. Dugmore. 2016. "Early Warning Signals of Social Transformation: A Case Study from the US Southwest." *PLoS One* 11 (10): e0163685.

Stodder, Ann L.W., Anna J. Osterholtz, Kathy Mowrer, and Jason P. Chuipka. 2010. "Processed Human Remains from the Sacred Ridge Site: Context, Taphonomy, Interpretation." In *Animas-La Plata Project, Volume XV: Bioarchaeology*, edited by Elizabeth M. Perry, Ann L.W. Stodder, and Charles A. Bollong, 279–415. Phoenix, AZ: SWCA Environmental Consultants.

Titiev, Misha. 1968. *Old Oraibi: A Study of the Hopi Indians of Third Mesa*. New York: Kraus Reprint.

Turner, Christy G., II, and Jacqueline A. Turner. 1999. *Man Corn: Cannibalism and Violence in the Prehistoric American Southwest*. Salt Lake City: University of Utah Press.

White, Tim D. 1992. *Prehistoric Cannibalism at Mancos 5MTUMR-2346*. Princeton, NJ: Princeton University Press.

Whitehead, Neil L. 2004. "On the Poetics of Violence." In *Violence*, edited by Neil L. Whitehead, 55–78. Santa Fe, NM: SAR Press.

Whitehead, Neil L., and Sverker Finnström. 2013. *Virtual War and Magical Death: Technologies and Imaginaries for Terror and Killing*, Neil L. Whitehead and Sverker Finnström, eds. Cultures and Practice of Violence Veries: Durham, NC, and London: Duke University Press.

Whiteley, Peter. 2008. "The Discourse of Cannibalism at Awat'ovi." In *Social Violence in the Prehispanic American Southwest*, edited by Patricia Crown and Deborah L Nichols, 184–215. Tucson: University of Arizona Press.

Wilcox, David R., and Jonathan Haas. 1994. "The Scream of the Butterfly: Competition and Conflict in the Prehistoric Southwest." In *Themes in Southwest Prehistory*, edited by George J. Gumerman, 211–238. Santa Fe, NM: SAR Press.

PART 2

Europe, Eurasia, and Africa

6

Poetics of the House

Changing Realities of Body and Person in Aksumite Mortuary Practice

DILPREET SINGH BASANTI

Every creature, once born, will seek to live until it cannot. Yet that creature may not always be what we suppose. In our society, the subject is clear: it is whatever is beneath the skin. In other cultures, however, the body may not be a simple shell and a person may extend beyond their ostensible confines to create other kinds of entities, such as collectives, hybrids, ghosts, ancestors, nations, deities, and so on. Since these entities defy our standards of skin as a marker of the real, we may see them as only "socially defined" (i.e., not really "real"), but in the processes of their formation they are not dissimilar from the relationships between swarms of cells, constituent proteins and amino acids, bacteria, and other living forms that compose the body. The body, while seemingly whole, is actually several creatures interacting and held together by the skin (which is itself a swarm of cells constantly replaced). The interactions of the body become so tightly wound that their constituents lose their independence, allowing a new and greater entity to emerge. The interactions between people, though looser, may also create such creatures, in the sense that those entities acquire their own existence and then begin to drive the mechanics of biology/society around them. The body cannot define the form of these new creatures but must instead be utilized in other ways to write and rewrite the relationships that make such arrangements possible. Through this process, interactions generate creatures, and those creatures spin realities.

Through simple social rites or poetic acts, societies bind the body's buzzing swarms into different creatures based on the relationships they most value.

DOI: 10.5876/9781646420612.c006

Thinking through "poetics" pushes us to move from looking at symbols and symbolic performances only for their supposed referents or functional outcomes and to instead see how those symbols are used in enacting a larger, meaningful social order (Whitehead 2002; 2004, 67–68). Here, the way poetic acts amplify meaning gives them power to rearrange interactions and reconfigure realities. This generative nature of poetics can help us understand the shared values people are trying to enact as reality, so that every iteration or departure becomes a meaningful event.

This chapter uses this idea of the poetic to explain a sequence of events that occurred in the ancient Aksumite kingdom (AD 50–700) in northern Ethiopia. An Aksumite community that buried its dead in a cemetery known now as the Northern Stelae Field (NSF) found itself in tension as it negotiated between two burial rites: group burial around stelae and burials in individual sarcophagi. It is not immediately clear why these rites should have been seen as antagonistic to each other but looking at how stelae burial produced shared meanings among Aksumites can reveal the challenge posed by sarcophagi—these were the "poetics of the house."

For the NSF community, the primary entity of the stelae tradition was the group, rather than the individual. The stelae, as harbors for collective burial and social memory, were much more instrumental in creating the group than was the individual body. This newly made group-actor was something akin to a "social house." This was not true with the introduction of sarcophagus burial, which appears to have unraveled these prior relationships. Rites and symbolisms of stone, house, body, and memory that defined the poetics of the house set the terms for how sarcophagus burial could be understood. This chapter thus begins by considering the relationship bodies have to actors through theories of personhood. It then moves to looking at the importance of poetics in establishing those relationships and what that meant for the way of life that was challenged by the prospect of sarcophagus burial at Aksum.

BODIES OUT OF PERSONS

Theories of personhood challenge our ideas of how bodies relate to actors in the archaeological record. Anthropologists first studied personhood to help push against long-ingrained ideas of the impartible individual as the basic acting "person" in a society. Early on, Marcel Mauss explained how people in Puebloan societies of the southwest United States did not always operate as individual actors but instead derived their roles from predetermined ideas of the kind of "person" they were supposed to be (Mauss 1985). Mauss describes how the society had a limited number of forenames, each of which came with a defined role that individuals were supposed to act out. According to Mauss, these roles were set out along with a number of other practices to help define one's position in a clan, so that the "role of all of them is to really act out . . . the prefigured totality of the life of the clan" (Mauss 1985, 6). The status of the clan as the basic acting unit reconfigured individual personhoods, so that the basic persons were already there and simply wrapped themselves in newly made bodies at birth.

Later studies of personhood elaborated a range of ways that bodies relate to social actors. "Fractal" (Wagner 1991) or "dividual" (Strathern 1988) personhoods examined persons as constituted from different elements distributed throughout a network of relationships. Societies in Melanesia, for example, saw people as temporarily dividing themselves to give to others in ceremonial gift-exchanges, and would themselves become authored in these exchanges with others (Strathern 1988). These ideas were taken to mortuary archaeology to explain how the fragmentation, circulation, and eventual deposition of bodies portrayed a sense of "dividual" personhood (Chapman 2000; Duncan and Schwarz 2014; Jones 2005). Individual personhoods were also found outside of Western contexts, though with variable relationships with the body (Wilkinson 2013). Other studies examined configurations of body and person in animal/human relations, especially when considering mortuary contexts of mixed depositions. Viveiros de Castro (1998, 2004) explains that in Amerindian society, people and animals are made of essentially the same internal "stuff"—a single soul instead of separate ones—which means that putting on a jaguar's body is all that is required to change a person into a jaguar. Drawing inspiration from these ideas, Conneller has examined the transformations of people to deer in the mortuary practices at Starr Carr through the wearing of deer masks (Conneller 2004). In another study, the mixing of bear bones with human skeletons in Upper Paleolithic Siberian graves helped enact a reality in which bears and humans shared a common personhood (or "bearhood") (Losey et al. 2013). The "body" here was modified in a way that captures the closeness of the relationships between ancient peoples and animals that were key to their societies, blurring the distinction between the two. Other relational approaches have looked at how animals, objects, or landscapes could also become persons (Argent 2010; Bray 2009; Hill 2013; Wilkinson 2013). Still, in other worlds, the person may be a group or lineage, so that bodies actually restrict people from what they really are and must be dried out, defleshed, and reused in other ways to free the spirit and allow group members to retain a presence of the departed (Bloch 1971; Crossland 2013; Hertz 1960). These new ancestors and ghosts then dictate the pace of society around them and define the personhood of the group.

In all these examples, the varied understandings of personhood point to different sets of interactions that were important in defining the central actor and the subsequent reality that their bodies take on. It is quite easy to see these cases as simply "social" interpretations of an objective biology—different viewpoints of a body we all see and know—and thereby dismiss the realities of societies all over the world. For us, biology is real and self-evident, defined by the skin. Yet the skin may not be the paramount marker of the creature and there are other types of actors that may extend beyond the skin. Groups, for example, are often seen as simple accumulations or collections of things merely existing together, so that the individual in the body comes to be seen as "biological" as compared to the group, which is "social" and "skinless." Yet in biology, early life is thought to have arisen from interactions between amino acids, which took on new structural, biochemical, and functional repertoires through their own emerging properties. Over time, those interactions formed increasingly complex entities, including biochemical layers separating internal and external environments: a cell wall (Dyson 1985; Eigen and Schuster 1979; Hoffmeyer 2008; Hordijk, Hein, and Steel 2010; Kauffman 1986, 1993). In this sense, interactions create entities that emerge their own properties, and so we can consider cases of "skinless" creatures as a more nascent form of such development—the creature is something that is always coming into form, and it is not clear where, in the scale of ever-tightening interactions and interdependencies, it becomes a "being." Ant colonies are one example: it is the entire colony that is the organism rather than the individual ant, as it is ant colonies that reproduce other ant colonies rather than individual ants (Gordon 2010). As part of this organization, individual ants are written to be sterile. These dynamics of reproduction are then an emergent property of the entire group, and the entire ant colony is the creature or central actor. If we focus on how interactions may processually create such entities, then human social groups, such as families or kin groups, may also be actors themselves. Human social groups are far more ephemeral arrangements, so individual members retain autonomy, but this does mean that groups have their own form: Individuals are defined partly by their membership to a group, rather than solely by their own properties. In this way, in societies where group personhood is prized, it is the group that acts, and the reality of the body then acquires a different form. Our Western delineation of the skin as defining the "creature" then fails to define the actual actor.

MULTIPLE ONTOLOGIES OF THE BODY AND THE POETIC

Cultures are not necessarily defined by a single reality of the body, however; multiple understandings of the body or personhoods may be in play simultaneously, sometimes in contradiction (Graham 2009; Harris and Robb 2012; Tarlow 2010). If realities are generated by social relationships, then they are constantly coming into being, and shifting and negotiating with other realities as social relationships themselves are continuously renegotiated. Bodies are therefore always in flux and it is through poetics they may be bound as specific realities at any given moment.

Annemarie Mol gives us an example: in her ethnography of atherosclerosis (the hardening and restriction of arteries) at a Dutch university hospital, she shows how bodies can be seen as different creatures depending on social context (Mol 2002). Bodies move from being machines on operating tables that doctors perform surgery on to social beings who require phone calls to their family. When a body is lying on a dissection table, Mol notes that a cloth covers its face to afford dignity, so that one sense of the creature can remain social while the other is worked on (Mol 2002, 126). The body then takes on two realities—one is a social creature; the other is a machine with a malfunctioning part inside. Both of these understandings of the body are already embedded in society and in material culture (Harris and Robb 2012), but it is the rite that snaps them into place at a given time. The transformation of the body from human to machine is done by unraveling the previous relationships (as friend, family member, etc.) and rewriting a new one with the doctor, and it is the symbolic placing the cloth that both enacts one reality while retaining a possibility for the other. These realities then impact procedure and practice, as the pathology technician has to fill the belly and thorax, sew up the body, clean the blood, and dress it up in a way that the families can say goodbye while only seeing one version of the creature. This action functions as a poetic: The cloth is a symbol, but how it is placed gives it a power to rearrange the creature into a specific medical body.

Mol's study helps demonstrate how a simple social rite (placing a cloth) can carry meaning far larger than itself, and thereby gain a power to bind different realities to the body. In archaeology, this turns our attention from looking at symbols for their referents to trying to understand how they were used to enact a larger social order (Whitehead 2002). Rituals such as placing the cloth may appear meaningless in the archaeological record, or could be seen to represent some exotic religious belief, but they may actually be poetic expressions that act on the body to produce persons beyond the physical shell.

These considerations ease our taken-for-granted ideas on the motivations behind body-processing. Such acts may be small, but they are generative, producing realities much larger than themselves. At ancient Aksum (AD 50–700) in northern Ethiopia, one community found itself in tension between two different treatments of the body: stelae and sarcophagus burial. Understanding this tension requires us to investigate relationships between body and person produced through such burial rites.

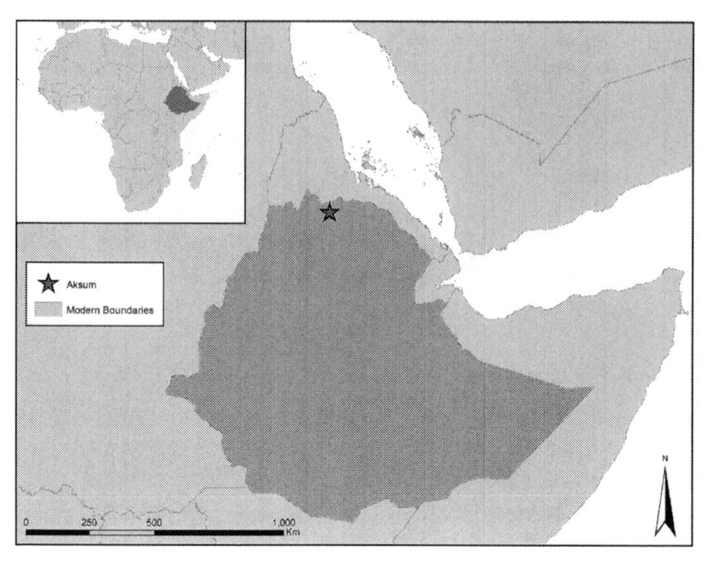

FIGURE 6.1. Aksum, northern Ethiopia.

THE CASE STUDY

BACKGROUND TO THE AKSUMITE KINGDOM

The metropolis of Aksum was the capital of an ancient kingdom in the Tigray region of northern Ethiopia (AD 50–700) (figure 6.1). Aksum originally grew along local African trade routes (Phillipson 1998) but soon became an economic and military power (Fattovich 2010; Kobishchanov 1979; Munro-Hay 1991; Sergew 1972). After Aksum conquered the port city of Adulis on the coast of modern-day Eritrea, the Aksumite Empire became middleman to the Red Sea trade that linked the Mediterranean and Indian Ocean worlds. The Aksumites interacted with the populations of Rome, Gaul, India, South Arabia, the Middle East, and Central Asia, perhaps reaching as far as China (Fattovich 2010; Phillipson 1998; Seland 2014; Sutton 1989). The *Periplus Maris Erythrae*, a Greek trading manual in use from the first and second centuries AD, contains the earliest references to Aksum's participation in the trade (Casson 1989). The empire declined sometime in the seventh and eighth centuries, but subsequently became an important source of heritage for the social and political traditions of northern Ethiopia (Buxton 1970; Finneran 2007; Tamrat 1972; Phillipson 2012).

Today, the small town of Aksum (also spelled "Axum") houses the ruins of the former kingdom. The most famous of these remains are the large and elaborate funerary stelae found in the Northern Stelae Field (NSF) (Littmann 1913;

FIGURE 6.2. Stela 2, an Aksumite storied stela.

Munro-Hay 1989; Phillipson 1997, 2000). Prior to a conversion to Christianity in the fourth through sixth centuries, the community that buried their dead in the NSF erected rough stones over their graves. These early stelae stood only a few meters in height, but later stelae were larger, more elaborate monuments. At least six stelae standing between 15 and 33 m tall and weighing several hundred tons were carved in the impression of multistoried "houses." This house symbolism takes the form of multiple stories of inscribed windows and representations of timber frames—also known as "monkey heads"—that jut out just past the stone façade of domestic Aksumite architecture (figure 6.2). It is unknown how the stelae fit into the polytheistic religion of the time outside of their chronological co-occurrence. Further south and west is another stelae cemetery known as the Gudit Stelae Field (GSF), which contains simpler stelae thought to mark the interments of less-wealthy Aksumites (Munro-Hay 1989; Tarakegn 1997). These are the best-investigated features in Aksum, where archaeology has otherwise been minimal. Other areas of stelae are scattered around the larger vicinity of Aksum, with many more still to be recorded.

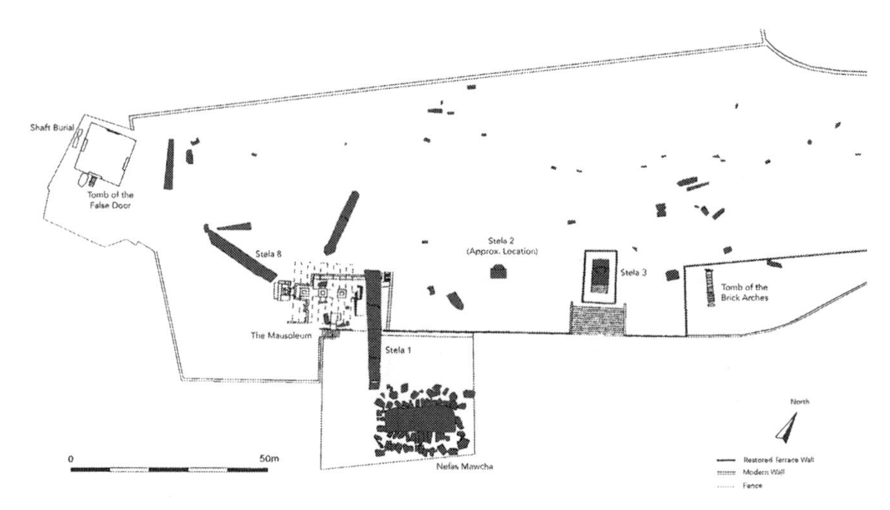

FIGURE 6.3. Plan map of Stela Park area, western edge of the NSF. (From Munro-Hay 1989. Used with permission from BIEA.)

TENSIONS AT THE NORTHERN STELAE FIELD

The end of the stelae tradition in the NSF came suddenly. The NSF is generally thought to have originated at its northeastern edge and expanded southwards and then westward. This hypothesis is based on the fact the stelae were made larger going westwards and from a few observations on ceramic development (Munro-Hay 1989). Two larger tombs, the Mausoleum and the Tomb of the Brick Arches, are both located in the later portions of this field (figure 6.3). Two radiocarbon dates from the Mausoleum and seven dates from the Tomb of the Brick Arches roughly indicate third- to fourth-century AD dates (Phillipson 2000).

Based on the hypothesized east–west expansion of the field, the last storied stela the NSF community carved would have been Stela 1. Stela 1 was the largest stela ever hewn at Aksum, standing about 33 m high and weighing up to 520 tons (Phillipson 1994). However, this stela collapsed when the Aksumites tried to raise the monument, as the bulk was too heavy for the 2 m basal stem protruding into the soil. The impact was immediate, and the Aksumites did not erect any more stelae in this field. Instead, these Aksumites built the Tomb of the False Door at the western edge of the NSF. The tomb was built with a smaller and more simplified chamber design than the tombs of before, and inside rests a single, empty sarcophagus. It is likely that the idea of sarcophagus burial came from Aksum's wide-ranging connections, particularly those from the eastern Mediterranean (Finneran 2007, 193).

The end sequence of the NSF then suggests there was some incongruence and friction between stelae and this new use of sarcophagus burial. This opposition derived from the materiality of the rites involved in the two practices, and that power was defined through the poetics of the house.

Person and Body in the Poetics of the House

The poetics of the house are the social rites that took place around stelae burial and seem to have generated a shared sense of meanings that anchored group or collective personhoods. Interments in the NSF often occur in groups and tend to cluster around stelae. This practice may actually extend beyond the NSF and characterize Aksumite society more generally. In one well-recorded example from the GSF, two individuals were originally buried before a stela was raised and followed by five later interments (Tarakegn 1997, 153). Excavations in the NSF took place before the advent of modern recording procedures and it is consequentially difficult to describe the burials with the same level of clarity, but the available data seem to display the same general pattern of burial in groups (Munro-Hay 1989). These groups appear to be quite small (3–10 individuals), suggesting they are some sort of kin group, family, or social house. These groups could be much larger, however, if the shaft graves in the NSF held multiple interments that did not register in previous excavations.

Human remains recovered through excavations at Aksum in general tend to be disarticulated, fragmentary, commingled, and many times burnt. In at least three cases in the NSF, bodies were simply tossed into graves (Munro-Hay 1989, 100–101). Grave cuts were sometimes too narrow to hold even a flexed burial, suggesting either a lack of concern with body placement or a hasty interment. There also appears to be selective curation of cranial and long bones; for example, eight skulls were recorded at the bottom of Chamber 2 in Shaft Tomb A (Munro-Hay 1989, 324). Selective curation is often a strong indicator of secondary burial (Beckett and Robb 2006; Robb 2016; see also Tarakegn 1997), but it is unknown to what extent this practice was widespread at Aksum beyond a few possible examples. The reuse of tombs or burial plots for multiple interments where new burials would disrupt the old could also explain the condition of many remains at the NSF. Some of these instances can be explained by looting, but the general frequency and widespread number of such disarticulated remains suggests other factors were also involved, which is doubled by the fact that disarticulated remains are also found in numerous trenches where looter's tunnels were not present. Other natural factors, particularly runoff and soil retention in the clays, could have impacted the preservation of skeletal materials, though it does not help that Aksumites placed the NSF in one of the more vulnerable areas at the foot of Beta Giyorgis and Mai Qoho hills where water rushes down

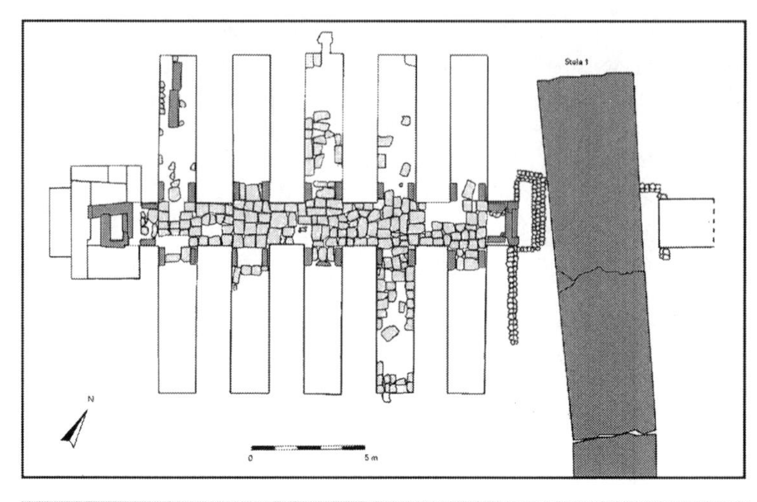

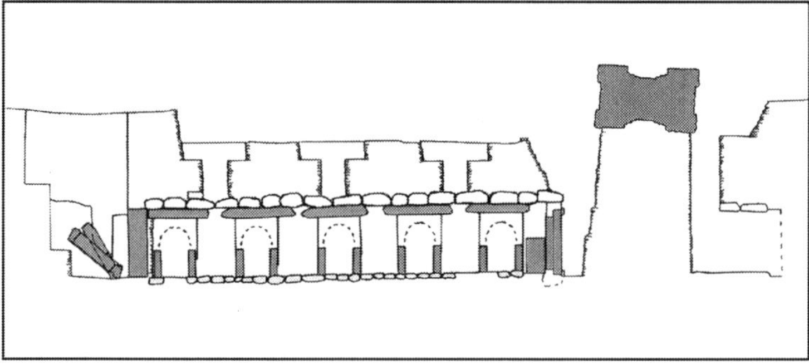

Figure 6.4. Plan (top) and profile (bottom) of the Mausoleum tomb. (From Phillipson 2000. Used with permission from BIEA.)

to the central reservoir. Overall, there seems to be a lack of concern with preserving individual bodies.

The ephemerality of human remains contrasts with the durability of the elaborate stelae and tombs at NSF. The NSF is host to two known monumental tombs that housed multiple interments. The Tomb of the Brick Arches has only been partly excavated, but the tomb appears to be laid out in multiple burial chambers with two loci each, though human remains are strewn into the entry chambers (Phillipson 2000). The other tomb, the Mausoleum, is the largest tomb in the NSF. This tomb is laid out with ten chambers along a central passageway (figure 6.4). Unfortunately, the tomb was reentered multiple times, as recently as the eighteenth century, and it is consequentially unknown how many of the 9+ individuals discovered here were placed in Aksumite times (Phillipson 2000, 217). Looking at the architectural features, both the Tomb of the Brick Arches and the Mausoleum are designed with multiple chambers and appear to be egalitarian in the sense that no chamber is set apart from any other. The general symbolism of the tomb layout then appears to espouse a collectivist orientation to personhood at this time. Domestic contexts at Aksum are not well-enough investigated to examine the relationship between mortuary symbolism and daily life, but the rites of stelae burial seem to have produced ideals of group personhood.

Additionally, the stelae are implicated in rites of social memory. Social memory is often seen as facilitating cohesion among social groups (Connerton 1989; Rowlands 1993; Van Dyke and Alcock 2003). Social groups such as families need to be defined in some way and veneration of a common ancestor is often the norm across Africa and elsewhere (Calhoun 1981; Fortes 1965; Goody 1962; Kopytoff 1971). Inscribed bowls found at the base plates of the storied stelae have been interpreted as spaces for the placement of ablutions and offerings (Fattovich 1987, 43; Phillipson 1994, 194), apparently in periodic ancestry or commemoration rites. These bowls mimic ceramic vessels of a Greek-Roman design, and we can speculate that these types of pots may have also been placed in front of stelae at certain times. Secondary burial is also often implicated in ancestor veneration rites (Hertz 1960). These ancestry rites would have been symbolic, but also poetic, in the sense that they configure the relationships of the group. The ensuing interactions then created a new creature in the "ancestor" that would help to inspire the actions of its living family. The ancestor would then also be perpetuated and would help to perpetuate the social house. In other worlds, these creatures could be ghosts, spirits, or other forms: skinless but existent directors of society. It is unknown how and to what extent ancestors were indeed important to Aksumites and the NSF community, but the importance of social memory in organizing the NSF social groups more generally is implied by the material culture.

It is here that we can reconsider the house symbolism of the stelae. Since the stelae allowed the possibility for group burial, secondary burial, offerings, and commemoration rites, and a locus for associations of ancestry, we must then think of the house symbolism as part of this poetic. In this sense, the house symbolism is a manifestation of the shared meaning of collectivity produced through the poetics of the house. More important, the house symbolism helped amplify those meanings. This is not dissimilar from other "house societies," where the house is often taken as a symbol for a group that is itself a social and moral person (Beck 2007; Gillespie 2001; Joyce and Gillespie 2000). In house societies, it is the house that is the creature perpetuating itself—even as individual members live and die, the "house" continues to organize individuals and sustain itself through time. Just as body defines the individual person in our culture, it is the house that is the metaphorical body of the social group (or the body that is the individual "house" of our "selves"). The idea that the association between house and stelae may be present in earlier monuments and only become amplified with explicit symbolisms is hinted at by two stelae that carry protoforms of the house symbolism (Littmann 1913, see Stela 7 and 34). Today, local Aksumite tour guides also believe that the house symbolism is also present in the Mausoleum, which they argue was designed to look like a storied stela. The profile of the tomb superficially resembles a storied stela (figure 6.4), but the more intriguing support comes from the internal plaster designed to look like solid nepheline syenite (Phillipson 2000, 176)—the same granite from which the stelae were carved. In this case, the Mausoleum was meant to look like solid rock—and not just any rock, but the inside of the storied stela. The social group that was buried there wanted to be buried inside the walls of a storied stelae and the house it symbolized. This use of stone symbolism was therefore much akin to Mol's placing of the cloth in that it helped define the Aksumite social house in death and amplified the sense of group personhood.

These iterations of stelae burial therefore generated a sense of grouphood that defined the poetics of the house. In this case, individual bodies would become more ephemeral either through ritual action in ancestry rights or a lack of concern with their preservation. In these burials, bones mixed together or simply disappeared, helping to diffuse a sense of personhood in the collective. House members themselves may live and die, and even over a generation the social group could look radically different than they did in the beginning. It was the stelae that anchored them in continuity and that were instrumental in facilitating the performances by which the Aksumite social house was born, reborn again and again, and perpetuated through time. Consequentially, the Aksumites focused their efforts on the stelae and these mortuary features that helped to keep them as families in their deaths.

The Shift to Sarcophagus Burial

It was also through the poetics of the house that sarcophagus burial obtained its significance. The sarcophagus found in the Tomb of the False Door used similar symbolisms of stone but generated a different reality to the Aksumite body (figure 6.5). It is difficult to think of sarcophagus burial as representative of separate religious tradition, given its infrequent occurrence at Aksum, but the poetics of the house can tell us how this departure from normal burial practice became significant.

Stone, which helped to define collective bodies of the stelae tradition, now defined individual creatures in sarcophagi. No stelae ever marked the Tomb of the False Door. Pottery, coinage, and other features of the tomb likely indicate a late

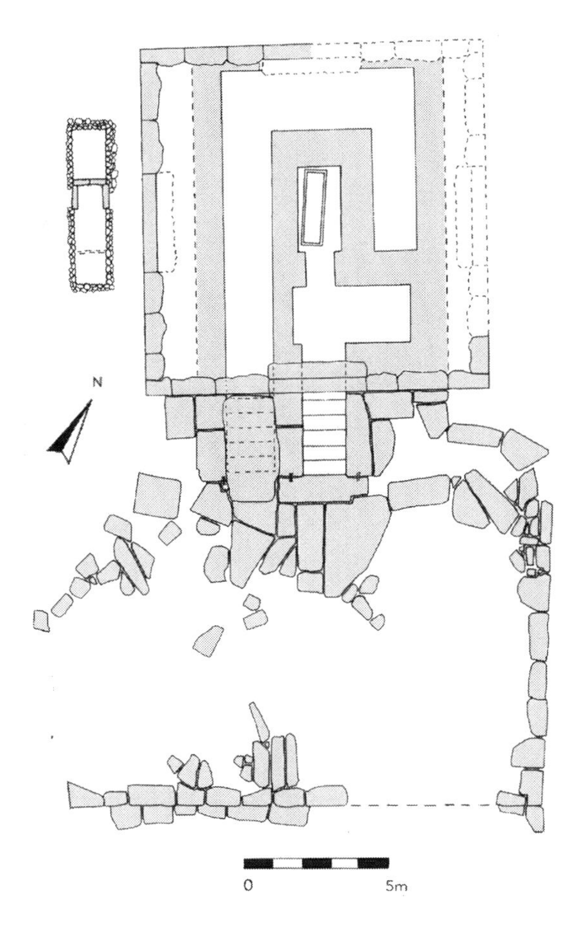

FIGURE 6.5. Plan map of the Tomb of the False Door. (From Munro-Hay 1989. Used with permission from BIEA.)

fourth- or early fifth-century date (Munro-Hay 1989, 105–110, 157). Inside, an entry vestibule leads to a burial chamber holding a single sarcophagus burial: the only case of an individual being buried alone at Aksum (figure 6.6). No skeletal remains were found with the sarcophagus, and a multitude of rationales why can be provided, but the sarcophagus itself seems to indicate a shift in focus towards a greater preservation of the body. The sarcophagus, though now empty, is a more individualizing feature that strongly defines the body in comparison to the multichambered tombs of before. The properties of durability and longevity inherent to stone now generated a reality that prized individual personhoods, unraveling prior relationships of the family and social house. The ability of the sarcophagus to do so came in reference to the poetics of the house, which defined the role of stone symbolism to bound bodies and set the terms for tension when the practice was imported.

FIGURE 6.6. Sarcophagus burial in the Tomb of the False Door.

As a departure from the normal burial modes of the poetics of the house, the sarcophagus then put individual and collective personhoods into tension. Collectivist and individualist orientations of personhood may exist together, however, as can multiple realities to the body (Fowler 2016; Harris and Robb 2012; Tarlow 2010). But this did not happen in the NSF community, and it was by the poetics of the house that the sarcophagus became oppositional. The idea that group and individual personhoods were in tension is supported by another burial near the Tomb of the False Door. Located just 2 m west of the Tomb of the False Door is a single shaft grave (Munro-Hay 1989, 110–113) (figure 6.5). This grave is associated with the tomb by proximity, alignment, and ceramic typology, and likely had to come soon after or it would have been destroyed by the tomb's construction. It is unknown whether this grave was supposed to house a single interment or multiple interments. The immediate explanation for this burial is that it was someone (or someones) originally intended to be buried inside the tomb in association with the individual of the sarcophagus before this was not allowed. We can speculate that this led to the altered chamber design of the tomb, resulting in the unusual closed chamber. In this case, the sarcophagus burial evoked strong memories in a similar but different way from the stelae tradition—memories that arose from the same desire of family members trying to stay together, but now amplified by the tension of having to remain apart.

The tensions between these personhoods then help explain why the fall of Stela 1 was such a disaster in the particular way it was. The poetics of the house entailed a stronger set of group relationships that configured human emotion, obligation, motivation, and concern, and therefore became an inextricable part of the Aksumite social order. The life of the stelae was fundamentally entwined with the life of the social house, given its role in preserving such relationships. When Stela 1 fell, those relationships unraveled—giving up the stelae meant the NSF community could not just change one aspect of burial but an entire set of rites that weaved realities of how they could interact and relate to each other. Sarcophagi generated new relationships between body and person based on the importance of stone in the poetics of the house. Bodies that would once mix in stone tombs so that families became one were now bound apart as sarcophagi. The social house was no longer performed, and so it ceased to be, leaving its constituent members to adopt ways of life (and ways of death) that did not yet mean anything to them and what they had prized up to that time.

CONCLUSIONS

The shift from stelae to sarcophagi entailed wider changes in the social order that signal different relationships between body, personhood, and the possibilities for social interaction. The poetics of the house generated a sense of group personhood for the NSF community, one akin to a social house. These poetics involved group burial, rites of social memory/ancestry, possible secondary burial, and the use of house and stone symbolisms. Stone became an especially important symbolism that helped bind the reality of the dead body and created "group bodies" (stone houses) in stelae burials. Based on these values, the NSF Aksumites focused more on the construction of elaborate monuments that amplified group identity than on preserving individual bodies—many of which received hasty burial or were perhaps intentionally processed postmortem in ancestry rites. While broken bodies may initially be seen as violent, here they came from rites of family and togetherness, and so the preservation of individual bodies was less important than those mortuary features that helped to generate and regenerate the social house.

The rite of sarcophagus burial, on the other hand, produced an individual creature. The stone symbolism that bounded collective bodies of the stelae tradition was now tailored to an individual as a sarcophagus. Outside of the Tomb of the False Door is another interment perhaps originally intended to be buried inside the tomb with the individual of the sarcophagus before this was no longer allowed—demonstrating that maintaining the social group was indeed an important source of tension and that these rites were seen as incongruous. Part of the disaster of Stela 1 then, from the perspective of NSF community, was the unraveling of family relationships and dynamics of interaction that defined Aksumite social life up to that time.

There are no reasons why this particular story needed to play out as it did, as multiple realities of person and body (including group and individual) often exist simultaneously. But Whitehead's notion of the poetic as generative helps to explain how the sarcophagus burial became meaningful as an oppositional act. Normally, the analysis of these two burial practices and tension would suggest two competing cultural or religious traditions. Examples of sarcophagi, however, have been too few to rely on this idea—only four in total have been found at Aksum. While Christian associations of the sarcophagus may be present, it also seems the sarcophagus acquired its meaning in reference to the poetics of the house. Stelae burial created a "group" creature, but the poetics by which it did so meant that sarcophagus burial had to generate an "individual" creature. The story of the stelae rite and the fall of Stela 1 is then a story of families trying to keep themselves together through times of change, and how their actions imbued all their material world with meaning, possibility, and strife.

As a short epilogue: the Aksumite social house did not die, however. Four kilometers north of Aksum are two further Christian tombs that were once mounted by basilica churches and thought to date later in time. One tomb is empty but the other contains the three additional sarcophagi. The sarcophagi still seem to be individualizing material features, but this group burial implies a different configuration of collectivist and individualist orientations to personhood than seen at the Tomb of the False Door. At first glance, it appears stone lost its strength, but perhaps not, as sarcophagus burial was soon abandoned completely. No other instances of sarcophagi are known. Instead, Christians were soon buried together at churches, many times again as families who may disinter bones of deceased family members to rebury as one—a practice that continues today. A tradition of rock-hewn churches would arise, so that symbolisms of stone remain important to the poetics of burial places. Material culture, while different, still produces a shared sense of group personhood, which is still predominantly rooted in the family in northern Ethiopian social life today. The material configurations of the great urban Addis Ababa do inch many towards more individual living, but not completely. The fall of Stela 1 did not then totally dissolve the Ethiopian social house, which continuously reorganized itself through sweeping histories of change. And so too did the Aksumite house, once born, continue to live.

ACKNOWLEDGMENTS

The author would like to thank Anna Osterholtz, Amanda Logan, David Phillipson, Calen Ryan, and three anonymous reviewers for their comments and suggestions. The author would also like to thank the British Institute in Eastern Africa (BIEA) for use of figures 6.3, 6.4, and 6.5. Copyright remains with the BIEA.

REFERENCES

Argent, Gala. 2010. "Do the Clothes Make the Horse? Relationality, Roles and Statuses in Iron Age Inner Asia." *World Archaeology* 42 (2): 157–174.

Beck, Robin A., Jr., ed. 2007. *The Durable House: House Society Models in Archaeology*. Carbondale, IL: Southern Illinois University Press.

Beckett, J., and John Robb. 2006. "Neolithic Burial Taphonomy, Ritual and Interpretation in Britain and Ireland: A Review." In *Social Archaeology of Funerary Remains*, edited by R. Gowland and C. J. Knüsel, 57–80. Oxford, UK: Oxbow Books.

Bloch, Maurice. 1971. *Placing the Dead: Tombs, Ancestral Villages and Kinship Organization in Madagascar*. New York: Seminar Press Ltd.

Bray, Tamara L. 2009. "An Archaeological Perspective on the Andean Concept of Camaquen: Thinking through Late Pre-Columbian Ofrendas and Huacas." *Cambridge Archaeological Journal* 19 (03): 357–366.

Buxton, David Roden. 1970. *The Abyssinians*. London: Thames and Hudson.

Calhoun, C. J. 1981. "The Authority of Ancestors: A Sociological Reconsideration of Fortes's Tallensi in Response to Fortes's Critics." *Man* 15 (2): 304–319.

Casson, Lionel. 1989. *The Periplus Maris Erythraei*. Princeton, NJ: Princeton University Press.

Chapman, J. 2000. *Fragmentation in Archaeology: People, Places and Broken Objects in the Prehistory of Southeastern Europe*. London: Routledge.

Conneller, Chantal. 2004. "Becoming Deer: Corporeal Transformations at Star Carr." *Archaeological Dialogues* 11 (1): 37–56.

Connerton, P. 1989. *How Societies Remember*. Cambridge, UK: Cambridge University Press.

Crossland, Zoë. 2013. *Ancestral Encounters in Highland Madagascar*. Cambridge, UK: Cambridge University Press.

Duncan, William N., and Kevin R. Schwarz. 2014. "Partiable, Permeable, and Relational Bodies in a Maya Mass Grave." In *Commingled and Disarticulated Human Remains: Working Toward Improved Theory, Method, and Data*, edited by Anna J. Osterholtz, Kathryn M. Baustian, and Debra L. Martin, 149–172. New York: Springer.

Dyson, Freeman. 1985. *Origins of Life*. Cambridge, UK: Cambridge University Press.

Eigen, Manfred, and Peter Schuster. 1979. *The Hypercycle*. Berlin: Springer.

Fattovich, Rodolfo. 1987. "Some Remarks on the Origins of the Aksumite Stelae." *Annales d'Ethiopie* 14 (1): 43–69.

Fattovich, Rodolfo. 2010. "The Development of Ancient States in the Northern Horn of Africa, c. 3000 BC–AD 1000: An Archaeological Outline." *Journal of World Prehistory* 23 (3): 145–175.

Finneran, Niall. 2007. *The Archaeology of Ethiopia*. Routledge: London.

Fortes, Meyer. 1965. *Some Reflections on Ancestor Worship in Africa*. Oxford: Oxford University Press.

Fowler, Chris. 2016. "Relational Personhood Revisited." *Cambridge Archaeological Journal* 26 (3): 397–412.

Gillespie, Susan D. 2001. "Personhood, Agency, and Mortuary Ritual: A Case Study from the Ancient Maya." *Journal of Anthropological Archaeology* 20: 73–112.

Goody, Jack. 1962. *Death, Property and the Ancestors: A Study of the Mortuary Customs of the LoDagaa of West Africa*. Stanford, CA: Stanford University Press.

Gordon, Deborah M. 2010. *Ant Encounters: Interaction Networks and Colony Behavior*. Princeon and Oxford: Princeton University Press.

Graham, Emma-Jayne. 2009. "Becoming Persons, Becoming Ancestors: Personhood, Memory, and the Corpse in Roman Rituals of Social Remembrance." *Archaeological Dialogues* 16: 51–74.

Harris, Oliver J. T., and John Robb. 2012. "Multiple Ontologies and the Problem of the Body in History." *American Anthropologist* 114 (4): 668–679.

Hertz, Robert A. 1960 [1907, 1909]. *Death and the Right Hand: A Contribution to the Study of the Collective Representation of Death*. Translated by Rodney Needham and Claudia Needham. Glencoe, IL: The Free Press.

Hill, Erica. 2013. "Archaeology and Animal Persons: Toward a Prehistory of Human-Animal Relations." *Environment and Society: Advances in Research* 4: 117–136.

Hoffmeyer, Jesper. 2008. Biosemiotics : An Examination into the Signs of Life and the Life of Signs. Scranton, PA: University of Scranton Press.

Hordijk, Wim, Jotun Hein, and Mike Steel. 2010. "Autocatalytic Sets and the Origin of Life." *Entropy* 12: 1733–1342.

Jones, A. 2005. "Lives in Fragments?: Personhood and the European Neolithic." *Journal of Social Archaeology* 5 (2): 193–224.

Joyce, Rosemary A., and Susan D. Gillespie, eds. 2000. *Beyond Kinship: Social and Material Reproduction in House Societies*. Philadelphia: University of Pennsylvania Press.

Kauffman, Stuart A. 1986. "Autocatalytic Sets of Proteins." *Journal of Theoretical Biology* 1: 1–24.

Kauffman, Stuart A. 1993. *The Origins of Order : Self-Organization and Selection in Evolution*. New York: Oxford University Press.

Kobishchanov, Yuri M. 1979. *Axum*. University Park: Pennsylvania State University Press.

Kopytoff, Igor. 1971. "Ancestors as Elders in Africa." *Africa* 41 (02): 129–142.

Littmann, Enno. 1913. *Deutsche Aksum-Expedition*. Berlin: Greimer.

Losey, Robert J., Vladmir I. Bazaliiskii, Angela R. Lieverse, Andrea Waters-Rist, Kate Faccia, and Andrzej W. Weber. 2013. "The Bear-Able Likeness of Being: Ursine Remains at the Shamanka II Cemetery, Lake Baikal, Siberia." In *Relational Archaeologies*, edited by Christopher Watts, 65–96. London and New York: Routledge.

Mauss, Marcel. 1985. "A Category of the Human Mind: The Notion of the Person; the Notion of the Self." In *The Category of the Person: Anthropology, Philosophy, History*, edited by M. Carrithers, 1–25. Cambridge and New York: Cambridge University Press.

Mol, Annemarie. 2002. *The Body Multiple: Ontology in Medical Practice*. Durham, NC: Duke University Press.

Munro-Hay, Stuart C. 1989. *Excavations at Aksum*. London: Thames and Hudson.

Munro-Hay, Stuart C. 1991. *Aksum: An African Civilization of Late Antiquity*. Edinburgh: Edinburgh University Press.

Phillipson, David W. 1994. "The Significance and Symbolism of Aksumite Stelae." *Cambridge Archaeological Journal* 4 (02): 189–210.

Phillipson, David W. 1997. *The Monuments of Aksum*. Addis Abada, Ethiopia, and London: British Institute in Eastern Africa.

Phillipson, David W. 1998. *Ancient Ethiopia: Aksum, Its Predecessors and Successors*. London: British Museum Press.

Phillipson, David W. 2000. *Archaeology at Aksum, Ethiopia, 1993–7*. London: British Institute in Eastern Africa.

Phillipson, David W. 2012. Foundations of an African Civilisation: Aksum and the Northern Horn, 1000 BC–AD 1300. Woodbridge, Suffolk, and Rochester, NY: James Currey.

Robb, John. 2016. "What Can We Really Say about Skeletal Part Representation, MNI and Funerary Ritual? A Simulation Approach." *Journal of Archaeological Science Reports*.

Rowlands, Michael. 1993. "The Role of Memory in the Transmission of Culture." *World Archaeology* 25 (2): 141–151.

Seland, Elvind Heldaas. 2014. "Archaeology of Trade in the Western Indian Ocean, 300 BC–AD 700." *Journal of Archaeological Research* 22 (4): 367–402.

Sergew, Hable Selassie. 1972. *Ancient and Medieval Ethiopian History to 1270*. Addis Abada, Ethiopia: United Printers.

Strathern, M. 1988. *The Gender of the Gift. Problems with Women and Problems with Society in Melanesia*. Berkeley: The Unviersity of California Press.

Sutton, J.E.G. 1989. "Aksum, the Erythraen Sea, and the World of Late Antiquity: A Foreword." In *Excavations at Aksum*, edited by Stuart C. Munro-Hay, 1–6. London: Thames and Hudson.

Tamrat, Taddesse. 1972. *Church and State in Ethiopia, 1270–1527*. Oxford Studies in African Affairs. Oxford: Clarendon Press.

Tarakegn, Ayele. 1997. "The Mortuary Practices of Aksumite Ethiopia with Particular Reference to the Gudit Stelae Field (GSF) Site." PhD, University of Cambridge, UK.

Tarlow, Sarah. 2010. *Ritual, Belief, and the Dead Body in Early Modern Britain and Ireland.* Cambridge, UK: Cambridge University Press.

Van Dyke, Ruth M., and Susan E. Alcock, eds. 2003. *Archaeologies of Memory*. Oxford: Blackwell Publishers.

Viveiros de Castro, Eduardo. 1998. "Cosmological Deixis and Amerindian Perspectivism." *The Journal of the Royal Anthropological Institute* 4 (3): 469–488. doi: 10.2307/3034157.

Viveiros de Castro, Eduardo. 2004. "Perspectival Anthropology and the Method of Controlled Equivocation." *Tipití: Journal of the Society for the Anthropology of Lowland South America* 2 (1): 3–22.

Wagner, R. W. 1991. "The Fractal Person." In *Big Men and Great Men: The Personifications of Power*, edited by M. Godelier and M. Strathern, 159–173. Cambridge, UK: Cambridge University Press.

Whitehead, Neil L. 2002. *Dark Shamans: Kanaimà and the Poetics of Violent Death*. Durham, NC: Duke University Press.

Whitehead, Neil L, ed. 2004. *Violence*. Santa Fe, NM: SAR Press.

Wilkinson, Darryl. 2013. "The Emperor's New Body: Personhood, Ontology, and the Inka Sovereign." *Cambridge Archaeological Journal* 23 (3): 417–432.

7

Smiting Pharaohs

The Poetics of Violence and Power in Ancient Egypt

ROSELYN A. CAMPBELL

Although many people would like to believe that violence happens because "bad" people do bad things simply by virtue of being bad, some of the most egregious examples of violence have been perpetrated in the name of virtue, honor, and noble ideals (Eller 2010, 11). Violence has been used as a legitimate, accepted, and even expected tool of power and control by rulers in complex societies through time and space. Whitehead's (2004; 2007, 6) work on the poetics of violence has noted that such violent "performances" derive their meaning from the purposeful use of culture- and context-specific ritual, symbolism, and ideology. The violent and often public manipulation of human bodies by rulers provides a vivid reification of identities, social mores, and ideologies. When interpreting evidence of violence in archaeological remains, it thus becomes all important to understand the way that the participants would have viewed the violent act.

It is not simply the violent act itself that exploits and manipulates these cultural reference points, however; the way that a human body is processed before, during, and after an act of violence also draws upon cultural ideas of desecration and preservation, justice and injustice, what is appropriate and what is inappropriate, to reinforce, obscure, or complicate the meaning of the violence itself. Victims of violence may be mutilated and displayed, ritually destroyed, or buried with honor. Both the violent act itself and the treatment of the body are processes fraught with cultural meaning that, when conducted by ruling powers, can manipulate symbols and ideology for a variety of purposes. In this light, this chapter assesses examples of

DOI: 10.5876/9781646420612.c007

state-sanctioned, violent manipulation of the human body in ancient Egypt, both before and after death, and the way that such bodily processing was used as a tool of power and control.

POETICS AND PROCESSING BODIES

As John Carman has pointed out, violence "is something of which all human beings seem to be capable, and at the same time an attribute of humanity that we would choose to deny" (Carman 1997, 2). Recent scholarship has yielded noteworthy studies analyzing and contextualizing violence in past cultures throughout the world (Knüsel and Smith 2013; Martin and Frayer 1997; Martin, Harrod, and Pérez 2012; Porter and Schwartz 2012; Ralph 2013; Redfern 2017). Intraspecies violence has existed for at least as long as modern *Homo sapiens* has walked the planet, and the occurrence, and indeed prevalence, of violence in seemingly every human society through time has led many scholars to suggest that violence is in some way an integral part of the biological makeup of humankind (Berger and Trinkaus 1995; Eller 2010; Turpin and Kurtz 1997; Zollikofer et al. 2002). The question of whether humans are biologically predisposed toward violence is a complex one, and has been the subject of much heated debate (Thrift 2007; Turpin and Kurtz 1997; Whitehead 2004). However, focusing on *why* humans are violent tends to prioritize biological mandates, often ignoring or minimizing the social and cultural contexts that determine *how* and *when* violence occurs (Turpin and Kurtz 1997; Whitehead 2007). The circumstances under which killing may be called murder, justice, punishment, or reward are entirely culturally mandated (Turpin 1986, 1995; Turpin and Kurtz 1997). One man's murder may be another man's righteousness, justice, or kindness. This is a central point of Neil Whitehead's discussion of the poetics of violence, where he notes that we must understand violence as "a legitimate and socially constructive cultural performance" (2004, 60). Acts of violence for political or social purposes do not simply affect the corporeal body, but rather, target the individual and collective psyche, and are embedded in the ritual and symbolism of the culture in which they take place (Pérez 2012, 15). Thus we find instances of evisceration of pregnant women and forced cannibalism of family members during the 1994 genocide in Rwanda, and removal of feet and hands of prisoners in the civil war in Sierra Leone, techniques that were carefully calculated to inspire horror and fear in the populace and to encourage compliance, obedience, and concepts of belonging and not belonging to certain groups (Pérez 2012; Whitehead 2004). Killing with hammers, mallets and other everyday implements in the ethnic cleansing of Bosnia provided both a method of killing that was convenient, and a way to inspire fear and horror by causing death with ordinary objects that were relatively harmless under ordinary circumstances (Pérez 2012; Whitehead 2004). The causing of death in these modern examples is almost subsidiary to the performance; using mundane objects, or excessive violence, to mutilate and cause pain to individual victims, attacks and obliterates their identities in symbolic ways.

When applying the concept of poetics to the violent processing of human bodies, we must consider the complex cultural context in which all violent performances are enmeshed, not only in the present but in past cultures as well. What was violent to the ancient Egyptians may not have been viewed as violent to the Aztecs, or to us, and vice versa. With this in mind, then, let us consider how the Egyptians viewed violence, and how and why violent processing of bodies was used or not used within this society. In particular, I focus here on the use and performance of violence by, or at the behest of, the Egyptian king.

THE VIOLENT KING

As the apex of Egyptian religious, political, and cultural society, the ancient Egyptian king was expected to employ violence if necessary for the preservation of the Egyptian way of life, or in other circumstances as he deemed fit (Bestock 2017; Davis 1992; Emery 1974; Hall 1986; O'Connor 2011; Wengrow 2006; Wilkinson 2001, 2013). Because the Egyptian king was also a representative of the gods, and a god himself, all state-sanctioned violence was implicitly violence that also affected the spiritual realm. As a semidivine king and the earthly embodiment of the god Horus, the Egyptian king was responsible for maintaining *ma'at* (usually translated as "order," referring to cosmic order, balance, and maintenance of the status quo) against the forces of chaos, or *isfet*, embodied by the god Seth (Dunand and Zivie-Coche 2005). Just as Horus had fought and defeated Seth to claim his rightful place as heir to the throne of Egypt, so the Egyptian king was tasked with continuing the struggle against the ever-present forces of *isfet* (Dunand and Zivie-Coche 2005; Gardiner 1932). Subjugation of the forces of evil and chaos (often as personified by enemy soldiers) was integral to the ideology of the kingship in ancient Egypt. Anyone who threatened *ma'at* had to be punished or eliminated to restore balance (Dunand and Zivie-Coche 2005). In such cases, violence would be viewed as not only the legitimate and right thing to do, but the absolute duty of the king to preserve the world and Egyptian society.

PERFORMING VIOLENCE

Public display of the king's performance of such ideologically charged violence would have been an invaluable way to demonstrate his virulence, strength, and right to rule Egypt. Pérez discusses the nature of violence, particularly when enacted by a ruling power, as a socially constructed performance with a carefully selected target audience and, in many cases, a specifically chosen victim. Violence as a tool of control is meaningless without an audience, and thus acts of violence that are intended to manipulate and control spectators are enacted as if on a stage, with "props" (or tools to carry out the violent act) and a method of killing and/or processing that has been calculated to elicit the most powerful response (Pérez 2012). Killing an enemy in secret may stop that particular enemy but will not preclude others from similar actions; disposing of an enemy in front of numerous witnesses, however, and wreaking destruction on the body, sends a much more public and widespread message. Public sacrifice and execution provide a visceral understanding not only of the fate of those who resist the established authority, but also the power of the ruling figures (Carter 2013). Several texts reference the public, gruesome display of the corpses of defeated enemies by the Egyptian king (Filer 1997; Muhlestein 2008, 2011). By allowing these bodies to publicly decay, rather than having them properly buried according to Egyptian tradition, the Egyptian king simultaneously proclaimed his total destruction of the enemy and his power to keep the soul of the deceased from entering the afterlife.

The mode of death is often integral to the performance of violence. In cases of corporal punishment and execution, the mode of death may be calculated to make an example of the transgressor and dissuade others from repeating the crime. The technique used depends in part on the main goal of the killing; if dominance over a prisoner or enemy was intended, a particularly violent method of killing would be most effective to highlight the victim's helplessness and annihilate the perceived source of rebellion or crime. By not only killing but utterly destroying one defeated enemy leader, the Egyptian king symbolically (and magically, to some degree) destroyed all enemies in that group, not just in that one moment but for all eternity.

In other cases, it may be enough to simply cause death in the most expedient way, for example in cases where court officials or retainers were killed to accompany a deceased leader into the afterlife. Even when the cause of death was major trauma, such as the blunt-force trauma to the cranium used to kill at least some of the individuals destined to accompany the rulers of Ur to the afterlife, the injury was obscured and the body arranged as if the trauma had never occurred (Baadsgaard, Boutin, and Buikstra 2012; Baadsgaard et al. 2011). The practice of human sacrifice in ancient Egypt has been much debated, due largely to the apparent absence of perimortem traumatic injury on the individuals, though all other features of the burials perfectly fit the patterns for sacrificial victims accompanying a ruler into the afterlife (Kaiser 1985; Morris 2007). It may be that we must uncouple our modern association of major trauma with human sacrifice, and instead look to the ways that the ancient Egyptians perceived the ritual of sacrifice. Perhaps the ritual was not even viewed as violence but rather as a meaningful, and perhaps necessary, honor for those destined to dwell near their lord for all eternity.

The processing of the body after death provides an additional avenue for messages of power and domination. Disarticulation, mutilation, and annihilation of a corpse or representative of a person may be used to symbolize social and political victory and total power over both physical and spiritual life and death, while preservation of a body allowed rebirth into the eternal afterlife (Pérez 2012; Robben 2000; Varner 2013). In a culture that poured such effort into preparations for death, and that devoted so many resources to ensure that the deceased would enter the afterlife with every comfort they had enjoyed in life, manipulation of the corpse would have been a particular concern. The Egyptians believed that in order to successfully enter the afterlife, the body of the deceased had to be preserved, giving rise to some of the most elaborate mummification rituals the world has seen (Grajetzki 2003; Ikram and Dodson 1998). Some of the earliest-known Egyptian religious texts provide spells for avoiding fragmentation of the body, both in this life and the next (Allen 2015; Eyre 2002; Faulkner 2007). Damage to the body, before or after death, could have eternal consequences, and thus the threat of unwanted postmortem processing would have been a particularly powerful tool of power.

At a casual glance, the performance of violence in ancient Egypt seems to have most commonly occurred in art and text. Images of the king, poised to smash the heads of enemy captives, are carved and painted on monuments and objects across Egypt. This so-called "smiting motif" was used by Egyptian rulers as early as the Predynastic Period (c. 5300–3000 BC), and conveys a powerful image of the mighty pharaoh about to smash the heads of subdued enemy prisoners or rulers. Some texts (such as the Amada Stela of Amenhotep II) seem to indicate that the pharaoh occasionally killed defeated rulers with his own hands (Filer 1997; Muhlestein 2011). Other authors have addressed the textual and artistic references to capital punishment (Tyldesley 2000), execution of enemies (Bestock 2017; Davis 1992; Hall 1986), and warfare (Darnell and Manassa 2007; Spalinger 2005). Muhlestein (2011) presented a diachronic perspective of possible evidence for violent killing in ancient Egypt (see also Muhlestein 2008, 2015), but did not analyze human remains beyond a brief summary of possible cases of sanctioned violence.

Physical evidence of state-sanctioned violence is more scarce, a fact that has led many researchers to treat artistic and textual evidence of violence either in a positivist way (i.e., the images and descriptions of violence are an accurate representation of real events) or apologetically (the images of violence had little to no bearing on actual use of violence). The reality is certainly far more complex and nuanced, though a complete discussion is beyond the scope of this chapter. Some types of violence are more difficult to identify than others. While execution (Anonymous 2012) was almost certainly enacted on living human victims as well as in royal imagery, physical evidence of such practices has been difficult to identify with certainty. There is some evidence to suggest that state-sanctioned human sacrifice also occurred in the early stages of Egyptian state formation (Crubézy and Midant-Reynes 2005; Petrie 1925). Manipulation of the body of enemies, such as display of the corpse or the taking of trophies from defeated enemies, was certainly practiced during some periods (Bietak 2012; Forstner-Müeller et al. 2012).

Given the remarkable preservation of human remains from ancient Egypt, and the centuries of archaeological work conducted in Egypt, there is surprisingly little physical evidence of state-sanctioned violence against living (or even dead) victims. This is interesting in and of itself, as it suggests that while the Egyptians were perfectly willing to depict and enact violence in a variety of contexts and mediums, some evidence for violence in the physical world may have been actively concealed, and the bodies of the victims were processed as if the violence had not occurred (or were simply destroyed entirely). In some cases, postmortem processing was certainly intended to obscure violence. The most obvious example of this is the mummy of King Ramses III. Though ancient Egyptian legal records indicate that an assassination plot was hatched against the king, and the perpetrators caught and convicted, the plot was long believed to have been unsuccessful due to the absence of any clear wounds to the king's mummy (Peet 2005). More recent analysis with computed tomography and radiography, however, has revealed that the king's throat was cut, violently and deeply, and the wound carefully covered with bandages during the mummification process (Hawass et al. 2012; Redford 2002). This finding reiterates an important point about Egyptian beliefs about life after death: if a successful transition into the afterlife was desired, the body needed to be preserved in the best condition possible, unblemished and fully functional (Assman 2005; Ikram and Dodson 1998). Physical evidence of state-sanctioned violence in ancient Egypt, then, might only be displayed in particular circumstances. Thus, in cases of retainer sacrifice (i.e., individuals killed to accompany and serve their deceased ruler in the afterlife), there would be no need to highlight the occurrence of violence. Destruction of these individuals would impair their ability to serve their king in the afterlife, such that even if they were violently killed, the evidence of violence may have been purposely obscured in the postmortem processing of these remains, though we cannot discount the effects of taphonomy on evidence of violence.

The question of whether victims of state-sanctioned violence were willing or reluctant deserves mention here, however unanswerable in archaeological material. It may be that the willingness of the victim could affect the way that the remains were processed after death; perhaps willingness to die along with one's ruler was rewarded with a proper burial, while the (presumed) unwillingness of a convicted criminal to die was punished by obliteration of the remains. However, in ancient Egypt (as in other ancient cultures), the act of sanctioned violence was part of an established system, with physical and spiritual obligations that needed to be fulfilled. The *process* of the violence, be it sacrifice, execution, or some other form of violence, was more important than the individual actors. While the quiescence of the victim may have had some impact on how the remains were processed, it seems to have been more or less irrelevant in comparison to the crucial process or ritual that needed to be completed. The processing of the body was part of the ritual, and had to be carried out in a culturally determined manner for the requisite obligations to be fulfilled.

Due to the lengthy history of Egyptian civilization, a comprehensive discussion of state-sanctioned violence and processing of human remains would require several volumes, and such is not the intent here. Instead, I focus on specific and clear examples of state-sanctioned violence, and the ways that the processing of the bodies from these rituals was designed to display or hide this violence in accordance with Egyptian ideals about kingship and *ma'at*. In particular, three cases are assessed: human sacrifice, execution, and trophy-taking.

HUMAN SACRIFICE IN EGYPT

The Egyptian belief in an afterlife much like an idealized earthly life encouraged individuals to take items with them to the grave, ranging from simple pots in poorer burials to the elaborate and costly funerary assemblages of the pharaohs (Assman 2005; Dodson and Ikram 2008; Grajetzki 2003; Ikram and Dodson 1998). Sometimes these grave goods seem to have included human lives as well, perhaps as simply another form of burial goods intended to accompany the pharaoh into the afterlife.

Evidence for sacrificial burial derives almost exclusively from Abydos in southern Egypt and, to a lesser degree, Saqqara in northern Egypt. The kings of the newly unified Egypt during the period now known as the Early Dynastic Period (c. 3000–2686 BC, including the First and Second Dynasties) encircled their royal tombs and separate funerary enclosures (of uncertain use but most likely for funerary rituals) with a row (or rows) of simple burials, a practice that then ceased and did not reappear in the same form for the rest of Egyptian history (Morris 2007; Petrie 1900, 1925; Shaw 2004).[1] These subsidiary burials are characterized by their orderly and discrete organization around a royal tomb and/or royal funerary enclosures, and typically include few grave goods (Morris 2007; Petrie 1900,

[1] All dates derived from Shaw (2004).

1925). When grave goods are present, they may include vessels, jewelry, tools, weapons, or sometimes items associated with the profession of the deceased (e.g., small boats or paints) (Morris 2007). Yet the apparent haste with which the graves were constructed—Petrie believed that the long walls had been laid out together and then the space between simply divided by partitions of mudbrick (Petrie 1900, 1925)—seems to suggest that expediency and haste were more important for these tombs than individual display. Though there is little evidence of perimortem lethal trauma, based on the observation that the (sometimes hundreds of) individuals surrounding the royal tombs of this period in Abydos appear to have been deposited all at the same time rather than over a period, many scholars have postulated human sacrifice (Kaiser 1985; Morris 2007; Petrie 1900, 1925; Wengrow 2006).

The subsidiary burials at Abydos were mainly excavated in 1922 by W. M. Flinders Petrie, who unlike many of his contemporaries, took copious notes and excavation photographs, and published his findings regularly (Petrie 1900, 1925). A first glance at Petrie's excavation notes and some of his photographs seems to indicate that these skeletons might seem to be relatively normal burials of the Early Dynastic Period in Egypt; as was standard for most burials of the time, the bodies were generally placed in a flexed position, unwrapped (artificial mummification was barely beginning at this time period), with a few grave goods such as ceramic vessels and stone or copper tools (Grajetzki 2003; Ikram 2015; Petrie 1900, 1925). A closer examination, however, reveals several interesting aspects. According to Petrie's excavation notes and photographs, one individual had his or her legs tied together, and then tied to the thighs. The head was also raised when the body was uncovered. Another was found with the right leg raised, and during excavation Petrie propped up the leg with bricks to preserve this position for the excavation photo. Several individuals had one arm that appears twisted or flung to the side, as if the body had been flung into the pit with little care (Petrie 1925).

Unfortunately, the cause of death for these individuals has proved difficult or impossible to determine. Many of the burials were heavily looted and disturbed even before Petrie began his excavations (Petrie 1900, 1925). As was fairly standard practice for the time, Petrie retained only the crania that he felt were of interest, and reburied the postcranial remains (thus rendering them difficult to access, given the complexities of obtaining excavation permits for Abydos, and in Egypt in general) (Petrie 1925). The crania that he retained were distributed to museums, mostly in the United Kingdom (Petrie 1900, 1925), where they are currently under study by this author. Some individuals do show evidence of perimortem lethal trauma, and some do not. Of course, we cannot dismiss the possibility that soft-tissue trauma was the cause of death. Petrie's suggestion that the individuals were stunned and then buried alive (Petrie 1925) should be taken with a healthy dose of skepticism, falling, as it does, well within the tradition of Woolley's rather melodramatic contemporary interpretation of the funerary scenes at the royal tombs in Ur (Molleson and Hodgson 2003; Woolley and Burrows 1934).

The subsidiary graves at Macramallah's Rectangle in Saqqara, believed to date to Egypt's First Dynasty, are similar in many ways to those at Abydos, and show additional evidence of social stratification as demonstrated by the quality (e.g., stone or alabaster dishes in some graves vs. clay vessels in others) and quantity of grave goods (Morris 2007). The location of each burial also seems to have been a statement of status; Morris notes that the richest subsidiary sacrificial burials at Macramallah's Rectangle were those nearest and to the right of the proposed location of the king's body (i.e., to the king's right if he was facing the same direction as the sacrificial victims), while farther burials contained fewer and lower-quality grave goods. Many of the sacrificial victims were young adult males, but adult females were also interred in the subsidiary graves, as were children (though since only the crania were retained from the original excavations, determination of sex was not always possible or reliably accurate) (Morris 2007).

Despite the absence of clear causes of death in most cases, retainer sacrifice seems the most likely explanation for these subsidiary burials. The simultaneous closure of all subsidiary burials around a single royal tomb argues against the later practice of individually constructed tombs for officials that were utilized at different times as their owners died naturally (Dodson and Ikram 2008; Grajetzki 2003; Reisner 2011). The social and political landscape of the Early Dynastic Period provides textbook conditions for human sacrifice, based on comparisons from clear human sacrifice in societies from around the world (Cameron 1987; Kuhrt 1987; Morris 2007; Sagan 1985, 1993; Shannon 2002; Walker 1989). The new rulers of Egypt were faced with unifying a diverse range of cultural groups clustered along hundreds of miles of the Nile Valley, and the death of each of these rulers would have drawn the nascent Egyptian state closer to the ever-looming threat of chaos (Hoffman 1979; Kemp 2005; Midant-Reynes 2000; O'Connor 2011; Shaw 2004; Wengrow 2006; Wilkinson 2001). The ultimate control of the ruler over life and death would have been displayed to powerful effect by mass human sacrifices (Morris 2007). This form of conspicuous consumption solidified the ruler's position and encouraged the populace to accept the new political system.

The processing of these bodies in these subsidiary tombs bears particular mention. In cases of human sacrifice throughout the world, the mode of death, and the way the remains are processed after death, depends in part on the purpose of the sacrifice: is the point of the sacrifice to cause death and thus liberate or give that individual's life force to something else, or is the point of the sacrifice to embark on a journey into the afterlife with a deceased ruler or important person? In the case of the Central and South American human sacrifices, rituals often involved much bloodshed and pain, because part of the purpose was to share or release the sacrificed individual's life force, often with the sacrificer or victor (Benson and Cook 2001; Geller 2011; Klaus, Centurión, and Curo 2010; Read 1998). Such rituals have left clear markers on the human remains that are easily identifiably as state-sanctioned, ritualized violence (Klaus, Centurión, and Curo 2010).

Yet not all sacrifices are the same. If the main goal of the killing is conspicuous consumption and power over life and death, as is often the case for retainer sacrifice (i.e., the sacrifice of members of the court, often including officials, wives and concubines, and servants or slaves), it may be unnecessary to utterly destroy the sacrificial victims, since the purpose is at least partly to display the ruler's ultimate power over life and death. Death may simply be another stage in a journey, a threshold that must be crossed, rather than a glorification of violence and power. In such situations, it may even be undesirable to obliterate or "damage" the victim, since doing so could inhibit the ability of the victim to serve his or her ruler in the afterlife. For example, the sacrifices at the Royal Tomb at Ur were not really focused on causing death at all; rather, the purpose was to create a moment in time that would persist for eternity (Baadsgaard et al. 2011; Baadsgaard, Monge, and Zettler 2012; Molleson and Hodgson 2003). While the human sacrificees at Ur were still violently killed (Baadsgaard et al. 2011; Baadsgaard, Monge, and Zettler 2012), care was taken to arrange the bodies in such a way that the violent aspects of their death were hidden or at least not emphasized. To some degree, this seems to also be the case in Egypt. While the position of the bodies in the Abydos and Saqqara subsidiary burials seems to hint at some sort of coercion and perhaps even careless deposition of the bodies themselves, the corpses do not appear to have been ritually manipulated, damaged, or displayed after death. It seems that the focus was on preparing to follow the leader into the afterlife, rather than on the violence of death itself. Death may have even been considered somewhat of a necessary side effect of remaining loyal to the king for all eternity. Whatever the rituals practiced before death, violence was not overtly or explicitly displayed in the processing of the remains after death.

Perhaps the reason for this nonviolent processing lies in the identity of those buried in these subsidiary burials. The fact that these individuals all received some type of mortuary treatment (i.e., a tomb and generally some grave goods) seems to indicate some level of respect (Petrie 1900, 1925). The inclusion of typically Egyptian artifacts in some of the graves supports the hypothesis that the interred, at least in death, were identified as Egyptians (Morris 2007; Petrie 1900, 1925). It seems that they were accorded some degree of honor, based on the inclusion of grave goods and the proximity to the royal tombs and enclosures, as well as the overall health of the individuals (Keita and Boyce 2006). The king exercised his divine control over life and death by decreeing that these individuals accompany him into the afterlife, but this was the extent of the message. Further violent processing of the remains was not necessary, and manipulation or display would likely have been viewed as undesirable. The bodies of those serving the king in the afterlife needed to be intact to better serve their lord, and the populace that was not sacrificed had already been convinced that dictating who lived and who died was a royal prerogative. In fact, the Egyptians may not have viewed this practice as violent at all, but simply a way to extend service to the king into the afterlife.

EXECUTION

In contrast to the relatively nonviolent processing of sacrificial victims (however violent their actual demise may have been), execution as a state-sanctioned violent practice took a very different approach. While evidence for execution is mostly limited to textual records, the nature of these records (e.g., legal documents rather than ritualistic religious texts) suggests that execution was indeed practiced for a variety of reasons. A few texts contain brief and often oblique references to capital punishment, which was seemingly only enforced in cases of robbery of royal tombs or regicide (Muhlestein 2011, 2015; Tyldesley 2000). Interference with the divine cult (e.g., robbery of temple property) also elicited severe punishments, and some scholars believe that punishment for such offenses included mutilation and destruction of the perpetrator's body by fire, in life or after death (Muhlestein 2008, 2011, 2015; Willems 1990). Such a punishment would have lasting effects beyond death; without a body, the deceased would not be able to enter the afterlife, and his or her spirit would be doomed to wander restlessly between worlds for all eternity (Assman 2005; Grajetzki 200; Hornung 1993; Ikram and Dodson 1998). It is interesting, but unsurprising, that so few physical remains of executed individuals have been found from ancient Egypt. Ideologically, the purpose of any execution, as a state-mandated punishment, was to punish the transgressor for disrupting *ma'at* in some way. Perhaps there are so few obviously executed individuals in archaeological contexts because the bodies were ritually destroyed to symbolize the complete power and dominance of the Egyptian king, and the restoration of *ma'at*.

Execution was, of course, one of the most serious punishments that could be meted out in the earthly realm, and seems to have been retained for offenses against the Egyptian concept of *ma'at*: in practical terms, this generally meant offenses against the king (as the divine incarnation of the god Horus) and the gods, such as rebellion, robbery of royal tombs, or theft of sacred or royal property (Muhlestein 2011; Tyldesley 2000). Two distinct types of execution appear to have been practiced in ancient Egypt: capital punishment and execution of war captives.

Capital Punishment

According to legal accounts, individuals found guilty of tomb robbery in the New Kingdom (c. 1550–1069 BC) seem to have been impaled (Muhlestein 2011; Tyldesley 2000). There is some evidence that as early as the Middle Kingdom, Senwosret I impaled those who desecrated the temple at Tod (south of modern Luxor), but most references to impalement derive from the New Kingdom, particularly the Ramesside period (Muhlestein 2011). This punishment is explicitly recorded for royal tomb robbers in Papyrus Amherst, which also describes the interrogation of suspects (which included beating suspects on the soles of their feet) and sentences of impalement for the conspirators found guilty of robbing royal tombs (Muhlestein 2011; Peet 2005). The hieroglyphic determinative for impalement, accompanying the phrase *diw Hr tp Xt* ("to put on top of stakes" according to Muhlestein 2011, 54) does appear to unambiguously show a figure being (or about to be) impaled atop a stake (figure 7.1) (Peet 2005).

The texts do not record whether the offenders were dead or still alive when impaled, and thus it is possible (if perhaps unlikely) that death occurred in a different manner, and impalement served as a highly visible performance of social and criminal justice. These transgressors may or may not have been alive when they were placed on stakes, but either way the public display of their bodies would have served as a grisly reminder of the consequences of such crimes (Muhlestein 2011; Tyldesley 2000). The decay and subsequent fragmentation of the body would have rendered the deceased incapable of entering the afterlife, a fate far worse than death in the Egyptian mindset. In this case, it seems likely that beyond the impalement, the bodies were purposely not processed, or were processed in a way that effectively removed them from the world of the living and the dead, and perhaps even from memory.

Isolated textual references may hint that drowning and burning were also used as forms of capital punishment (Muhlestein 2011, 2015; Tyldesley 2000; Willems 1990). Death by burning or drowning would have been a particularly powerful punishment because the body would be destroyed or lost, thus eliminating any possibility of an afterlife for the accused (Muhlestein 2011, 2015; Willems 1990). Muhlestein mentions punishment for those responsible for the decay of the Temple of Tod during the Middle Kingdom, who were subject to "flaying, beheading, and burning" (Muhlestein 2015, 245), while Willems notes that "the enemies [responsible for desecrating the temple] have been placed on the brazier" (Willems 1990, 41). Tyldesley also notes references to burning as punishment for vandalism of a temple, theft of state property, and rebellion against the king, and notes that such executions were likely held in public locations to serve as grim reminders of the consequences of such serious crimes (Tyldesley 2000). Death by burning, as a way of destroying someone utterly and thus precluding any chance to enter the afterlife,

FIGURE 7.1. The hieroglyphic determinative depicting what appears to be an individual being (or about to be) impaled. (Hieroglyph typed using the JSesh program: fair use; Rosmorduc 2014.)

would almost certainly be considered a fate worse than death, and the author of this account may have thus been attempting to reinforce the severity and magnitude of the crime. However, without more direct textual references or (in an ideal but somewhat unlikely scenario) archaeological or bioarchaeological evidence of such practices, it is difficult to say whether these dramatic punishments were enforced in real life.

Execution of War Captives

While war captives were almost certainly executed, probably publicly, there is little physical evidence to support this assessment. Textual records note numerous cases of not only execution of defeated enemies, but display of the bodies. Enemy leaders were more likely to be brutally executed than other, lower-ranking captives; after a particularly triumphant campaign in the Levant, Amenhotep II records on the Amada Stela that he brought seven defeated princes back to Thebes, tied to the prow of his boat, before displaying their bodies at Thebes and Gebel Barkal (the verb tense in this account is unfortunately ambiguous regarding whether the princes were slain before or after they were brought back to Thebes) (Filer 1997). There is also some textual evidence suggesting that captives may have been publicly executed in Thebes after victorious campaigns (Muhlestein 2011). The viceroy Djehutymose subdued a rebellion during the reign of Akhenaten, and on a stela at Buhen, Djehutymose boasted that he placed some of the captured rebels "atop a stake," likely indicating public impalement (Darnell and Manassa 2007). Whether the victims were alive or already deceased upon impalement cannot be determined, but this practice seems to have been quite rarely used as punishment for rebels (Darnell and Manassa 2007). One of the Amarna letters (EA 101) seems to suggest that a rebellious Amorite king was captured and executed by the forces of Amenhotep III (Darnell and Manassa 2007; Muhlestein 2011).

Physical evidence of such executions, however, is extremely limited. The most famous, and perhaps only known example, was that of a bound and decapitated individual who seems to have been part of a foundation deposit for the Temple of Mut in Luxor (Anonymous 2012). Foundation deposits, intended to dedicate or bless a new construction project and buried near or under part of the structure, are common throughout Egypt, but no other known examples include human remains. This individual was bound and decapitated and placed beneath a temple pillar, presumably to dedicate the temple and demonstrate Egypt's total victory over enemies (Anonymous 2012). The posture of the body calls to mind the familiar images of defeated captives, bound and beheaded, dating to as early as the Early Dynastic Period. By rendering the enemy impotent, both physically and ideologically by fragmentation of the body, and by interring the body in a ritual space, the Egyptian king was demonstrating his eternal victory over the forces of *isfet* (in this case, personified by the deceased individual).

TROPHY-TAKING

Trophy-taking has long been used by cultures around the world for a variety of purposes, though perhaps the most common form of trophy-taking is intended to provide a physical marker or count of victory (Andrushko, Schwitalla, and Walker 2010; Finucane 2008, Forstner-Müeller et al. 2012; Tung 2008, 2012; Zimmerman 1997). While trophy-taking in Egypt has often been overlooked, tantalizing evidence of such practices has emerged not only in the artistic record but also in archaeological contexts.

Enemy soldiers who were already dead (or perhaps were dying) were likely mutilated; Egyptian reliefs frequently show piles of severed hands or genitalia that are used to tally the number of defeated enemy soldiers in a graphic display of victory (Bestock 2017; Darnell and Manassa 2007). For example, the walls at the mortuary temple of Medinet Habu (built by Ramses III during his reign from 1184 to 1153 BC) in modern Luxor show piles of severed hands and male genitalia that had been collected from defeated enemy soldiers as a way of enumerating the defeated enemy, and a depiction of King Horemheb defeating Asiatics and Sea People shows at least two fallen soldiers whose right hands had already been severed (Darnell and Manassa 2007). The removal of what was likely the sword hand for most soldiers (or even a depiction of such mutilation) would have magically rendered the victim mutilated and weakened.

Though such practices have often been viewed as purely symbolic, physical evidence has emerged in a few cases. Perhaps the most obvious confirmation that trophy-taking was indeed practiced in Egypt is in the collection of severed hands found at Tell el Dab'a in late 2011 (Bietak 2012; Forstner-Müeller et al. 2012). In front of a Second Intermediate Period (c. 1650–1550 BC, though these dates are currently being revised) palace, Bietak and his team found two pits; inside each pit was a single right hand (Bietak 2012). Two more pits were found from an (unspecified) earlier building phase, containing an additional fourteen hands in total. Bietak notes that some of the hands "were of extraordinary size and robustness" (Bietak 2012, 43). Perhaps these hands were presented as offerings, tokens of victory, at or near the temple (Bietak 2012). While the ostensible purpose for collecting these hands was to count the fallen enemy soldiers, even removal of a hand (the right hand seems to have been favored) from a living victim would have minimally made the victims a less effective or ineffective soldier, and could easily have caused death from infection and blood loss (Bietak 2012). Obviously the severing of genitalia from soldiers would have similar effects, though such trophies are less likely to survive in the archaeological record. In an ideological sense, both the male hand and genitalia were strongly linked to new life and fertility, and the removal of these organs would also disallow the revivification of the deceased enemy's spirit (Cooney 2010, 224).

Whether the king personally cut off these grisly trophies or not is somewhat irrelevant, because according to Egyptian ideology, it was the king who was ultimately responsible for subduing all enemies, restoring *ma'at*, and by extension, collecting the spoils and trophies of war. Since the hands were derived (presumably) from enemy soldiers, the rest of the bodies were likely left on the battlefield to decay or be retrieved by survivors. The deposition of the hands in front of the palace at Tell el Dab'a suggests that they may have been intended as a foundation deposit, or perhaps as a dedicatory offering in gratitude to the gods for the triumph of Egyptian forces. In this respect, it could be argued that these hands were processed as objects, since Egyptian kings often offered up the spoils of war as gratitude for victory in battle. At the same time, the hands were not objects, but were parts of human beings who were viewed as the forces of *isfet*, and thus may be considered as a symbolic combination of execution and (non-retainer) human sacrifice in the pursuit of *ma'at*.

WHEN IS VIOLENCE VIOLENT?

It seems clear from the examples discussed here that the ancient Egyptians were no more and no less violent than any other civilization throughout history. The Egyptian king was expected to, and apparently did, use violence in specific, culturally defined circumstances. These violent rituals manipulated Egyptian ideas and beliefs as they manipulated human bodies, creating the most powerful message for a specific context. As Whitehead has noted, violence in such cases was not an aberration at all, but a legitimate and socially expected course of action (Whitehead 2004, 60). The legitimacy of the violence depended on the context and the actors involved; presumably the slaughter of a fellow human being by an ordinary citizen was viewed differently, both practically and mythologically, from the king's slaughter of a real and/or symbolic enemy of Egypt.

Yet paradoxically, in some cases the processing of the remains of what may seem the most violent rituals (such as execution or human sacrifice) has rendered these practices almost invisible to modern eyes. If we fail to consider the ancient Egyptian ideology of kingship, life after death, and beliefs about the proper way the world should operate, we may miss the evidence for these practices altogether. For the Egyptians, violence affected both the physical and the spiritual worlds, and the processing of the body of a victim of violence was directly influenced by the purpose and context of the violence. The bodies of defeated enemies had to be rendered impotent not only in this world but the next, and a variety of methods of mutilation and destruction ensured that the corpse could not return as a vengeful spirit.

Conversely, the bodies of those who seem to have been sacrificed to accompany their ruler into the afterlife were treated with some level of respect, not only in the placement of their graves but in the inclusion of grave goods to take into the afterlife (Morris 2007; Petrie 1900, 1925). While we may view any form of human sacrifice as violent and radical, the Egyptians may have viewed this practice as a nonviolent and necessary component of a royal burial. Perhaps this explains the lack of obvious lethal trauma on some of the human remains from these graves; the perpetrators may have taken care to choose a relatively painless or quick method of inducing death (and thus, perhaps, archaeologically invisible), since the point of the ritual was not suffering but rebirth and renewal in the next world. It could perhaps even be theorized that the preservation of the bodies of victims, as in cases of human sacrifice, constituted cultural acceptance of the practice. Both the violence of death and the subsequent preservation of the bodies were part of a larger ritual, firmly grounded in Egyptian beliefs about the role of the king and the afterlife.

CONCLUSION

As Whitehead (2004, 65) noted, "violence cannot be treated as extracultural." If we are to understand how, when, and why violence and violent processing is practiced in particular circumstances, we cannot divorce such acts from their deep cultural backgrounds. The ancient Egyptians expected the king to employ what we would consider violence in a variety of specific situations, and the application of these violent rituals enforced ideas about the workings of the world and what it meant to be Egyptian. By damaging and mutilating the human body, or minimally, by causing death, the Egyptians conveyed messages of inclusion and exclusion, and enacted and reenacted rituals of both sacred and mundane significance. Processing of the human bodies involved in these rituals was fraught with religious and social meaning. Although this study has focused on ancient Egypt, the intent is also to highlight the differences and similarities in the ways that humans use violent processing as a tool of social, political, and economic power and control, and how processing of human remains associated with violent rituals may display, continue, or obscure this violence (Krohn-Hansen 1994). Perhaps, if we can gain a greater understanding of how cultures in the past understood, used, and even celebrated violence, we can begin to evaluate the patterns and effects of violence within our own society, where proximity and familiarity may obscure the broad patterns.

REFERENCES

Allen, James P. 2015. *The Ancient Egyptian Pyramid Texts*. 2nd ed. Atlanta, GA: SBL Press.

Andrushko, Valerie A., Al W. Schwitalla, and Phillip L. Walker. 2010. "Trophy-Taking and Dismemberment as Warfare Strategies in Prehistoric Central California." *American Journal of Physical Anthropology* 141 (1): 83–96.

Anonymous. 2012. "Hopkins in Egypt Today." http://pages.jh.edu/~egypttoday/2012/index2012.html, May-June 2012.

Assman, Jan. 2005. *Death and Salvation in Ancient Egypt*. Translated by David Lorton. Ithaca, NY: Cornell University Press.

Baadsgaard, Aubrey, Alexis T. Boutin, and Jane Buikstra, eds. 2012. *Breathing New Life into the Evidence of Death: Contemporary Approaches to Bioarchaeology*. Advanced Seminar Series. Santa Fe, NM: SAR Press.

Baadsgaard, Aubrey, Janet Monge, Samantha Cox, and Richard L. Zettler. 2011. "Human Sacrifice and Intentional Corpse Preservation in the Royal Cemetery of Ur." *Antiquity* 85 (327): 27–42.

Baadsgaard, Aubrey, Janet Monge, and Richard L. Zettler. 2012. "Bludgeoned, Burned, and Beautified: Reevaluating Mortuary Practices in the Royal Cemetery at Ur." In *Sacred Killing: The Archaeology of Sacrifice in the Ancient Near East*, edited by A. Porter and G. M. Schwartz, 125–158. Winona Lake, IN: Eisenbrauns.

Benson, Elizabeth P., and A. G. Cook, eds. 2001. *Ritual Sacrifice in Ancient Peru*. Austin: University of Texas Press.

Berger, Thomas D., and Erik Trinkaus. 1995. "Patterns of Trauma among the Neandertals." *Journal of Archaeological Science* 22 (6): 841–852.

Bestock, Lauren. 2017. *Violence and Power in Ancient Egypt: Image and Ideology before the New Kingdom*. London: Routledge.

Bietak, Manfred. 2012. "The Archaeology of the 'Gold of Valour.'" *Egyptian Archaeology* 42: 32–33.

Cameron, A. 1987. "The Construction of Court Ritual: The Byzantine Book of Ceremonies." In *Rituals of Royalty: Power and Ceremonial in Traditional Societies*, edited by D. Cannadine and S.R.F. Prince, 106–136. Cambridge, UK: Cambridge University Press.

Carman, John. 1997. "Introduction: Approaches to Violence." In *Material Harm: Archaeological Studies of War and Violence*, edited by John Carman, 1–23. Glasgow, UK: Criuthne Press.

Carter, Michael J. 2013. "'Persuade the People': Violence and Roman Spectacle Entertainment in the Greek World." In *The Archaeology of Violence: Interdisciplinary Approaches*, 158–168. New York: State University of New York Press.

Cooney, Kathlyn M. 2010. "Gender Transformation in Death: A Case Study of Coffins from Ramesside Period Egypt." *Near Eastern Archaeology* 73: 224–237.

Crubézy, É., and B. Midant-Reynes. 2005. "Les sacrifices humains à l'époque prédynastique: l'apport de la nécropole d'Adaïma." In *Le sacrifice humain en Égypte ancienne et ailleurs*, edited by J.-P. Albert and B. Midant-Reynes, 58–81. Soleb, Sudan.

Darnell, J. C., and C. Manassa. 2007. *Tutankhamun's Armies: Battle and Conquest During Ancient Egypt's Late 18th Dynasty*. New York. Wiley.

Davis, Whitney. 1992. *Masking the Blow: The Scene of Representation in Late Prehistoric Egyptian Art*. Berkeley: University of California Press.

Dodson, Aidan, and Salima Ikram. 2008. *The Tomb in Ancient Egypt*. London: Thames and Hudson.

Dunand, Françoise, and Christiane Zivie-Coche. 2005. *Gods and Men in Egypt: 3000 BCE to 395 CE. David Lorton*. Ithaca, NY, and London: Cornell University Press.

Eller, Jack David. 2010. *Cruel Creeds, Virtuous Violence: Religious Violence across Culture and History*. Amherst, NY: Prometheus Books.

Emery, Walter B., ed. 1974. *Archaic Egypt: Culture and Civilization in Egypt Five Thousand Years Ago*. London: Penguin Books.

Eyre, C. 2002. *Cannibal Hymn: A Cultural and Literary Study*. Liverpool, UK: Liverpool University Press.

Faulkner, R. O. 2007. *The Ancient Egyptian Pyramid Texts*. Stilwell, KS: Digireads.com.

Filer, J. M. 1997. "Ancient Egypt and Nubia as a Source of Information for Violent Cranial Injuries." In *Material Harm: Archaeological Studies of War and Violence*, edited by John Carman, 47–74. Glasgow, UK: Cruithne Press.

Finucane, Brian. 2008. "Trophy Heads from Nawinpukio, Perú: Physical and Chemical Analysis of Huarpa-era Modified Human Remains." *American Journal of Physical Anthropology* 135 (1): 75–84.

Forstner-Müeller, I., M. Bietak, M. Lehmann, and C. Reali. 2012. "Report on the Excavations at Tell el Dab'a 2011." http://www.auaris.at/html/index_en.html.

Gardiner, Alan Henderson. 1932. *Late Egyptian Stories*. Bruxelles: Fondation egyptologiwue Reine Elisabeth.

Geller, P. L. 2011. "The Sacrifices We Make of and for Our Children: Making Sense of Pre-Columbian Maya Practices." In *Breathing New Life into the Evidence of Death: Contemporary Approaches to Bioarchaeology*, edited by Aubrey Baadsgaard, Alexis T. Boutin, and J. Buikstra, 79–105. Santa Fe, NM: SAR Press.

Grajetzki, Wolfram. 2003. *Burial Customs in Ancient Egypt: Life in Death for Rich and Poor*. 2nd ed. London: Duckworth.

Hall, Emma Swan. 1986. *The Pharaoh Smites His Enemies: A Comparative Study*. München: Deutscher Kunstverlag.

Hawass, Zahi, Somaia Ismail, Ashraf Selim, Sahar N. Saleem, Dina Fathalla, Sally Wasef, Ahmed Z. Gad, Rama Saad, Suzan Fares, Hany Amer, Paul Gostner, Yehia Gad, Carsten M. Pusch, and Albert R. Zink. 2012. "Revisiting the Harem Conspiracy and Death of Ramesses III: Anthropological, Forensic, Radiological, and Genetic Study." *BMJ: British Medical Journal* 345, doi: https://doi.org/10.1136/bmj.e8268.

Hoffman, Michael A. 1979. *Egypt before the Pharaohs: The Prehistoric Foundations of Egyptian Civilization*. Cairo: The American University in Cairo Press.

Hornung, Erik. 1993. *Der Eine Und Die Vielen*. Darmstadt: WBG Academic.

Ikram, Salima. 2015. *Death and Burial in Ancient Egypt*. Cairo: The American University in Cairo Press.

Ikram, Salima, and Aidan Dodson. 1998. *The Mummy in Ancient Egypt: Equipping the Dead for Eternity*. New York: Thames and Hudson.

Kaiser, W. 1985. "Umm el-Qaab: Nachuntersuchungen im früheitlichen Königsfriedhof. 2. Vorbericht." *Mitteilungen des Deutschen Archäologischen Instituts, Abteilung Kairo* 38: 211–269.

Keita, S O.Y., and A. J. Boyce. 2006. "Variation in Porotic Hyperostosis in the Royal Cemetery Complex at Abydos, Upper Egypt: A Social Interpretation." *Antiquity* 80 (307): 64–73.

Kemp, Barry. 2005. *Ancient Egypt: Anatomy of a Civilization*. New York: Routledge.

Klaus, Haagen C., C. Centurión, and M. Curo. 2010. "Bioarchaeology of Human Sacrifice: Violence, Identity and the Evolution of Ritual Killings at Cerro Cerillos, Peru." *Antiquity* 2010: 1102–1122.

Knüsel, C. J., and Martin J. Smith, eds. 2013. *The Handbook of the Bioarchaeology of Human Conflict*. New York: Routledge.

Krohn-Hansen, Christian. 1994. "The Anthropology of Violent Interaction." *Journal of Archaeological Research* 50 (4): 367–381.

Kuhrt, A. 1987. "Usurpation, Conquest, and Ceremonial: From Babylon to Persia." In *Rituals of Royalty: Power and Ceremonial in Traditional Societies*, edited by D. Cannadine and S. R. F. Prince, 20–55. Cambridge, UK: Cambridge University Prss.

Martin, Debra L., and David W. Frayer, eds. 1997. *Troubled Times: Violence and Warfare in the Past*. Volume 3: *War and Society*. New York: Routledge.

Martin, Debra L., Ryan P. Harrod, and Ventura R. Pérez. 2012. *The Bioarchaeology of Violence*, University Press of Florida, Gainesville.

Midant-Reynes, Beatrix. 2000. *The Prehistory of Egypt: From the First Egyptians to the First Pharaohs*. Malden, MA: Wiley-Blackwell.

Molleson, Theya, and Dawn Hodgson. 2003. "The Human Remains from Woolley's Excavations at Ur." *Iraq* 65: 91–129.

Morris, Ellen F. 2007. "Sacrifice for State: First Dynasty Royal Funerals and the Rites at Macramallah's Rectangle." In *Performing Death: Social Analyses of Funerary Traditions in the Ancient Near East and Mediterranean*, edited by Nicola Laneri, 15–38. Chicago, IL: University of Chicago Press.

Muhlestein, Kerry. 2008. "Royal Executions: Evidence Bearing on the Subject of Sanctioned Killing in the Middle Kingdom." *Journal of the Economic and Social History of the Orient* 51 (2): 181–208.

Muhlestein, Kerry. 2011. "Violence in the Service of Order: The Religious Framework for Sanctioned Killing in Ancient Egypt." *Near Eastern Archaeology* 78 (4): 244–251.

Muhlestein, Kerry. 2015. "Sacred Violence: When Ancient Egyptian Punishment was Dressed in Ritual Trappings." *Near Eastern Archaeology* 78 (4): 244–251.

O'Connor, David. 2011. *Abydos: Egypt's First Pharaohs and the Cult of Osiris*. London: Thames and Hudson.

Peet, T. E. 2005. *The Great Tomb Robberies of the Twentieth Egyptian Dynasty: Being A Critical Study, with Translations and Commentaries, of the Papyri in Which These Are Recorded*. Eastford, CT: Martino Publishers.

Pérez, Ventura R. 2012. "The Politicization of the Dead: Violence as Performance, Politics as Usual." In *The Bioarchaeology of Violence*, edited by Debra L. Martin, Ryan P. Harrod, and Ventura Pérez, 13–28. Gainesville: University Press of Florida.

Petrie, Flinders. 1900. *The Royal Tombs of the First Dynasty, 1900–1901. Edited by Francis L. Griffith*. London and Boston: Egypt Exploration Fund.

Petrie, W. Flinders. 1925. *Tombs of the Courtiers and Oxyrhynkhos*. London: British School of Archaeology in Egyypt and Egyptian Research Account.

Porter, A., and G. M. Schwartz, eds. 2012. *Sacred Killing: The Archaeology of Sacrifice in the Ancient Near East*. Winona Lake, IN: Eisenbrauns.

Ralph, S., ed. 2013. *The Archaeology of Violence: Interdisciplinary Approaches*. Albany: State University of New York Press.

Read, K. 1998. *Time and Sacrifice in the Aztec Cosmos*. Bloomington: Indiana University Press.

Redfern, Rebecca. 2017. *Injury and Trauma in Bioarchaeology: Interpreting Violence in Past Lives*. Cambridge, UK: Cambridge University Press.

Redford, S. 2002. *The Harem Conspiracy: The Murder of Ramesses III*. DeKalb, IL: Northern Illinois University Press.

Reisner, George Andrew. 2011. *The Development of the Egyptian Tomb down to the Accession of Cheops*. Whitefish, MT: Literary Licensing.

Robben, A.C.G.M. 2000. "The Assault of Basic Trust: Disappearances, Protest, and Reburial in Argentina." In *Cultures Under Siege: Collective violence and Trauma*, edited by A.C.G.M. Robben and M. M. Suárez-Orozco, 70–101. Cambridge, UK: Cambridge University Press.

Rosmorduc, Serge. 2014. JSesh Documentation. http://jseshdoc.qenherkhopeshef.org. Accessed May 4, 2018.

Sagan, Eli. 1985. *At the Dawn of Tyranny: The Origins of Individualism, Political Oppression, and the State*. New York: Knopf.

Sagan, Eli. 1993. *Cannibalism: Human Aggression and Cultural Forms*. Santa Fe, NM: FirstDrum.

Shannon, U. 2002. "Private Armies and the Decline of the State." In *Violence and Politics: Globalization's Paradox*, edited by K. Worcester, S. A. Bermanzohn, and M. Ungar, 32–47. New York: Routledge.

Shaw, I. 2004. *The Oxford History of Ancient Egypt. New edition*. Oxford: Oxford University Press.

Spalinger, A. 2005. *War in Ancient Egypt*. Oxford, UK: Blackwell Publishing.

Thrift, N. 2007. "Immaculate Warfare? The Spatial Politics of Extreme Violence." In *Violent Geographies: Fear, Terror, and Political Violence*, edited by Derek Gregory and Allan Pred, 273–294. New York: Routledge.

Tung, Tiffiny A. 2008. "Dismembering Bodies for Display: A Bioarchaeological Study of Trophy Heads from the Wari Site of Conchopata, Peru." *American Journal of Physical Anthropology* 136 (3): 294–308.

Tung, Tiffiny A. 2012. *Violence, Ritual, and the Wari Empire: A Social Bioarchaeology of Imperialism in the Ancient Andes*. Gainesville: University Press of Florida.

Turpin, Jennifer. 1986. "Rape as a Social Problem." In *The Austin Rape Crisis Center Training Manual* 1–35. Austin, TX: Austin Rape Crisis Center.

Turpin, Jennifer. 1995. *Reinventing the Social Self: Media and Social Change in the Former Soviet Union*. Westport, CT: Praeger.

Turpin, Jennifer, and Lester R. Kurtz, eds. 1997. *The Web of Violence: From Interpersonal to Global*. Urbana: University of Illinois Press.

Tyldesley, Joyce. 2000. *Judgement of the Pharaoh: Crime and Punishment in Ancient Egypt*. London: Weidenfeld and Nicolson.

Varner, E. R. 2013. "Violent Discourses: Visual Cannibalism and the Portraits of Rome's 'Bad' Emperors." In *The Archaeology of Violence*, edited by S. Ralph, 121–142. Albany: State University of New York Press.

Walker, Phillip L. 1989. "Cranial Injuries as Evidence of Violence in Prehistoric Southern California." *American Journal of Physical Anthropology* 80 (3): 313–323.

Wengrow, D. 2006. *The Archaeology of Early Egypt: Social Transformations in North-East Africa, c. 10,000 to 2,650* BC. Cambridge, UK: Cambridge University Press.

Whitehead, Neil L. 2004. "On the Poetics of Violence." In *Violence*, edited by Neil L. Whitehead, 55–78. Santa Fe, NM: SAR Press.

Whitehead, Neil L. 2007. "Violence and the Cultural Order." *Daedalus* 136 (1): 40–50. doi: 10.2307/20028088.

Wilkinson, Toby A.H. 2001. *Early Dynastic Egypt*. Revised edition. London and New York: Routledge.

Wilkinson, Toby A.H. 2013. *The Rise and Fall of Ancient Egypt*. New York: Random House Trade Paperback.

Willems, H. 1990. "Crime, Cult and Capital Punishment (Mo'alla Inscription 8)." *The Journal of Egyptian Archaeology* 76: 27–54.

Woolley, Leonard, and E. R. Burrows. 1934. *Ur Excavations. Volume II: The Royal Cemetery: A Report on the Predynastic and Sargonid Graves Excavated between 1926 and 1931*. London: British Museum, and Philadelphia, PA: University of Pennsylvania.

Zimmerman, Larry J. 1997. "The Crow Creek Massacre: Archaeology and Prehistoric Plains Warfare in Contemporary Contexts." In *Material Harm: Archaeological Studies of War and Violence*, edited by John Carman, 75–94. Glasgow, UK: Cruithne Press.

Zollikofer, Christoph P. E., Marcia S. Ponce de León, Bernard Vandermeersch, and François Lévêque. 2002. "Evidence for Interpersonal Violence in the St. Césaire Neanderthal." *Proceedings of the National Academy of Sciences of the United States of America* 99 (9): 6444–6448.

8

Social Memory and Mortuary Practices in Neolithic Anatolia

MARIN A. PILLOUD, SCOTT D. HADDOW, CHRISTOPHER J. KNÜSEL,
CLARK SPENCER LARSEN, AND MEHMET SOMEL

The Neolithic is a cultural designation that is generally associated with the domestication of plants and animals. In the Near East, its earliest origins appear with plant domesticates beginning at 10,700 cal BP (Fuller, Willcox, and Allaby 2012; Willcox 2012). The earliest domestication of ungulates in this region is thought to have occurred in an area extending from southeastern Anatolia to Iran between 8500 and 7000 BC (Vigne 2008; Zeder 2008, 2011). Concomitant with this domestication of plants and animals comes the development of settled life and agglomerated villages that signal a changing relationship with the "built environment" (Watkins 2006; Zeder 2015, 5), thus constituting the broad changes associated with the "Neolithic Revolution" (*sensu* Childe 1936). Recently, researchers have addressed the variability within this process and moved away from the simplistic notion of a "revolution." Instead, research is focused on how *neolithization* occurred in a nonlinear fashion (Sterelny and Watkins 2015).

While this radical cultural change likely varied greatly in time and place, the "Neolithic package" has been defined as a cultural construct that included domesticated plants and animals, as well as similarities in artifacts, settlement type, and symbolic representation (Çilingiroglu 2005; Özdoğan 2010). The initial development of this package can be seen in the *core* area, extending from the Levant to Anatolia, where it paused for nearly two millennia before moving to the Aegean basin (Brami 2015), and paused again for another two millennia before progressing further outward (Özdoğan 2008, 2011). This substantial pause allowed for a protracted period

DOI: 10.5876/9781646420612.c008

of development of Neolithic culture (Düring 2013). As neolithization spread westwards and out of the core area, it adapted and changed, although much of what came later could find its origin in this initial *core* area (Özdoğan 2010). Of particular interest is the similarity in mortuary practices seen early on in this core area, which included intramural burial and, in many cases, some manner of secondary manipulations of skeletal elements, to include cranium/skull removal and caching and/or disturbances of previous interments. While these practices had their root in earlier preagricultural societies in the Levant during the Natufian, they become more widely spread during the Neolithic in the Near East (Kuijt 1996). Then, as the Neolithic transitions to the subsequent Chalcolithic and the "Neolithic package" moves westward, these practices become less visible in the archaeological record (Özdoğan 2010). The development and growth of these practices from the Natufian to the Neolithic point to an intimate association with death and the dead, an association that may have been critical in maintaining social stability during the transition to agriculture. These mortuary practices may have served as a means of reinforcing social memory, which may have been critical in the rise of socioeconomic complexity and the interaction between these communities and the landscape and its resources.

While much work has been done on the Neolithic and Natufian periods in the Levant, less research has focused on Anatolia as a key location in the development of the Neolithic (see Watkins 2016). In this study, the role of mortuary practices in creating and reinforcing social memory during the process of neolithization in Anatolia is explored at the sites of Körtik Tepe, Çayönü, Boncuklu, Aşıklı Höyük, Çatalhöyük, Tepecik-Çiftlik, and Köşk Höyük (figure 8.1). These sites have well-documented burial practices, whereas several other impressive sites show no evidence for burial practices or have revealed few human remains (Lichter 2016). The sites discussed here cover the region extending from southeastern Anatolia to central Anatolia and span a period of over 5,000 years (from approximately 10,400 to 5000 cal BC). The inclusion of several sites in this region permits intersite comparison of mortuary practices during the development of the Neolithic.

MORTUARY PRACTICES AND SOCIAL MEMORY

The advent of domesticated animals and plants resulted in broad sociocultural and biological changes. During the Neolithic, human populations experienced shifts in economy, landscape management, sanitary conditions, and social structure. In addition to increases in skeletal indicators of stress, the period saw reductions in height and skeletal robusticity, and craniofacial and dental changes in relation to dietary changes (Meiklejohn and Babb 2011; Larsen 1995; Pinhasi and Meiklejohn

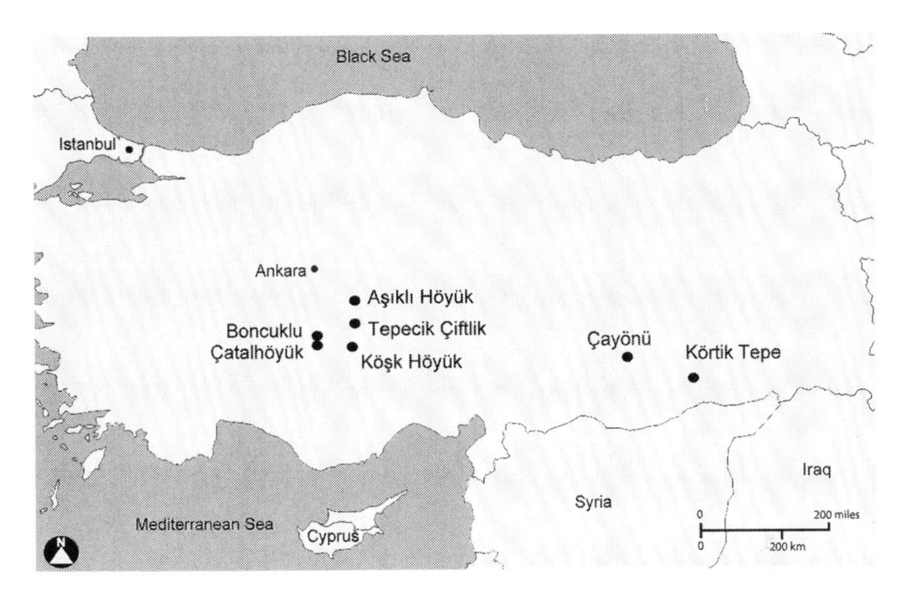

FIGURE 8.1. Location map of sites discussed in text.

2011). One way of mitigating the uncertainty of these changes would have been to create social cohesion through repetitive ritual that was an extension of practices that characterized hunter-gatherers in preceding periods. Burial practices would have served as a means of providing such an outlet, and as a way of maintaining ritual, as it is through repetition that memories are generated and maintained, and social structure is reinforced (Haddow and Knüsel 2017; Joyce 2001; Kuijt 2001).

In this discussion, the term "mortuary practices" is used to refer to the activities surrounding the deposition of the deceased. While debate continues over how elaboration of these practices can reveal aspects of social structure and social complexity of the once-living population (Binford 1971; Brown 1995; Parker Pearson 1982; Saxe 1970), the goal here is to identify patterns that highlight the role of social memory in the development of Neolithic societies, and in constructing and maintaining social organization. There is no implicit direct correlation between treatment of the dead and social relations amongst the living, but instead a connection between the two that is explored here at greater depth. The position taken in this discussion is in line with that of Kuijt (2001), who argues that during the Pre-Pottery Neolithic of the Near East social organization was *linked* to mortuary practices and ritual (specifically the practice of skull removal), which was in turn linked to use of space and social memory.

Social memory can be defined as the transmission of group experience through material culture and ritualized performance (Peterson 2013), which can exist as a long-term phenomenon that persists for more than a few generations (Meskell 2003). In much the same way that Whitehead (2004a, 2004b) argued that violence was an extended ritual that could imbue power and convey deep social meaning (i.e., linked to social memory), it is argued here that mortuary practice can have a similar effect in communicating social memory. Further, this postmortem manipulation of the dead can be equated to displays of violence that serve as expressions of culture involving the dead, those manipulating them, and those observing (Whitehead 2007). Therefore, these extended mortuary practices that involve processing human remains over time serve as a means to create and enforce a shared social experience, which could have implications for the construction of social structure. In this discussion, there is a focus on mortuary practices as a means of creating and transmitting social memory. This focus is on the *persistence* of such practices through time (beginning in the Natufian and continuing through the Neolithic). This long-term consideration of mortuary practices is different from the actual amount of time invested in practices and extended mortuary rites (e.g., individual time spent on primary versus secondary burial treatments).

To explore the construction and maintenance of social memory in Neolithic Anatolia, the biocultural background of several sites (Körtik Tepe, Çayönü, Boncuklu, Aşıklı Höyük, Çatalhöyük, Tepecik-Çiftlik, and Köşk Höyük) is summarized with a focus on archaeological evidence for the adoption of domesticated plants and animals and contemporary mortuary practices, including intramural and extramural burial, the practice of removing and/or decorating heads (or skulls),[1] and evidence for defleshing of the dead. As there is much debate over how the term "secondary burial" is used in the archaeological literature (see Knüsel 2014), and it is rarely explicitly defined, this study instead documents whether there is evidence for multiple individuals being interred in the same location. Also recorded, where possible, is the total number of remains in each site. These sites are briefly presented below in temporal order (earliest to latest); these findings are also outlined in table 8.1.

Körtik Tepe

Körtik Tepe is a Pre-Pottery Neolithic site located near the Turkish border with Syria that is composed of circular mudbrick structures (Erdal 2015). The site was

[1] While it is recognized that there are specific anatomical terms to differentiate between the cranium (bony framework of the head minus the mandible) and skull (cranium and mandible), the anthropological literature can often be vague in terms of what skeletal elements were actually involved in these mortuary treatments. Therefore, the terms "head," "skull," and "cranium" are used very broadly here, and outside of their anatomical definition in order to reflect what is reported in the literature.

Table 8.1. Summary of evidence for domestication and mortuary practices of Neolithic Anatolian sites*

		Domestication			*Burial Practices*					
Site	*Dates of Occupation (cal BC)*	*Plant*	*Animal*	*Approximate number of skeletons recovered*	*Intramural*	*Extramural*	*Decorated skulls*	*"Head" removal*	*Defleshing*	*Multiple individuals*
Körtik Tepe	10,405–9280	No	No	~800	Yes	Yes	Painted and plastered cranial and postcranial remains	No	Yes	?
Çayönü	10200–8270	Yes	Yes	~600	Yes	Yes	No	Yes	?	Yes
Boncuklu	8500–7500	Yes	Further work needed	>100	Yes	Yes	No	Yes	No	Yes
Aşıklı Höyük	8200–7300 (9000?)	Yes	Proto-domestication	~90	Yes	No	No	No	No	Yes
Çatalhöyük	7100–5950	Yes	Yes	~600	Yes	Rarely	Only one plastered skull	Yes	?	Yes
Tepecik-Çiftlik	7000–5500	Yes	Possible	~170	Yes	Yes	No	No	No	Yes
Köşk Höyük	6200–5500	Yes	Yes	?	Yes	No	Yes	Yes	No	?

* References provided in the text.

occupied in the tenth millennium BC (Özkaya and Coşkun 2009), and has recently been radiocarbon dated to between 10,405 and 9280 years cal BC (Benz et al. 2012). The site has not revealed evidence for the adoption of domestication and the majority of plant and animal remains appear to be wild (Arbuckle and Özkaya 2006; Riehl et al. 2012;).

Approximately 800 individuals have been recovered from the site, making it one of the largest skeletal samples dating to this time and region. Burials of infants, children, and adults of both sexes have been recovered from beneath the floors of these structures, and in open spaces between them. Some of the human remains from this site show evidence of painting and plastering and also multiple cut marks, which Erdal (2005) argues represents ritual defleshing prior to interment.

Çayönü

The site of Çayönü is in southeastern Anatolia and dates to approximately 10,200–8270 cal BC (Yakar 2011). Much of the architecture at this site represents domestic structures with a few designated for public use (Özdoğan 1999). Six subphases have been identified, characterized by trends in building layout: Round Building, Grill Building, Channeled Building, Cobble-Paved Building, Cell Plan Building, and Large Room Building (Özdoğan 1999). These phases represent a gradual transition from curvilinear architectural patterns to rectangular building structures. Both wild and domesticated plants were exploited on site (van Zeist and De Roller 1994). Pigs were likely in a stage of protodomestication (Ervynck et al. 2001), whereas ungulates appear to have been domesticated throughout the occupation of the site (Hongo et al. 2009).

Çayönü contains both intramural and extramural burials in early aceramic phases of occupation (Özdoğan 1999). In the later aceramic phases, remains were predominantly placed in a large public space referred to as the "Skull Building" (Beyer-Honca 1995, Özbek 1988). This so-called charnel house was in use for some time and contained remains of infants and children, and both adult males and females. Within this building were isolated skulls, "decapitated" skeletons, and evidence of burnt remains, in addition to possible shelves to store skeletal elements (Özdoğan 1999). In the later phases of occupation (PPNC), inhabitants returned to burying their dead in primary inhumations beneath the floors of the houses (Pearson et al. 2013), and there was evidence of both single and multiple burials throughout the occupation sequence (Özdoğan 1999). A total of around 600 individuals have been recovered from the site (Özbek 1992; Pearson et al. 2013), although this number is a broad estimate, as there are many secondary burials, isolated skulls, and disarticulated limbs reported in the literature, which makes an exact calculation of interred individuals difficult.

Boncuklu

The site of Boncuklu Höyük in the Konya Plain dates to ca. 8500–7500 cal BC (Bayliss et al. 2015). It is composed of small curvilinear buildings (15–20 m^2) made of mud brick. Based on the size of these structures, it is likely that they could have accommodated only two to three adults and several children, and they are hypothesized to have been occupied by nuclear families (Baird 2012). There is evidence of repeated reconstruction of structures in the same location (Baird 2012).

Faunal remains include bird, fish, as well as an assemblage dominated by cattle/aurochs and boar/pig, with only a small number of sheep and goats. Further work is required to determine whether these remains represent wild or domestic species (Baird et al. 2012). There are, however, the remains of domesticated crops, including emmer and free-threshing wheat, hulled barley, and possibly einkorn wheat (Baird et al. 2012).

The Boncuklu burials are located beneath the house floors and some show evidence of "head" removal (Bayliss et al. 2015). There are also single burials found extramurally in the midden areas, in addition to "heads" without bodies, and group burials (Mustafaoğlu 2015). Skeletal analyses are ongoing; however, the number of individuals recovered thus far is likely to be under 100.

Aşıklı Höyük

Aşıklı Höyük is located on the bank of the Melendiz River in the Cappadocia region, and dates between 8200 and 7300 cal BC (Esin 1998). More recently, deeper layers have been recovered that push back the dates of occupation to approximately 9000 cal BC, making Aşıklı one of the earliest villages in central Anatolia (Stiner et al. 2014). Plant remains are found throughout the site, including large quantities of hackberry (Quade et al. 2014), as well as other seeds, nuts, pulses, and grasses (Stiner et al. 2014). Analyses of cereal remains in the upper levels provide evidence for the domestication and cultivation of crops (van Zeist and de Roller 1995), along with wild gathered fruits and nuts (Özbaşaran 2011a). Wild animals were hunted throughout the occupation of the site. However, there is a trend towards more reliance on caprines in later levels, as well as evidence for maintaining large numbers of caprines on site and selective culling and stabling of these animals (Stiner et al. 2014). These findings are in line with earlier studies that described sheep and goat remains at Aşıklı Höyük as being in a state of protodomestication (Esin and Harmanakaya 1999).

Habitation sequences are more pronounced in Aşıklı Höyük, where buildings were planned, and the original layout of earlier structures was preserved throughout later phases of construction. Habitations do not share walls but instead have spaces between them, ranging from 1 m to 1.5 m wide to as narrow as 30–35 cm (Esin et al. 1991). Deeper levels of the site have semisubterranean oval structures, similar to those at Boncuklu, while rectangular buildings gradually came to be predominant over the centuries of occupation; they are similar to those seen later at Çatalhöyük (Özbaşaran 2011a).

To date, close to 90 individuals have been found beneath the floors of habitations. The majority were placed in a flexed position, but some were extended (Esin and Harmanakaya 1999). Most burials were single primary interments, although there were some cases of double burials (Esin et al. 1991). The burial assemblage is composed of both sexes and a range of ages.

Çatalhöyük

The Neolithic component of Çatalhöyük occupies a mound of approximately 13 ha that reaches a height of nearly 21 m (Hodder 2002), with radiocarbon dates between 7100 and 5950 cal BC (Bayliss et al. 2015; Marciniak et al. 2015). There is archaeological evidence for the domestication of sheep and goats (Russell and Martin 2005) and, to a lesser extent, cattle. Other faunal remains include wild animals, such as aurochsen (Russell et al. 2013). Plant material includes domesticated glume wheat, barley, and pulses, as well as various wild plants such as almonds, acorns, hackberry, plums, and tubers (Fairbairn, Near, and Martinoli 2005). The site is arranged as an agglomeration of densely packed mudbrick buildings. Adjacent structures shared walls, and there were no windows or doors for entry; instead, buildings were entered through holes in the roofs via ladders. Houses typically consisted of a single central room surrounded by smaller storage rooms. Within this central room was an oven, above which was the ladder to enter the structure (Hodder 2006a).

To date, nearly 600 skeletons have been recovered from Çatalhöyük. The most common burial location was beneath the plastered platforms of the central room of houses, with a preference for interment under northern and eastern platforms, especially of adults (Boz and Hager 2013; Mellaart 1962, 1967). There seems to be no distinctive patterning by adult age or sex with regard to burial location or orientation (Hamilton 2005), or in the number and type of grave goods (Nakamura and Meskell 2013). The vast majority of interments in Çatalhöyük are primary undisturbed single interments beneath platforms (Boz and Hager 2013). The skeletons are found in flexed positions and tend to have limited grave goods. In many instances, however, platforms were reopened to inter additional individuals (figure 8.2). The stratigraphy of these interments is often complex, and it can be difficult to reconstruct the sequence of individual burial events, but in some cases it is clear that skeletal elements were intentionally removed or rearranged during subsequent interment events (Haddow et al. 2016).

FIGURE 8.2. Example of multiple (group) burial from Çatalhöyük. (Image courtesy of the Çatalhöyük project.)

At Çatalhöyük there are several instances of primary burials found with elements of the skull (i.e., cranium and mandible) missing. These skeletons are otherwise largely complete and fully articulated, including the small bones of the hands and feet, and in most cases the first cervical vertebra is present and in articulation. In addition to "headless" bodies, there are isolated crania found in a variety of depositional contexts throughout the site (Haddow and Knüsel 2017). In one instance an adult cranium and mandible was plastered and painted red before being interred with an adult female in a primary burial (Boz and Hager 2013).

Initial studies of cut marks showed only one case with clear cut marks on the atlas vertebra of a primary adult burial lacking the cranium and mandible (Andrews, Molleson, and Boz 2005). However, cut-mark evidence has recently been revisited in a master's thesis and the number may be as high as 19 individuals with cut marks, with only one cut mark on the cervical vertebrae and the rest elsewhere on the body (Barmettler 2016). These findings require further assessment, but the results do speak to the degree of postmortem processing and the complexity of mortuary practices. To achieve this level of skeletal manipulation (limb and head removal) with little or no evidence of cut marks, some manner of postmortem defleshing (either through extensive natural decomposition, or intentional human intervention) would likely have been required (Pilloud et al. 2016).

Tepecik-Çiftlik

Tepecik-Çiftlik is a settlement site that is estimated to have been occupied between 7000 and 5500 cal BC, based on stratigraphy and limited available radiocarbon dates (Bıçakçı, Godon, and Çakan 2012). The site shows evidence of domesticated plants (Bıçakçı 2010) and potential evidence for domesticated animals (sheep, goats, cattle) (Bıçakçı 2004). Burials in the Neolithic levels are spatially related to the houses and contain intramural as well as extramural burials. There is evidence for both primary and secondary burials and the reuse of certain burial areas over time (Bıçakçı, Godon, and Çakan 2012). Over 170 individuals have been unearthed from the various Neolithic levels. Additionally, a large mass grave was found in level five that contained at least 42 individuals of both sexes and all ages (Büyükkarakaya and Erdal 2014).

Köşk Höyük

Köşk Höyük has two levels that date to 6200–5500 cal BC and 5300–4800 cal BC, respectively (Arbuckle, Öztan, and Gülçur 2009). The site represents the transition from late Neolithic to the Chalcolithic (Arbuckle 2012). This study is predominantly concerned with the earlier, Neolithic level. In this level, there is evidence for domesticated plants and animals (Arbuckle 2012; Arbuckle, Öztan, and Gülçur 2009).

Within Köşk Höyük, individuals are buried beneath the house floors (Naumann et al. 1984). There have been two "headless" skeletons recovered (Özbek 2009a), in addition to 13 plastered skulls, and six unplastered skulls, making it the largest assemblage of plastered "heads" found in Central Anatolia. The plastered skulls were of both males and females and included one child (Özbek 2009b). In later Neolithic levels, individuals were buried in jars beneath the house floors (Bacvarov 2007; Özbaşaran 2011b). Based on the current literature, the total number of burials recovered at Köşk Höyük could not be determined.

THE CONSTRUCTION OF MEMORY

While there is variation across these sites, there are general patterns that emerge (see table 8.1). Intramural interment was practiced at all of the sites discussed here, although extramural burials also occurred at some sites, and many show evidence of some form of secondary mortuary treatment, including the collection and curation of crania, and sometimes painting and plastering of crania and other bones. Of great interest is the fact that this form of mortuary practice was adopted *before* the advent of domestication of plants and animals. Körtik Tepe is the earliest site in this discussion and, as of yet, does not contain evidence for the domestication of plants and animals. The site does show evidence of intra- and extramural burial as well as possible defleshing and secondary skeletal treatments. There also exist precursors of these mortuary practices in the Levant during the Natufian within settled communities, which date to before the broad adoption of the domestication of plants and animals. Several Natufian sites show evidence for intramural burials, secondary burials, and multiple interments (e.g., Belfer-Cohen 1988; Boyd 1995; Byrd and Monahan 1995; Noy 1989). Additionally, within Anatolia during the Epipaleolithic, at the site of Pınarbaşı, there is evidence to suggest cranial removal of an adult male interment (Baird et al. 2013). These findings suggest that mortuary practices persisted prior to, and through, the early development of the Neolithic. Practices that extend before and after the adoption of domestication perhaps served as a means to ease social tensions and maintain an egalitarian social structure as part of the hunter-gatherer past. The intensification and reaffirmation of these hunter-gatherer mortuary practices during the Neolithic hint at their importance in the early process of neolithization. These practices begin to subside in the following Chalcolithic period as populations gradually adapt to living in more densely populated communities with emerging social differentiation and status differences, which perhaps could no longer be repressed via ritual practice.

The burial rites outlined here speak to the level of intimacy and involvement Neolithic Anatolian peoples had with death through the extended relationship they had with the dead. This intimate connection was manifested in two ways: (1) the selection of a limited number of individuals at a few sites for extended mortuary rites (e.g., skull removal, skull decoration, or decoration of infracranial elements) and (2) intramural burial. Both manifestations are explored further below.

The extended mortuary rites imply a link to the past and the deceased. The practice of skull removal has been argued by Testart (2008) to be evidence of violence and the taking of trophy heads, although this is largely rejected by other researchers (e.g., Belfer-Cohen and Goring-Morris 2009; Hodder 2009; Kuijt, Özdoğan, and Parker Pearson 2009). Many others have argued that these mortuary practices represent ancestor veneration (Garfinkel 1994; Kenyon 1953; Kuijt 2000), while others have argued that these practices represent a funerary ritual (as distinct from ancestor veneration or violence) as they are seen to involve adult males and females and children (Bonogofsky 2005; Kuijt 2008). The latter interpretation is promoted here (although, alternative possibilities are not completely discounted): these practices likely served as a ritual practice that functioned to maintain social continuity from preagricultural to agricultural communities. And, while not likely to be related exclusively to violent behaviors enacted on the living (i.e., the perimortem removal of skulls), the display of removing the head could be viewed along the same lines as is argued by Whitehead to be a meaningful cultural display full of social meaning.

The incorporation of intramural burial represents a similar link to the past and the dead that may be less obvious (Whitehead 2007). Not only does this practice intimately incorporate daily living and household activities to rituals associated with the dead, it creates a memory of the past that is both personal and social. Hodder argues that, within a collective social memory, some individuals were intended to be remembered through the recirculation of their remains, creating a sort of living archive that reinforced social memory and connections with the past (Hodder 2006b). In contrast, other individual remains did not actively participate in the lives of the living; they were forgotten and were not disturbed in their original location of interment. Alternatively, it is argued here that even the burials that remained untouched were not intentionally forgotten. Inhabitants were still living in the houses, just above these interred individuals. In order to keep them from being disturbed by subsequent burials and potentially other house activities, the memory of where these individuals were buried was maintained throughout the life cycle of the house. This life cycle likely varied by site, but, based on previously conducted dendrochronological and ^{14}C analyses, the average house at Çatalhöyük was occupied for 50–100 years (Cessford 2005).

In this discussion of mortuary practices during the transition to the Neolithic in Anatolia, it is important to highlight the fact that not every archaeological site had evidence of burials. Atakuman argues that the areas that did show evidence of burials may have served as centers for more intimate and locally based networks (Atakuman 2014). Other sites, without burials, may have become part of larger networks. This difference in interaction between sites could, in part, be related to the differences that are evident in mortuary practices at these sites. While there are elements that they all share (i.e., intramural burial), there is variation in how burial rites were executed. Some of this variation could also be related to temporal differences.

Ultimately, these mortuary practices were a means of reinforcing and creating social memory. These were shared experiences that acted to strengthen a "politics of memory" (Hodder 2006b). Extended mortuary rites, coupled with the cognitive mapping of intramural burial location, helped to create and reinforce social memory. It is this memory that would have helped the community deal with the changes in population density, economy, social structure, sanitary conditions, and regulations of power (i.e., scalar stress) that were newly emerging at this time (Hodder and Cessford 2004).

The importance of social memory in early agricultural sites can be linked to the expectation of resources in a "delayed-return system," an investment of time to ensure crops for humans and their animals. In contrast, hunter-gatherer groups are characterized by a system of "immediate return," which focuses on the present

(Hodder 2006b). The idea here is not that hunter-gatherers could not have developed the same relationship to the past—in fact, this relationship begins to change slightly prior to the advent of domestication (in the Natufian) and it is argued here that the two are linked. Changes in conceptualization of space, settled life, and immediacy of resources that preceded domestication set the stage for these delayed mortuary practices. With the further development of domestication in the Neolithic the use and maintenance of material culture created cues and reminders of the past to support a more stable "cognitive memory," as is illustrated in an intensification of these mortuary practices. It is this *materiality* that created and reinforced social memory (Hodder 2006b), and in some ways required it. Part of this "delayed-return" system led to stronger links to the past, through longer enduring links to ancestral dead (however they were defined), and repetitive practices to honor these dead (through the continued maintenance of their place of burial and, in some select cases, retention and manipulation of these remains by the living). The persistence of these mortuary practices over several generations attests to the effects of social memory, and its importance for the construction and maintenance of this egalitarian social structure over time.

Mortuary practices and displays of postmortem manipulation would have served to deemphasize differences between individuals while building community integration during this time of great cultural, social, and economic change, as Kuijt has argued for in the Levant during the Late Natufian and PPNA (Kuijt 1996, 2008). It is argued here that these practices extend into the Neolithic of Anatolia, and that egalitarianism was maintained through the continuation and intensification of these mortuary practices. Through these extended burial rites that involved the processing of remains for interment, identity and group organization could be maintained (Whitehead 2004b). As communities began to grow in the following Chalcolithic, such practices were lost and fully fledged social differentiation began to emerge. Thus, there is not a direct correlation between mortuary practices and social structure, but there is a connection between the two that is communicated through ritual, symbols, and memory.

CONCLUSIONS

Despite variation in the built environment of the sites reviewed here, with each representing different ways in which the Neolithic package was adopted over time, it appears that similar mortuary practices acted to reinforce social memory and maintain social stability in each of these differing circumstances. Ultimately, repetition over time and similarity in ritual mortuary treatments observed in Anatolia can be seen as a means for these societies to cope with the economic, social, and biological challenges they were facing as the Neolithic developed. These ritualized behaviors and social memory acted to create and maintain the social relations in the group as an extension of the practices adopted in the preceding hunting and gathering groups of the Natufian and Epipaleolithic, as they did in the Levant. These mortuary practices aided in the *neolithization* of the region and largely disappeared in the following periods as groups became increasingly socially differentiated.

REFERENCES

Andrews, Peter, Theya Molleson, and Başak Boz. 2005. "The Human Burials at Çatalhöyük." In *Inhabiting Çatalhöyük: Reports from the 1995–1999 Seasons*, edited by Ian Hodder, 261–278. Cambridge, UK: McDonald Institute for Archaeological Research.

Arbuckle, Benjamin S. 2012. "Animals and Inequality in Chalcolithic Central Anatolia." *Journal of Anthropological Archaeology* 31 (3): 302–313. doi: 10.1016/j.jaa.2012.01.008.

Arbuckle, Benjamin S., and Vecihi Özkaya. 2006. "Animal Exploitation at Körtik Tepe: An Early Aceramic Neolithic Site in Southeastern Turkey." *Paléorient* 32 (2): 113–136.

Arbuckle, Benjamin S., Aliye Öztan, and Sevil Gülçur. 2009. "The Evolution of Sheep and Goat Husbandry in Central Anatolia." *Anthropozoologica* 44 (1): 129–157.

Atakuman, Çiğdem. 2014. "Architectural Discourse and Social Transformation During the Early Neolithic of Southeast Anatolia." *Journal of World Prehistory* 27 (1): 1–42.

Bacvarov, Krun. 2007. "Jar Burials as Early Settlement Markers in Southeast European Neolithic." In *A Short Walk through the Balkans: The First Farmers of the Carpathian Basin and Adjacent Regions*. Società per la Preistoria e Protostoria della Regione Friuli-Venezia Giulia, Quaderno, edited by Michela Spataro and Paolo Biagi, 189–205. Trieste: Societa Preistoria Friuli.

Baird, Douglas. 2012. "The Late Epipaleolithic, Neolithic, and Chalcolithic of the Anatolian Plateau, 13,000–4000 BC." In *A Companion to the Archaeology of the Ancient Near East*, edited by D. T. Potts, 431–465. Oxford: Wiley-Blackwell.

Baird, Douglas, Eleni Asouti, Laurence Astruc, Adnan Baysal, Emma Baysal, Denise Carruthers, Andrew Fairbairn, Ceren Kabukcu, Emma Jenkins, and Kirsi Lorentz. 2013. "Juniper Smoke, Skulls and Wolves' Tails. The Epipalaeolithic of the Anatolian Plateau in its South-West Asian Context: Insights from Pınarbaşı." *Levant* 45 (2): 175–209.

Baird, Douglas, Andrew Fairbairn, Louise Martin, and Caroline Middleton. 2012. "The Boncuklu Project: The Origins of Sedentism, Cultivation and Herding in Central Anatolia." In *The Neolithic in Turkey, Volume 3*, edited by Mehmet Özdoğan, N. Başgelen and P. I. Kuniholm, 219–239. Istanbul: Arkeoloji ve Sanat.

Barmettler, Alexandra. 2016. "Funerary Practices at the Neolithic site of Çatalhöyük." MA, Department of Anthropology and Anthropological Museum, University of Zurich, Switzerland.

Bayliss, A., F. Brock, S. Farid, I. Hodder, J. Southon, and R. E. Taylor. 2015. "Getting to the Bottom of It All: A Bayesian Approach to Dating the Start of Çatalhöyük." *Journal of World Prehistory* 28: 1–26.

Belfer-Cohen, Anna. 1988. "The Natufian Graveyard in Hayonim Cave." *Paleorient* 14 (2): 297–308.

Belfer-Cohen, Anna, and A. Nigel Goring-Morris. 2009. "The Tyranny of the Ethnographic Record, Revisited." *Paléorient* 35 (1): 107–108.

Benz, Marion, Aytaç Coşkun, Irka Hajdas, Katleen Deckers, Simone Riehl, Kurt W. Alt, Bernhard Weninger, and Vecihi Özkaya. 2012. "Methodological Implications of New Radiocarbon Dates from the Early Holocene Site of Körtik Tepe, Southeast Anatolia." *Radiocarbon* 54 (3–4): 291–304.

Beyer-Honca, Mary Deirdre. 1995. "The Early Neolithic Mortuary Remains from Çayönü: Biological and Social Aspects of Living and Dying in a Village Community." PhD, Department of Anthropology, Indiana University.

Bıçakçı, Erhan. 2004. "Tepecik-Çiftlik: A New Site in Central Anatolia (Turkey)." *Architectura. Zeitschrift für Geschichte der Baukunst* 34: 21–26.

Bıçakçı, Erhan. 2010. "Tepecik-Çiftlik kazısı 2010 yılı çalışmaları." In *Kazı Sonucları Toplantısı*, edited by H. Donmez and O. Otgun, 69–89. Istanbul: Kültür Varlıkları ve Müzeler Genel Müdürlüğü.

Bıçakçı, Erhan, Martin Godon, and Yasin Gökhan Çakan. 2012. "Tepecik-Çiftlik." In *The Neolithic in Turkey*, edited by M. Özdoğan, N. Başgelen, and P. I. Kuniholm, 89–134. Istanbul: Archaeology and Art Publication.

Binford, Lewis R. 1971. "Mortuary Practices: Their Study and Potential." In *Approaches to the Social Dimensions of Mortuary Practices*, edited by J. A. Brown, 6–21. Washington, DC: Memoirs of the Society for American Archaeology, Number 25.

Bonogofsky, M. 2005. "A Bioarchaeological Study of Plastered Skulls from Anatolia: New Discoveries and Interpretations." *International Journal of Osteoarchaeology* 15 (2): 124–135.

Boyd, Brian. 1995. "Houses and Hearths, Pits and Burials: Natufian Mortuary Practices at Mallaha (Eynan), Upper Jordan Valley." In *The Archaeology of Death in the Ancient Near East*, edited by Stuart Campbell and Anthony Green, 17–23. Oxford: Oxbow Books.

Boz, B., and Lori D. Hager. 2013. "Living above the Dead: Intramural Burial Practices at Çatalhöyük." In *Humans and Landscapes of Çatalhöyük*, edited by Ian Hodder, 413–440. Los Angeles, CA: Cotsen Institute of Archaeology.

Brami, Maxime N. 2015. "A Graphical Simulation of the 2,000-year Lag in Neolithic Occupation between Central Anatolia and the Aegean Basin." *Archaeological and Anthropological Sciences* 7 (3): 319–327. doi: 10.1007/s12520-014-0193-4.

Brown, James. 1995. "On Mortuary Analysis—with Special Reference to the Saxe-Binford Research Program." In *Regional Approaches to Mortuary Analysis*, edited by Lane Anderson Beck, 3–25. New York: Plenum Press.

Büyükkarakaya, Ali Metin, and Y. S. Erdal. 2014. "New Data on Mortuary Practices from the Early Pottery Neolithic site of Tepecik-Çiftlik, Central Anatolia." 20th Annual Meeting of the European Association of Archaeology, Istanbul, Turkey.

Byrd, Brian F., and Christopher M. Monahan. 1995. "Death, Mortuary Ritual, and Natufian Social Structure." *Journal of Anthropological Archaeology* 14: 251–287.

Cessford, Craig. 2005. "Estimating the Neolithic Population of Çatalhöyük." In *Inhabiting Çatalhöyük: Reports from the 1995–1999 Seasons*, edited by Ian Hodder, 323–328. Cambridge, UK: McDonald Institute for Archaeological Research.

Childe, V. Gordon. 1936. *Man Makes Himself.* New York: New American Library.

Çilingiroglu, Çiler. 2005. "The Concept of 'Neolithic Package': Considering its Meaning and Applicability." *Documenta Praehistorica* 32: 1–13.

Düring, Bleda S. 2013. "Breaking the Bond: Investigating the Neolithic Expansion in Asia Minor in the Seventh Millennium BC." *Journal of World Prehistory* 26 (2): 75–100. doi: 10.1007/s10963-013-9065-6.

Erdal, Yilmaz Selim. 2015. "Bone or Flesh: Defleshing and Post-Depositional Treatments at Körtik Tepe (Southeastern Anatolia, PPNA Period)." *European Journal of Archaeology* 18 (1): 4–32.

Ervynck, A., K. Dobney, H. Hongo, and R. Meadow. 2001. "Born Free? New Evidence for the Status of *Sus scrofa* at Neolithic Çayönü Tepesi (Southeastern Anatolia, Turkey)." *Paléorient* 27 (2): 47–73.

Esin, Ufuk. 1998. "The Aceramic Site of Aşıklı and its Ecological Conditions based on its Floral and Faunal Remains." *Tuba-ar I*:95–103.

Esin, Ufuk., E. Bıcakci, M. Özbaşaran, N. Balkan-Atlı, D. Berker, and I. Yağmur. 1991. "Salvage Excavations at the Pre-Pottery Neolithic Site of Aşıklı Höyük in Central Anatolia." *Anatolica* 17: 123–174.

Esin, Ufuk, and S. Harmanakaya. 1999. "Aşıklı." In *Neolithic in Turkey: The Cradle of Civilization*, edited by Mehmet Özdogan and Nezih Basgelen, 115–132. Istanbul: Arkeoloji ve Sanat Yayinlari.

Fairbairn, Andrew, Julie Near, and Daniele Martinoli. 2005. "Macrobotanical Investigations of the North, South and KOPAL Area Excavations at Çatalhöyük East." In *Inhabiting Çatalhöyük: Reports From the 1995–1999 Seasons*, edited by Ian Hodder, 137–201. Cambridge, UK: McDonald Institute for Archaeological Research.

Fuller, Dorian Q., George Willcox, and Robin G. Allaby. 2012. "Early Agricultural Pathways: Moving Outside the 'Core Area' Hypothesis in Southwest Asia." *Journal of Experimental Botany* 63 (2): 617–633.

Garfinkel, Yosef. 1994. "Ritual Burial of Cultic Objects: The Earliest Evidence." *Cambridge Archaeological Journal* 4 (2): 159–188. doi: 10.1017/S0959774300001062.

Haddow, Scott D., and Christopher J. Knüsel. 2017. "Skull Retrieval and Secondary Burial Practices in the Neolithic Near East: Recent Insights from Çatalhöyük, Turkey." *Bioarchaeology International* 1 (1–2): 52–71.

Haddow, Scott D., Joshua W. Sadvari, Christopher J. Knüsel, and Rémi Hadad. 2016. "A Tale of Two Platforms: Commingled Remains and the Life-Course of Houses at Neolithic Çatalhöyük." In *Theoretical Approaches to Analysis and Interpretation of Commingled Human Remains*, edited by Anna J. Osterholtz, 5–29. New York: Springer.

Hamilton, Naomi. 2005. "Social Aspects of Burial." In *Inhabiting Çatalhöyük: Reports From the 1995–1999 Seasons*, edited by Ian Hodder, 301–306. Cambridge, UK: McDonald Institute for Archaeological Research.

Hodder, Ian. 2002. "Ethics and Archaeology: The Attempt at Çatalhöyük." *Near Eastern Archaeology* 65: 174–181.

Hodder, Ian. 2006a. *The Leopard's Tale: Revealing the Mysteries of Çatalhöyük*. New York: Thames and Hudson.

Hodder, Ian. 2006b. "Memory." In *Çatalhöyük Perspectives: Themes from the 1995–1999 Seasons*, edited by Ian Hodder, 183–195. Cambridge, UK: McDonald Institute for Archaeological Research.

Hodder, Ian. 2009. "An Archaeological Response." *Paléorient* 35 (1): 109–111.

Hodder, Ian, and Craig Cessford. 2004. "Daily Practice and Social Memory at Çatalhöyük." *American Antiquity* 69 (1): 17–40.

Hongo, Hitomi, Jessica Pearson, Banu Öksüz, and Gülçin Ilgezdi. 2009. "The Process of Ungulate Domestication at Cayönü, Southeastern Turkey: A Multidisciplinary Approach Focusing on *Bos* sp. and *Cervus elaphus*." *Anthropozoologica* 44 (1): 63–78.

Joyce, Rosemary A. 2001. "Burying the Dead at Tlatilco: Social Memory and Social Identities." *Archeological Papers of the American Anthropological Association* 10 (1): 12–26. doi: 10.1525/ap3a.2001.10.1.12.

Kenyon, Kathleen M. 1953. "Excavations at Jericho, 1953." *Palestine Exploration Quarterly* 85 (2): 81–96. doi: 10.1179/peq.1953.85.2.81.

Knüsel, Christopher J. 2014. "Crouching in Fear: Terms of Engagement for Funerary Remains." *Journal of Social Archaeology* 14 (1): 26–58. doi: 10.1177/1469605313518869.

Kuijt, Ian. 1996. "Negotiating Equality Through Ritual: A Consideration of Late Natufian and Pre-Pottery Neolithic A Period Mortuary Practices." *Journal of Anthropological Archaeology* 4: 313–336.

Kuijt, Ian, ed. 2000. *Life in Neolithic Farming Communities: Social Organization, Identity, and Differentiation*. New York: Kluwer Academic/Plenum Publishers.

Kuijt, Ian. 2001. "Place, Death, and the Transmission of Social Memory in Early Agricultural Communities of the Near Eastern Pre-Pottery Neolithic." In *Social Memory, Identity, and Death: Intradisciplinary Perspectives on Mortuary Rituals*, edited by M. S. Chesson, 80–99. Washington, DC: American Anthropological Association.

Kuijt, Ian. 2008. "The Regeneration of Life: Neolithic Structures of Symbolic Remembering and Forgetting." *Current Anthropology* 49 (2): 171–197.

Kuijt, Ian, Mehmet Özdoğan, and Mike Parker Pearson. 2009. "Neolithic Skull Removal: Enemies, Ancestors, and Memory." *Paléorient* 35 (1): 117–120.

Larsen, Clark Spencer. 1995. "Biological Changes in Human Populations with Agriculture." *Annual Review of Anthropology* 24: 185–213.

Lichter, C. 2016. "Burial Customs of the Neolithic in Anatalia: An Overview." *Der Anschnitt* 31: 71–83.

Marciniak, Arkadiusz, Marek Z. Barański, Alex Bayliss, Lech Czerniak, Tomasz Goslar, John Southon, and R. E. Taylor. 2015. "Fragmenting Times: Interpreting a Bayesian Chronology for the Late Neolithic Occupation of Çatalhöyük East, Turkey." *Antiquity* 89 (343): 154–176.

Meiklejohn, Christopher, and Jeff Babb. 2011. "Long Bone Length, Stature and Time in the European Late Pleistocene and Early Holocene." In *Human Bioarchaeology of the Transition to Agriculture*, 151–175. New York: John Wiley.

Mellaart, James. 1962. "Excavations at Çatal Hüyük, First Preliminary Report, 1961." *Anatolian Studies* 13: 43–103.

Mellaart, James. 1967. *Çatal Hüyük: A Neolithic Town in Anatolia*. New York: Thames and Hudson Ltd.

Meskell, Lynn. 2003. "Memory's Materiality: Ancestral Presence, Commemorative Practice and Disjunctive Locales." In *Archaeologies of Memory*, edited by R. M. Van Dyke and S. E. Alcock, 34–55. Malden, MA: Blackwell.

Mustafaoğlu, G. 2015. "Boncuklu Höyük." Paper presented at the conference Archaeogenomic Insights into Near Eastern Neolithic Populations. Middle East Technical University, Ankara.

Nakamura, Carolyn, and Lynn Meskell. 2013. "The Çatalhöyük Burial Assemblage." In *Humans and Landscapes of Çatalhöyük*, edited by Ian Hodder, 441–466. Los Angeles, CA: Cotsen Institute of Archaeology.

Naumann, Rudolf, Kenan Erim, Alba Palmieri, Manfred Korfmann, J. Cauvin, O. Aurenche, Afif Erzen, K. Tuchelt, H. Vetters, Keith DeVries, Richard Ellis, Nurettin Yardimci, J. J. Roodenberg, D. De Bernardi Ferrero, Clelia Laviosa, Önder Bilgi, Veli Sevin, Bedri Yalman, Oktay Aslanapa, Uğur Silistreli, Refik Duru, Vedat Idil, Harald

Hauptmann, J. Borchhardt, W. Müller-Wiener, W. Radt, Jale Inan, Crawford J. Greenewalt, and George F. Bass. 1984. "Recent Archaeological Research in Turkey." *Anatolian Studies* 34: 203–235. doi: 10.2307/3642864.

Noy, T. 1989. "Some Aspects of Natufian Mortuary Behavior at Nahal Oren." In *People and Culture in Change*, edited by Israel Hershkovitz. Oxford: BAR International Series.

Özbaşaran, Mihriban. 2011a. "Re-starting at Aşıklı." *Anatolia Antiqua* XIX: 27–37.

Özbaşaran, Mihriban. 2011b. "The Neolithic on the Plateau." In *The Oxford Handbook of Ancient Anatolia*, edited by Gregory McMahon and Sharon R. Steadman, 99–124. Oxford: Oxford University Press.

Özbek, Metin. 1988. "Culte des Crânes Humains â Çayönü." Round Table on Aceramic Neolithic in SE Turkey, Istanbul. *Anatolica* XV: 127–137.

Özbek, Metin. 1992. "The Human Remains at Çayönü." Proceedings of the 93rd Annual Meeting of the Archaeological Institute of America, Chicago, IL.

Özbek, Metin. 2009a. "Köşk Höyük (Niğde) neolitik köyünde kil sıvalı insan başları." *Edebiyat Fakültesi Dergisi* 26 (1).

Özbek, Metin. 2009b. "Remodeled Human Skulls in Köşk Höyük (Neolithic age, Anatolia): A New Appraisal in View of Recent Discoveries." *Journal of Archaeological Science* 36 (2): 379–386.

Özdoğan, A. 1999. "Çayönü." In *Neolithic in Turkey: The Cradle of Civilization*, edited by Mehmet Özdoğan and Nezih Basgelen, 35–63. Istanbul: Arkeoloji ve Sanat Yayinlari.

Özdoğan, Mehmet. 2008. "An Alternative Approach in Tracing Changes in Demographic Composition." In *The Neolithic Demographic Transition and Its Consequences*, edited by J. P. Bocquet-Appel and Ofer Bar-Yosef, 139–178. New York: Springer.

Özdoğan, M. 2010. "Westward Expansion of the Neolithic Way of Life: Sorting the Neolithic Package into Distinct Packages." Proceedings of the 6th International Congress on the Archaeology of the Ancient Near East. Wiesbaden.

Özdoğan, Mehmet. 2011. "Archaeological Evidence on the Westward Expansion of Farming Communities from Eastern Anatolia to the Aegean and the Balkans." *Current Anthropology* 52 (S4): S415-S430.

Özkaya, Vecihi, and Aytaç Coşkun. 2009. "Körtik Tepe, a New Pre-Pottery Neolithic A Site in South-Eastern Anatolia." *Antiquity* 83 (320). http://www.antiquity.ac.uk/projgall/ozkaya320/.

Parker Pearson, Michael 1982. "Mortuary Practices, Society and Ideology: An Ethnoarchaeological Study." In *Symbolic and Structural Archaeology*, edited by Ian Hodder, 99–113. Cambridge, UK: Cambridge University Press.

Pearson, Jessica, Matt Grove, Metin Özbek, and Hitomi Hongo. 2013. "Food and Social Complexity at Çayönü Tepesi, Southeastern Anatolia: Stable Isotope Evidence of

Differentiation in Diet according to Burial Practice and Sex in the Early Neolithic." *Journal of Anthropological Archaeology* 32 (2): 180–189.

Peterson, Rick. 2013. "Social Memory and Ritual Performance." *Journal of Social Archaeology* 13 (2): 266–283. doi: 10.1177/1469605312455768.

Pilloud, Marin A., Scott D. Haddow, Christopher J. Knüsel, and Clark Spencer Larsen. 2016. "A Bioarchaeological and Forensic Re-Assessment of Vulture Defleshing and Mortuary Practices at Neolithic Çatalhöyük." *Journal of Archaeological Science: Reports* 10: 735–743.

Pinhasi, Ron, and Christopher Meiklejohn. 2011. "Dental Reduction and the Transition to Agriculture in Europe." In *Human Bioarchaeology of the Transition to Agriculture*, edited by R. Pinhasi and Jay T. Stock, 451–474. Chichester, UK: Wiley-Blackwell.

Quade, Jay, Shanying Li, Mary C. Stiner, Amye Clark, Susan M. Mentzer, and Mihriban Özbaşaran. 2014. "Radiocarbon Dating, Mineralogy, and Isotopic Composition of Hackberry Endocarps from the Neolithic Site of Aşikli Höyük, Central Turkey." *Radiocarbon* 56 (4): S17-S2.

Riehl, Simone, Marion Benz, Nicholas J. Conard, Hojjat Darabi, Katleen Deckers, Hassan Fazeli Nashli, and Mohsen Zeidi-Kulehparcheh. 2012. "Plant Use in Three Pre-Pottery Neolithic Sites of the Northern and Eastern Fertile Crescent: A Preliminary Report." *Vegetation History and Archaeobotany* 21 (2): 95–106.

Russell, Nerissa, and L. Martin. 2005. "The Çatalhöyük Mammal Remains." In *Inhabiting Çatalhöyük: Reports from the 1995–1999 Seasons*, edited by Ian Hodder, 33–98. Cambridge, UK: McDonald Institute for Archaeological Research.

Russell, Nerissa, Katheryn Twiss, David C. Orton, and Arzu Demirergi. 2013. "More on the Çatalhöyük Mammal Remains." In *Humans and Landscapes of Çatalhöyük*, edited by Ian Hodder, 213–258. London: British Institute at Ankara.

Saxe, A. A. 1970. "Social Dimensions of Mortuary Practice." Unpublished PhD dissertation, University of Michigan, Ann Arbor.

Sterelny, Kim, and Trevor Watkins. 2015. "Neolithization in Southwest Asia in a Context of Niche Construction Theory." *Cambridge Archaeological Journal* 25 (03): 673–691.

Stiner, Mary C., Hijlke Buitenhuis, Güneş Duru, Steven L. Kuhn, Susan M. Mentzer, Natalie D. Munro, Nadja Pöllath, Jay Quade, Georgia Tsartsidou, and Mihriban Özbaşaran. 2014. "A Forager–Herder Trade-Off, from Broad-Spectrum Hunting to Sheep Management at Aşıklı Höyük, Turkey." *Proceedings of the National Academy of Sciences of the United States of America* 111 (23): 8404–8409. doi: 10.1073/pnas.1322723111.

Testart, Alain. 2008. "Des crânes et des vautours ou la guerre oubliée." *Paléorient* 34 (1): 33–58.

van Zeist, Willem, and Gerrit Jan De Roller. 1994. "The Plant Husbandry of Aceramic Çayönü, SE Turkey." *Palaeohistoria* 33/34: 65–96.

van Zeist, Willem, and Gerrit Jan de Roller. 1995. "Plant Remains from Aşıklı Höyük, a Pre-Pottery Neolithic Site in Central Anatolia." *Vegetation History and Archaeobotany* 4 (3): 179–185.

Vigne, Jean Denis. 2008. "Zooarchaeological Aspects of the Neolithic Diet Transition in the Near East and Europe, and their Putative Relationships with the Neolithic Demographic Transition." In *The Neolithic Demographic Transition and Its Consequences*, edited by J. P. Bocquet-Appel and O. Bar-Yosef, 179–205. Berlin: Springer.

Watkins, Trevor. 2006. "Neolithisation in Southwest Asia: The Path to Modernity." *Documenta Praehistorica* 33: 71–88.

Watkins, Trevor. 2016. "Anatolia as a Microcosm of the Neolithic Process." *Der Anschnitt* 31: 35–41.

Whitehead, Neil L. 2004a. "Introduction: Cultures, Conflicts, and the Poetics of Violent Practice." In *Violence*, edited by Neil L Whitehead, 25–54. Santa Fe, NM: SAR Press.

Whitehead, Neil L. 2004b. "On the Poetics of Violence." In *Violence*, edited by Neil L. Whitehead, 55–78. Santa Fe, NM: SAR Press.

Whitehead, Neil L. 2007. "Violence and the Cultural Order." *Daedalus* 136 (1): 40–50. doi: 10.2307/20028088.

Willcox, George. 2012. "The Beginnings of Cereal Cultivation and Domestication in Southwest Asia." In *A Companion to the Archaeology of the Ancient Near East*, edited by D. T. Potts, 163–180. Malden, MA: Blackwell.

Yakar, Jak. 2011. "Anatolian Chronology and Terminology." In *The Oxford Handbook of Ancient Anatolia*, edited by Gregory McMahon and Sharon R. Steadman, 56–96. Oxford: Oxford University Press.

Zeder, Melinda A. 2008. "Domestication and Early Agriculture in the Mediterranean Basin: Origins, Diffusion, and Impact." *Proceedings of the National Academy of Sciences of the United States of America* 105 (33): 11597–11604. doi: 10.1073/pnas.0801317105.

Zeder, Melinda A. 2011. "The Origins of Agriculture in the Near East." *Current Anthropology* 52 (S4): S221-S235.

Zeder, Melinda A. 2015. "Core Questions in Domestication Research." *Proceedings of the National Academy of Sciences of the United States of America* 112 (11): 3191–3198. doi: 10.1073/pnas.1501711112.

9

Mingled Bones, Mingled Bodies

Diversity in the Poetics of Death at Nabataean Petra, Jordan

MEGAN PERRY AND ANNA J. OSTERHOLTZ

The anthropological study of mortuary behavior provides rich information on social organization, identity, conceptions of death and the body, the meaning of material culture, and religion and ritual. The treatment of the deceased reflects larger societal concerns with concepts of the body and group identity. As a result, the corpse can undergo extreme levels of cleansing, dressing, decorating, prepping, preserving, dismembering, manipulating, displaying, interring, disinterring, reinterring, disinterring *again*, and resurrecting. Many societies consider the act of dismembering and disarticulating living bodies a violent act (Martin, Harrod, and Pérez 2013). Violent acts resulting in the physical disruption of living bodies, however, may be essential to life itself and the normal functioning of society (Martin and Osterholtz, chapter 5, this volume; Whitehead 2004, 2007). The same may be true with postmortem body manipulation. Indeed, the associations and meanings of corporeal disruption may change as soon as a once-living body is considered "dead"—even though the physical act of partitioning the body remains the same. While these acts may cease to be "violent" if they involve a deceased body versus one that is living, they remain imbued with meaning. The "poetics" of postmortem body manipulation creates a meaningful narrative of the relationships between and within the living and the dead, the manipulators and those being manipulated. However, unlike the poetics of Aristotle, postmortem dismemberment—reorganizing the physical manifestation of a human body—attains an "unnatural" quality, creating a narrative based on actions and realities that cannot exist in the real/living world (Alber et al. 2013).

DOI: 10.5876/9781646420612.c009

The power of integrating the living and the real with the dead and the unnatural through cycles of mortuary behavior not only emphasizes the social and cultural expectation that those in one group (the living, the real) will eventually belong to the other (the dead, the unnatural), but also how the social act of bodily manipulation serves to establish, maintain, and/or negotiate identity shared between these two worlds.

Here we explore the poetics of mortuary rituals involving corpse treatment at first-century AD Nabataean Petra. Petra's mortuary landscape still remains its most visible architectural feature, with intricately carved monumental tombs encircling the city center and lining varied approaches to the city. The bedrock hillocks within and outside of the city also are pockmarked with less-visible, less-ornate chamber tombs. A majority of the individuals within the tombs ended up within commingled assemblages, while others were left in their primary, articulated state. Does the presence of commingling and articulation reflect divergent mortuary narratives at Petra? Or are we simply seeing one step in the overall mortuary cycle, the process frozen in time due to unknown factors hindering access to the tombs?

ASPECTS OF NABATAEAN IDENTITY

The city of Petra served as the economic and religious center of the Nabataean kingdom, although the history and identity of the "Nabataeans" remains elusive. Textual sources identify the fourth-century BC Nabataeans as a nomadic group (Diodorus 1935, 2.48.2–5; 1954, 19.94.2–4) who gathered seasonally near a "rock" (Diodorus 1954, 19.95.1), perhaps referring to the "rock" (Grk. πέτρα, petra) where their capital was later established (see Graf et al. 2005; Graf, Schmid, and Ronza 2007). Historians and archaeologists grapple with characterizing Diodorus's Nabataeans, and how they relate to the monarchy established at Petra and the kingdom's actual inhabitants (Graf 1990; Knauf 1989, Macdonald 1991; Milik 1982). The kingdom's capital city during its florescence in the first centuries BC and AD reportedly had a cosmopolitan feel with many "foreigners" in residence (Strabo 1930, 16.4.24) and displays multiple cultural and stylistic influences on architecture and material culture (Anderson 2002; McKenzie 1990; Parr 1978; Patrich 1990). This cosmopolitanism has made characterizing Nabataean identity difficult, and some researchers argue the term "Nabataean" should be used only to identify residents of that political realm, not a distinct cultural group (Macdonald 1995).

Some scholars have explored whether aspects of a shared Nabataean identity may be expressed in ritual behaviors, including those related to death. While Nabataeans shared many cultural practices, there appears to be some individual agency in how these practices were performed. For instance, ritual feasting in large "dining halls" (*biclinia/triclinia*) associated with monumental façade tombs, temples, or other sacred contexts occurred regularly within the city (Haeckl, Jenni, and Schneider 2003; see also Strabo 1930, 16.4.26; Patrich 1990). However, these feasting events included only members of strongly cohesive groups (*marzēḥā*) based on family lineage, occupation, and/or worship of a particular deity or identification with a specific ancestor (Healey 2001; Nehmé 2013). Thus family and cultic ties had significant social importance beyond the larger polity and may have created intrapopulation heterogeneity in feasting behaviors.

The mortuary space served as the scene for similar practices emphasizing relations amongst family members and members of the *marzēḥā* even after death. It is clear from the inscriptions on Nabataean façade tombs at Medain Saleh that most tombs were built specifically to include only family members (Healey 1993; Wadeson 2013). Scattered inscriptions within some monumental Petra façade tombs also emphasize family ties, identifying the deceased as "X son of Y" or "Z daughter of A" (Healey 1993; Nehmé 2013). Very few epitaphs have been found on outer surfaces of the façade tombs at Petra, lost due to disintegration of the materials upon which they were painted or carved, or because they never existed in the first place. Regardless, the façade tombs in particular prominently existed in the world of the living, and city residents may have known through social memory to which family each tomb belonged. In fact, choices for the tombs' sculptural elements decorating relatively uniform tomb façades could have been linked to particular families (Sachet 2012). Similar to other ritual feasting, members of the family and the *marzēḥā* would have gathered for recurrent commemorative feasts for the dead within the dining halls or other spaces adjacent to the tombs (Perry 2016, 2017; Sachet 2010, 2012).

However, the ornate façade tombs, which are usually linked to members of the Nabataean royal family, Roman provincial officials, and other important personages, represent a different segment of society than the more numerous, less elaborate shaft chamber tombs that surround the city center and its environs. The 2012 and 2014 excavations of the Petra North Ridge, located along the city's northern urban edge, focused on four tombs (figure 9.1), recovering numerous articulated and commingled skeletal remains (total MNI = 114) along with intentional and accidental mortuary artifacts (Parker and Perry 2013, 2017; Perry 2016, 2017; Perry and Walker 2018). All tombs had similar construction, consisting of a tomb shaft cut into the bedrock averaging 2.5 m × 0.95 m wide and 2.9 m deep that opens into a rectilinear chamber with a surface area ranging from 7.3 m^2 to 40 m^2 (figure 9.2). The tomb chambers contain varied features for interment of the corpse, such as rectangular niches cut into the wall, rectangular shafts cut into the floor, or troughs/basins cut into the side or floor. A few articulated skeletons were found within some of these features, primarily in a wall niche or at the bottom of a rectangular shaft,

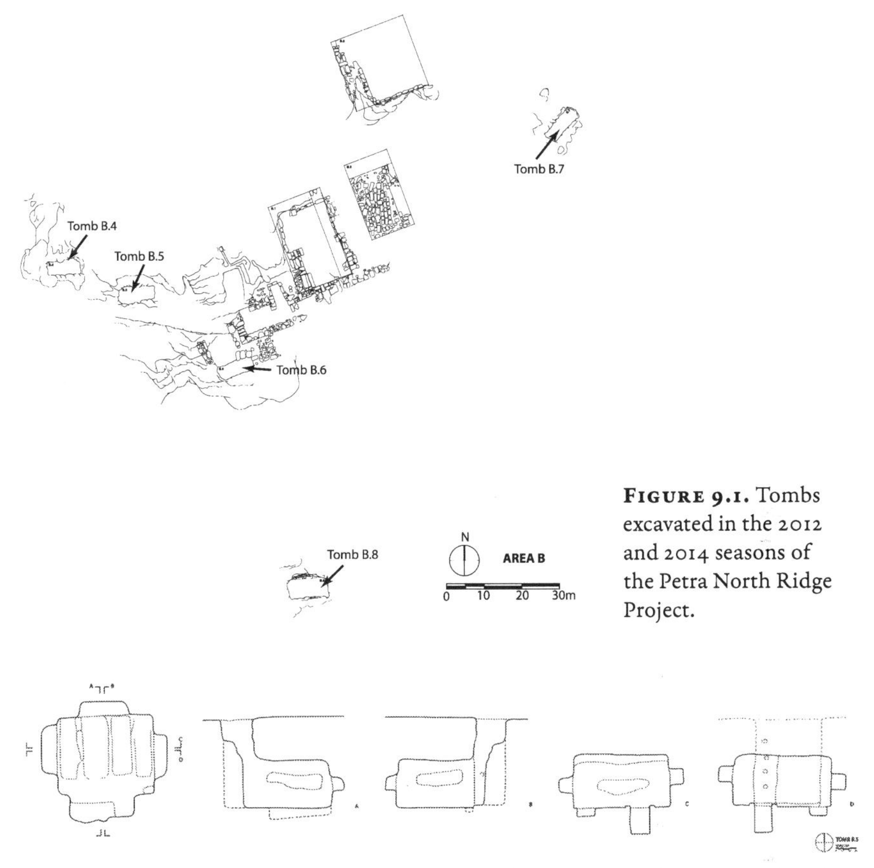

FIGURE 9.1. Tombs excavated in the 2012 and 2014 seasons of the Petra North Ridge Project.

FIGURE 9.2. Plan and sections of Tomb B.5, a typical tomb excavated on the North Ridge.

but others were found on top of or intermingled with commingled deposits. Other bodies were found partially articulated, with only the torso or legs in anatomical position and the rest of the remains presumably scattered among commingled deposits within the same layer. A majority of the skeletal remains within the tombs were found commingled, either within one of the floor features (troughs/basins or rectangular shafts) or directly on the chamber floor.

The shaft chamber tombs on the North Ridge existed in the world of the living through their close temporal and spatial proximity to adjacent late-first-century AD domestic structures and through evidence of interaction between family members and deceased ancestors. Archaeological evidence points to behaviors such as lighting incense, leaving behind the remains of funerary feasts and food offerings for the dead, and perhaps even playing games (Perry 2016, 2017). These tombs, similar to the façade tombs, have a basic homogeneity in their structure, but overall artifact assemblages suggest mortuary behaviors varied within each tomb. In addition, human activity in the tomb often resulted in the purposive creation of commingled assemblages. This likely signifies a lack of concern over maintaining individual corporeality at some point after death, unlike the mostly retained individual identities in the façade tombs. However, not all burials within a tomb ended up in commingled deposits, and some individuals have been left undisturbed in burial receptacles within the tomb. Are the primary burials in the chamber tombs important ancestors purposively left undisturbed, and do they reflect different poetic narratives than for those buried in the tombs? Or do they reflect one stage in a mortuary process resulting in eventual commingling that was never completed? Exploration of the commingled deposits based on element representation and stratigraphic information will assist in (1) distinguishing commingled deposits created from mortuary behaviors versus those resulting from tomb looting or natural processes, and (2) illuminating the poetics of body-processing of the purposive commingled deposits in the shaft chamber tombs at Petra.

IDENTIFYING MORTUARY-RELATED MANIPULATION

The mixture of articulated and commingled bodies within the two tombs implies that postmortem disturbances of human and/or natural origin occurred. That is, (1) humans interred the dead within the tombs, removing previous burials from the burial receptacles (niches, troughs, or shaft graves) for the placement of new individuals; (2) humans interred bones recovered from an external decomposition location (i.e., the interred bones were a secondary burial); (3) humans looted the tombs for valuables after they went out of use; and/or (4) natural forces such as fluvial intrusion displaced remains from their original primary or secondary disposition. It appears that, in most cases, bodies were interred initially as complete corpses, occasionally bedecked with jewelry or personal objects, and left to decompose. The postmortem processing could then progress along any of a number of trajectories:

1. The bodies would be left in their burial receptacle in a primary, articulated state.
2. The skeletal remains partially or completely devoid of soft tissue would be placed within another receptacle for communal burial.
3. The skeletal remains would be collected and brought to another tomb for secondary burial.
4. The skeletal remains would be displaced through tomb looting or natural processes.

Distinguishing human mortuary behaviors tied to the creation of commingled assemblages from those in the fourth trajectory provides the complementary data needed to understand why certain individuals would have different mortuary treatment at Petra.

First, simple stratigraphic assessment of each commingled deposit will help distinguish those likely resulting from behaviors extrinsic to the mortuary process, such as looting or natural events. Observations of stratigraphic indicators—natural fluvial and aeolian deposits in the form of laminations within soil profiles of stratigraphic deposits, versus disturbed strata—would differentiate assemblages left undisturbed after the tomb went out of ritual use from those disrupted due to other activities. The distribution of the skeletal remains themselves can also point to a cause for commingling. For example, a mostly articulated skeleton lying on a commingled deposit would suggest that the bones in that deposit were commingled during mortuary use of the tomb. On the other hand, retention of a few articulated body segments within the context of a commingled assemblage would indicate postmortuary processes, or at least a lack of concern for complete commingling. Density of skeletal elements within the assemblage also can be utilized, with the hypothesis that denser contexts are purposive, whereas those less dense resulted from looting or natural processes. One difficulty will involve identifying purposive commingled assemblages that were disturbed further by looting and/or natural factors.

In addition, representation of certain elements can provide some indication of the nature of the commingled deposit. MNI (minimum number of individuals) calculations for specific contexts within each tomb can be compared to those derived from specific hard, dense elements that usually survive natural taphonomic effects but that may not be well represented in assemblages moved from one place to another. Small elements, such as hand and foot phalanges, carpals, tarsals, and patellae, are more likely to be left behind during transportation from a primary processing location to a secondary burial location (e.g., an ossuary). Processing centers are therefore more likely to have better representation of smaller elements (Osterholtz, Baustian, and Martin 2012, 2014; Stodder et al. 2010). Lower MNI determinations for specific elements may also be indicative of trophy-taking (e.g., Osterholtz 2014) or the selective retention of some elements for ancestor veneration (e.g., Osterholtz et al. 2014). In general, complete representation of the small hand and foot bones is not necessarily expected, even in non-commingled contexts, due to other taphonomic factors that can impact their preservation. It is therefore a judgment call about what is meant by *good* or *poor* representation of the small elements, but one of the authors (Osterholtz) has typically used a standard of 30 percent: more than 30 percent of the expected number is considered to be *good* and below 30 percent is *poor*. While this is an admittedly arbitrary percentage, its conservativeness should also account for the loss of these elements due to other taphonomic impacts.

Skeletal remains from Petra were documented using a visual-feature-based recording system. The approach to analysis of the Petra North Ridge assemblage was based on methodology developed for the Sacred Ridge assemblage (Osterholtz and Stodder 2010; Stodder and Osterholtz 2010). In developing that methodology, the work of both bioarchaeologists (e.g., White 1992) and faunal analysts (e.g., Knüsel and Outram 2004) were consulted. Based on the high degree of fragmentation observed at Sacred Ridge, it was determined that standard techniques based on element completion (as outlined in Buikstra and Ubelaker 1994) for recording commingled MNI would be inadequate. This methodology outlined in Buikstra and Ubelaker calls for an estimation of the completeness of the element. When fragmentation is extreme, this is not sufficient. Instead, individual features of each element can be scored as present or absent based on the presence of at least 51 percent of the feature needed to score as "present." As an example, the femur was scored for multiple features including the greater trochanter, lesser trochanter, and neck, amongst others. These features were recorded using a visual recording form. The visual recording form was developed by Osterholtz for a few reasons: (1) to facilitate quick data entry, therefore making it functional in a time-sensitive situation; (2) to minimize data-entry errors through a visual inspection instead of identification of features by anatomical name; and (3) to create a permanent record of the overall representation of the element in time-sensitive situations such as field programs where remains are not permitted to leave the host country.

Counts of each skeletal feature recorded in the database were summed by tomb and specific contexts within each tomb using PROC MEANS in SAS. The MNI for each context was established by the element feature(s) with the maximum sum within that context. In addition, the maximum sums for elements from the hand and foot phalanges, the carpals, the tarsals, and the patellae were used to establish MNIs reflecting assemblage creation. Phalanx counts were established through summing the counts of complete, identifiable hand and foot phalanges in the sample provided by the SAS output (table 9.1). At this phase of analysis, MNI calculations took into consideration general age (adult vs. subadult) and sex differences within the sample. More detailed age analysis, particularly of the adults, may change our overall MNI calculations in the future.

RESULTS

Observations of the soil profiles, element density, and disposition of articulated and commingled remains distinguished deposits created through purposive bone caching in tomb receptacles, disturbance due to natural processes and looting, and one possible assemblage that was an extra-tomb secondary burial.

Table 9.1. MNI for each context within the Petra North Ridge tombs (B.4–B.7)

Context	Context #	Description	Total MNI	Percentage (%) of Total MNI			
				Carpals	Tarsals	Phalanges	Patellae
Tomb B.4 total*			16	13	16	15	59
B.4:10	34	Eastern wall niche B.4:11 (with 3 partially articulated skeletons)	4	11	5	3	38
B.4:13	37	Possibly intrusive infant burial in tomb shaft	1	0	0	0	0
B.4:16, B.4:17, B.4:22, B.4:23	35	All floor deposits (including 1 mostly articulated skeleton in B.4:22 and remains possibly washed from northern burial trough B.4:20)	10	36	34	24	85
B.4:15, B.4:18	16	Western burial trough B.4:21 (1 partially articulated skeleton)	1	0	0	5	100
Tomb B.5 total*			58	20	29	9	11
B.5:4	25	Fill overlying floor deposits	3	0	17	7	33
B.5:9, B.5:11, B.5:13, B.5:15, B.5:19	2	Commingled floor deposit in eastern sector of tomb with 2 partially articulated skeletons (mandible MNI = 14, everything else MNI~7)	14	4	5	4	7
B.5:12	23	Western niche B.5:25 (1 partially articulated skeleton)	1	25	7	5	100
B.5:17	22	Northern niche B.5:18 (1 partially articulated skeleton)	1	0	0	0	0
B.5:27, B.5:34, B.5:35	1	Floor shaft grave B.5:28	30	16	55	15	32
B.5:31	24	Floor shaft grave B.5:30 (1 partially articulated skeleton)	1	0	29	10	0

continued on next page

Table 9.1—*continued*

Context	*Context #*	*Description*	*Total MNI*	*Percentage (%) of Total MNI*			
				Carpals	*Tarsals*	*Phalanges*	*Patellae*
B.5:32, B.5:33	4	Floor shaft grave B.5:10	8	44	39	16	88
Tomb B.6 total*			24	11	11	29	31
B.6:6, B.6:21	9	Disturbed tomb fill with modern debris	1	0	43	5	0
B.6:23, B.6:27, B.6:33, B.6:34, B.6:40, B.6:41	6	Fill in southern deep shaft B.6:17 (includes series of 3 partially articulated burials)	5	37	44	42	60
B.6:24, B.6:28, B.6:31, B.6:39, B.6:43, B.6:44	10	Disturbed deposits from looted graves	15	2	19	3	27
B.6:36, B.6:37, B.6:38, B.6:42	5	Floor shaft grave B.6:19 (with 1 partially articulated burial at bottom)	3	0	17	5	0
Tomb B.7 total*			11	16	29	14	17
B.7:10, B.7:16, B.7:19, B.7:28, B.7:31	12	Floor shaft grave B.7:11	3	13	19	18	33
B.7:14, B.7:20	13	Floor shaft grave B.7:15	2	41	7	25	50
B.7:23, B.7:25, B.7:34	14	Floor shaft grave B.7:22	2	0	21	0	0
B.7:27, B.7:32	15	Floor shaft grave B.7:13 (with 1 partially articulated burial)	1	0	0	10	0
B.7:30, B.7:33, B.7:35	11	Floor shaft grave B.7:29 (with 1 mostly articulated burial)	3	27	45	17	67

* Tomb MNIs are based on the summed MNI of each tomb context

Tomb B.4

Much of the disruption of articulated burials in Tomb B.4 seemed to have occurred from natural processes. The northern trough B.4:20 did not contain any *in situ* bones, but B.4:17, the sand overlying the chamber floor in front of the niche, had a cluster of elements thought to have washed from the trough. Immediately to the south of B.4:17, within layer B.4:23, was a concentration of scattered human bones surrounding partially articulated elements (e.g., part of a vertebral column in one area and lower limbs and feet in another location), and in B.4:22 were additional commingled remains surrounding an almost complete articulated skeleton. The haphazard nature of the commingling, which seemed to have missed portions of the interred bodies, combined with the thinness of the scatter (with the possible exception of B.4:23), imply that the floor deposits were not purposive. In addition, while the skeletons interred in the eastern wall niche (B.4:11) remained generally articulated, a swath of remains extended out of the northern portion of the niche into the surrounding deposits (all designated as B.4:10). This scattering occurred when the tomb had been filled with nearly 0.75 m of soil, and thus was a later event than that which caused commingling of the floor deposits. Overall, analysis of the disposition of skeletal remains in the eastern wall niche B.4:11 and the northern trough B.4:20 presents a pattern where elements were "washed" out of their original place of burial at two different points in the tomb's history. One factor likely was a "window" opening found within the northwestern corner of B.4, where the northern and western troughs come together—the reason for this opening is unclear, but remnants of flat window glass found immediately in the corner indicate that during the tomb's use it would have provided protection for the tomb chamber. Damage to the glass, however, would have exposed the tomb interior to the elements, including fluvial intrusions from the flooding seasonal rains. These natural events displaced the remains within the northern trough, and likely can be implicated in the disturbance of the skeletal remains on the floor (which may have originally been placed in the troughs or on the floor). Laminations of waterborne silt within the soil layers surrounding the scattered bones would support this hypothesis. Eventually, seasonal rains would have displaced some of the remains in the eastern niche, likely originating from the tomb shaft, based on the direction of the scattering. At this point in the tomb's history, capstones that covered the opening of the wall niche had been displaced, exposing the burials to the elements.

The pattern of hand and foot bone and patella representation supports this scenario. The northern and western troughs have almost none of these elements, while they are strongly represented in the floor deposits. Therefore, these bones had been displaced from the troughs and redistributed across the floor due to the natural processes described above. The bones from the western niche B.4:11 are not well represented, and these small bones may have been lost due to oversight during excavation (despite the sifting of 100% of tomb deposits).

Tomb B.5

Tomb B.5 contains the largest MNI of the four discussed here. It also contains the only clearly purposive commingled deposits. The wall niches containing B.5:12 and B.5:17 and the easternmost shaft grave each had one articulated primary burial, although B.5:12 had an extra carpal and B.5:17 an extra tarsal. The eastern wall niche was completely empty. The westernmost shaft grave (B.5:28), containing B.5:27, B.5:34, and B.5:35, was densely filled with commingled remains, suggesting a purposive deposit. The use of this feature seems to change over time, with very densely packed remains with few artifacts in the lower stratum (B.5:35) and more artifacts and some partially articulated elements in the upper stratum (B.5:34). This floor shaft grave did not contain capstones, as did one other grave in the tomb (that also contained one of the primary burials), but it was sealed with loose silty sand that contained few human remains, implying the remains in this feature had not been disturbed once the tomb went out of use.

The most complicated assemblage appears to be represented by layers B.5:9, B.5:11, B.5:13, B.5:15, and B.5:19 at the eastern end of the tomb. Here, commingled skeletal remains were found tightly packed within two soil layers (B.5:15 and B.5:19). One almost intact, articulated skeleton was found at the higher of the two layers of these strata (B.5:15 Skeleton 1) and one other partially intact skeleton was recovered from the overlying stratum (B.5:9 Skeleton 1). The distinct transition between the two strata containing commingled remains would imply they had not been disturbed through environmental forces or tomb looting, and the presence of partially intact burials in the layers sealing the commingled deposits imply that they were created when the tomb was still in use.

The representation of hand and foot bones and patellae in the floor shaft grave B.5:28 differs notably from that in the floor deposits at the eastern end of the tomb. These bones are very well represented in B.5:28; that and their density imply that the original articulated skeletons had been interred within the tomb, carefully collected, and placed together within the shaft grave in a relatively short period of time. The skeletons probably were originally interred within other receptacles, such as the wall niches, which would explain the extra tarsal in one and extra carpal in another—apparently, the collection of elements for secondary burial was not 100 percent!

Unfortunately, floor shaft grave B.5:10 had been looted between the 2012 and 2014 excavation seasons, and thus the original disposition of the skeletal remains is unknown. The looted deposits were excavated as B.5:32 and B.5:33. Here, the representation of the carpals, tarsals, and patellae are high, similar to the representation in B.5:28, suggesting that it, too, was a receptacle for the bones from primary burials collected from within the tomb.

Tomb B.6

Looting likely caused commingling in most of the B.6 contexts. The deposits identified during excavation as B.6:6, B.6:21, B.6:24, B.6:28, B.6:31, B.6:39, B.6:43, and B.6:44 contained a scattering of human remains surrounding disturbed capstones that would have covered the floor shaft graves, and in the case of B.6:6 and B.6:21, modern garbage. This looting activity extended into the upper layer of floor shaft grave B.6:19, but did not reach the undisturbed articulated burial at the bottom of this shaft. The vertical sequence of three partially articulated skeletons surrounded by a few commingled remains in the deep shaft to the south of the tomb entrance (B.6:17) remains puzzling, and it is possible that repeated burial of each individual resulted in disturbance of the earlier interments.

Looting activity often results in displacement of elements from their original burial location. The high representation of phalanges, carpals, tarsals, and patellae within B.6:17 would suggest that, indeed, these skeletal remains had not been extensively disturbed after their interment, and the resulting slight commingling surrounding the partially articulated skeletons did not result in displacement of these elements from their original context. On the other hand, the poor representation of these elements in the other deposits in B.6, mostly under 30 percent, may indicate that the elements were left behind in the southern shaft, while the other bones were scattered around the tomb chamber, resulting in their disproportionate representation in this context. However, one would expect more displacement of the skeletons in the southern shaft grave if extensive looting had occurred. Another possibility is that the poor representation of hand and foot bones and patellae indicates the commingled deposits resulted from an extra-tomb secondary burial. However, the low density of these deposits and other clues outlined above would not support that these were commingled assemblages resulting from mortuary behavior, even secondary burial. Therefore, it appears that all interments in B.6 were primary, and no purposive commingling occurred. Furthermore, this looting activity seemed to have occurred in two stages: (1) one in antiquity, resulting in the disruption of B.6:24, B.6:28, B.6:31, B.6:39, B.6:43, B.6:44, and the upper layers of floor shaft grave B.6:19, after which fluvial and aeolian deposits built up within the tomb chamber; and (2) the second more recently, which had cleared a notable percentage of the tomb shaft fill and about a quarter of the way into the main chamber, and created the commingled deposits B.6:6 and B.6:21 that contained modern garbage.

Tomb B.7

Each of the five floor shaft graves in Tomb B.7 contained commingled remains. In each case, the elements were not densely concentrated, and that plus the lack of discernable strata in the soil would indicate this was not purposive commingling. Only a handful of skeletal elements were found in the soil overlying the opening of the floor graves, which may suggest that the disturbance, most likely looting, had occurred in antiquity before the graves were covered with soil; if so, perhaps the bones remain in their original floor shaft grave. In addition, there was a partial primary, articulated burial found at the bottom of two shaft graves, B.7:13 and B.7:29. Here, similar to floor shaft grave B.6:19, the looting had not significantly affected the bottom interment within these graves. It also appears that these burials likely were primary interments that retained their articulated state throughout the mortuary cycle, although the bottom interment in B.7:13 was more disturbed than B.7:29.

The mixed representation of hand and foot bones and patellae within the shaft graves is perplexing. Shaft graves B.7:13 and B.7:22 had very poor representation of these elements, while the others had fair to respectable proportions. All of the shaft graves had similar levels of disturbance, but it is possible that they experienced different taphonomic histories, resulting in the destruction of many of the elements (because of looters standing within a particular shaft grave, for example). In addition, it is possible that looting disturbance resulted in the transfer of bones from one shaft grave to another. Collection of taphonomic data in addition to potentially finding joins between fragmented artifacts within the different shaft graves should illuminate why shaft graves varied in representation.

DISCUSSION

Seasonal flooding and looting of the tombs explains most of the instances of commingling described above. Although a detailed study of bone taphonomy remains to be completed, the bones from all of the tombs had experienced varied post-depositional damage. Fragmentation was the primary issue, but also weathering and cortical and trabecular bone exfoliation and cracking typical for aqueous contexts. The tombs overall have a decent representation of hand and foot remains based on small-bone representation, suggesting that secondary burial, if occurring, was not a common practice. Breaking down the data by type of context (floor deposit, floor shaft with commingled remains only, floor shaft with commingled and primary

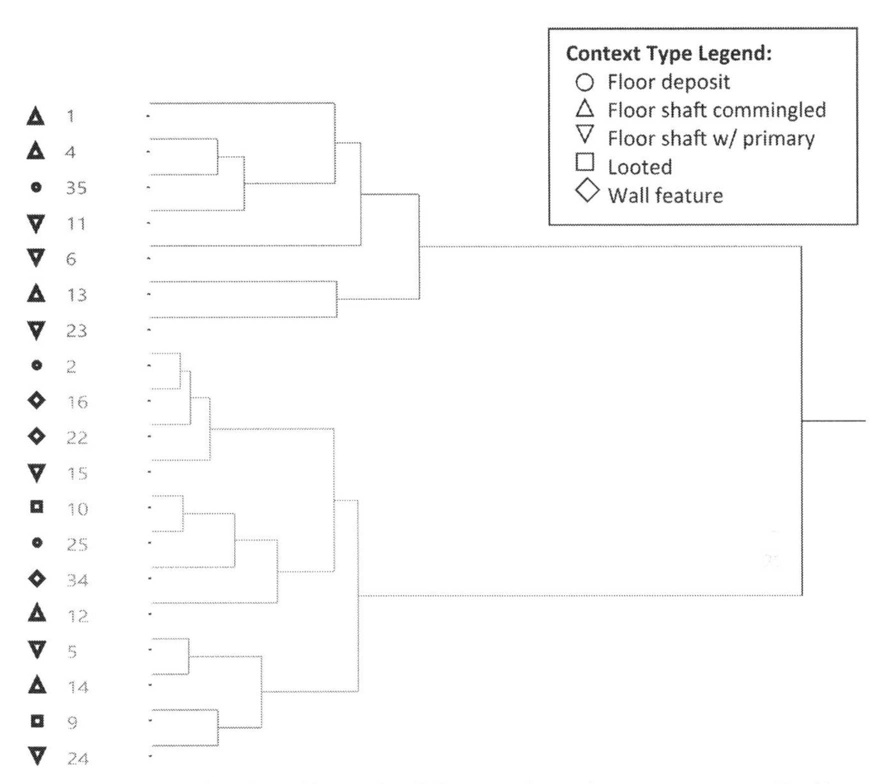

FIGURE 9.3. Results of Ward hierarchical cluster analysis of representation profiles (for carpals, tarsals, phalanges, and patellae) of each context in the Petra North Ridge Tombs (Descriptions of the numbered contexts can be found in Table 9.1). The different contexts separate into two separate groups: those with good representation (the upper cluster) and those with poorer representation (the lower cluster).

burial, looted, or wall feature) did not identify any distinct patterns in representation of hand and foot bones versus context type. To further explore any patterns of representation by context, the percentage of total MNI represented by carpals, tarsals, phalanges, and patellae were subjected to Ward hierarchical cluster analysis using JMP Pro 12.0. The data separated into two main clusters, those with better and worse representation (figure 9.3), with all of the wall features and looted contexts falling into the poor representation group, and the floor deposits and floor shaft graves of either type belonging to either cluster.

Only in B.5 was there evidence for mortuary-related commingled deposits created through intra- or extra-tomb secondary burial. The floor shaft graves B.5:28, containing B.5:27, B.5:34, and B.5:35, and B.5:10, containing B.5:32 and B.5:33, had a moderate appendage representation and both fell into the "good representation" cluster. On the other hand, the floor deposits of B.5:9, B.5:11, B.5:13, B.5:15, and B.5:19 had poor representation of hand and foot bones, and fell into the "poor representation" cluster. What happened to the hands and feet of these deposits if we assume that these bones were not brought from elsewhere? They could have been transported to the floor shaft graves B.5:10 and B.5:28. However, in that case a much higher representation of hand and foot bones than in the overall tomb would be expected within these contexts. The stratigraphic evidence from the B.5 floor deposit also suggests that they were deposited purposively while the tomb was in use rather than scattered and commingled due to looting or natural disturbances.

Even though commingling was not as widely practiced as originally conceived in Petra, there are instances in which it occurred. Some groups utilizing a particular tomb, such as Tomb B.5, added an additional step in mortuary-related body manipulation—combining the remains of their ancestors in a communal receptacle after the body had decomposed. This behavior also is hypothesized for Tomb F.1 that was excavated in the 2016 field season but not included in this analysis as the inventory of the bones had not been completed. The other tombs seemed instead to have buried decedents within a floor shaft grave on top of previously interred bodies. The relationship between individuals within each floor shaft grave cannot be ascertained from the available data, but the mix of ages and sexes seen in those in tomb B.7 imply they were not separated based on these demographic variables.

The variation in postmortem body manipulation at Petra implies the presence of two different poetic narratives communicated through mortuary ritual. The overriding framework clearly remains the emphasis on extended family ties between the deceased and between the living and dead members of the lineage that, through communal burial (or the living's expectation of communal burial), continues after death. Witnessing or participating in the interment of family members within the lineage's tomb and engaging in mortuary feasting with the family and the larger *marzēḥā* were active means for emphasizing these ties and fostering a group identity based at least partially on tomb inclusion.

The question remains why some families created an additional layer of postmortem body manipulation as part of the mortuary cycle. This behavior could have been largely practical. A tomb servicing a group with a larger population (and presumably unwilling or unable to fund and organize construction or purchase of another tomb) would have needed to remove primary interments for placement of new decedents. Only three out of four potential floor shaft graves were actually carved—the extent of the fourth at the chamber's eastern end (B.5:30) was merely outlined, by carving ca. 20 cm into the chamber floor. It is possible, then, that financial constraints prevented tomb expansion to fit with the size of the family and number of interments needed. However, keeping these now secondary intra-tomb burials within the spatial confines of the tomb, and symbolically within the family, remained a concern. Therefore, rectangular floor shaft graves such as B.5:28 and B.5:10 were reserved for archiving the ancestors' remains.

In addition, the approximately 12 individuals interred on the floor seemed to have been initially buried elsewhere outside of the tomb, but their skeletal remains were apparently recovered and placed within the tomb chamber—and were later topped with the corpses of two more individuals who were left in their primary state (although partially disturbed by later tomb activity of an unidentified nature). The original location of burial remains unclear from the available data. The Nabataean practice of secondary burial was commented on by the first-century AD geographer Strabo: "[The Nabataeans] have the same regard for the dead as for dung, as Heracleitus says: 'Dead bodies are more fit to be cast out than dung'; and therefore they bury even their kings beside dung heaps" (1930, XVI.4.24). Scholars have interpreted Strabo's description of casting out the bodies and leaving them beside dung heaps as leaving corpses exposed to the elements, after which, the bones presumably would be gathered. Published interpretations of this quote have noted that little archaeological evidence supports Strabo's description (Perry 2002; Wright 1969). However, the assemblage in B.5 implies there may be a small grain of truth in this text. Regardless of where and how far away the bodies in the B.5 floor context first decomposed, the interment of their bones within the confines of the family grave retained as much importance as those who had initially been interred within the tomb itself.

The "unnatural" disarticulation of the human bodies within these assemblages also allows the creation of a new identity that cannot physically exist in the natural world—that of a single corporate familial entity. The poetics of this behavior within the Nabataean cultural realm communicates to the community that family identity transcends that which is physically present in the world of the living to include those not corporeally animated, such as those who have attained the status of ancestor. In fact, it may communicate to us that the Nabataeans did not in fact distinguish between these two worlds, and that those not corporeally alive in a biological sense retained a "real" identity in the Nabataean concept of the natural world.

CONCLUSIONS

The above evidence suggests that mortuary behaviors on Petra's North Ridge means the deceased can either end up as part of a commingled deposit or left in a primary articulated state. Some families did not feel the need to collect the bones after decomposition of the body for burial of another, more recently deceased family member. This could have been because the tomb was considered sufficient for interment of that family group's size at the time the tomb was in use. Another possibility is that particular lineage moved from Petra. Finally, it could simply reflect diversity in mortuary processing by family or group identity, reflecting the homogeneity in Nabataean burial rites.

The North Ridge tombs (and particularly tombs B.6 and B.7) appear to have been first used in the first century BC and then went out of use in the late first/early second century AD. This late first-/early second-century date coincides with the Roman annexation of the Nabataean kingdom and construction of a northern city wall by the Nabataeans or Romans around this point. The construction of this wall puts the southern slope of the North Ridge, the location of these tombs, within the city. The later years of the cemetery also coincide with intensification of domestic settlements in the same sector of the ridge. The Romans, with their strict rules surrounding the location of graves and any activities related to body preparation outside of the city, could have implemented prohibitions against burial or tomb upkeep after the annexation, leaving some individuals in one stage of mortuary treatment. Therefore, it is possible that the primary intact burials discovered within the tombs could simply reflect mortuary cycles left incomplete due to the prevention of mourners tending to or continuing to use the tomb.

The varied mortuary programs at Petra illustrate an important element of Nabataean identity and interaction. As noted by Macdonald, "Nabataean" may better refer to a political or corporate entity, not an ethnic identity (Macdonald 1995). One way to express difference or subgroup identity may have been in mortuary processing, whereas spatial clustering of tombs within the city emphasized the individual groups' affiliation with the larger social and political construct of "Nabataean" Petra. At Petra, the act of body manipulation as shown through the gathering of remains into collective shaft tombs may have created as much meaning as the intentional non-manipulation of some bodies by other groups. Either way, social identity (both of the family group and the corporate identity of Petra) is negotiated and maintained.

Memory is also created through this manipulation and the consistent visiting of the tombs. The use of a glass panel in tomb B.4 is suggestive of rituals involving visiting the dead, experiencing the sights and scents of decomposition. This involvement of practice and action increases the power of mortuary processing to create identity and memory. Memory and revisiting in this way reinforce the relationship between the living and the dead as forms of veneration of the dead.

REFERENCES

Alber, J., S. Iversen, H. S. Nielsen, and B. Richardson. 2013. "Introduction." In *A Poetics of Unnatural Narrative*, edited by J. Alber, H. S. Nielsen, and B. Richardson, 1–15. Columbus, OH: Ohio State University Press.

Anderson, Björn. 2002. "Local Identities: References to Achaemenid Persian Iconography on Crenelated Nabataean Tombs." *Ars Orientalis* 32: 163–207.

Buikstra, Jane E., and Douglas H. Ubelaker, eds. 1994. *Standards for Data Collection from Human Skeletal Remains: Proceedings of a Seminar at the Field Museum of Natural History, Organized by Jonathan Haas*, edited by Hester A. Davis. *Arkansas Archeological Survey Research Series No. 44*. Fayettevilla, AR: Arkansas Archaeological Survey.

Diodorus Siculus. 1935. *Library of History*, Volume II: *Books 2.35–4.58*, translated by C. H. Oldfather. Cambridge, MA: Harvard University Press.

Diodorus Siculus. 1954. *Library of History*, Volume X: *Books 19.66–20*, translated by Russel M. Geer. Cambridge, MA: Harvard University Press.

Graf, David F. 1990. "The Origin of the Nabataeans." *Aram* 2: 45–75.

Graf, David F, Leigh-Ann Bedal, Stephan G. Schmid, and S. E. Sidebotham. 2005. "The Hellenistic Petra Project. Excavations in the Civic Center: Preliminary Report of the First Season, 2004." *Annual of the Department of Antiquities of Jordan* 49: 417–441.

Graf, David F, Stephan G. Schmid, and Elena Ronza. 2007. "The Hellenistic Petra Project: Excavations in the Qasr al-Bint Temenos Area: Preliminary Report of the Second Season, 2005." *Annual of the Department of Antiquities of Jordan* 51: 223–238.

Haeckl, U., H. Jenni, and C. Schneider. 2003. *Quellen zur Geschichte der Nabatäer. Textsammlung mit Übersetzung und Kommentar*. Freiberg: Universitätsverlag.

Healey, John F. 1993. *The Nabataean Tomb Inscriptions of Mada'in Salih*. Oxford: Oxford University Press.

Healey, John F. 2001. *The Religion of the Nabataeans: A Conspectus*. Leiden: Brill.

Knauf, E. A. 1989. "Nabataean Origins." In *Arabian Studies in Honor of Mahmoud Ghul*, edited by M. M. Ibrahim, 56–61. Weisbaden: Yarmouk University Publications.

Knüsel, C. J., and A. K. Outram. 2004. "Fragmentation: The Zonation Method Applied to Fragmented Human Remains from Archaeological and Forensic Contexts." *Environmental Archaeology* 9: 85–97.

Macdonald, M.C.A. 1991. "Was the Nabataean Kingdom a 'Bedouin State'?" *Zeitschrift des Deutschen Palästina-Vereins* 107: 102–119.

Macdonald, M.C.A. 1995. "North Arabia in the First Millennium BCE." In *Civilizations of the Ancient Near East*, edited by J. M. Sasson, J. Baines, G. Beckman, and K. S. Rubinson, 1355–1369. New York: Scribner and Sons.

Martin, Debra L., Ryan P. Harrod, and Ventura R. Pérez. 2013. *Bioarchaeology: An Integrated Approach to Working with Human Remains*. New York: Springer.

McKenzie, Judith. 1990. *The Architecture of Petra*. London: Oxford University Press.

Milik, J. T. 1982. "Origines des Nabatéens." In *Studies in the History and Archaeology of Jordan I*, edited by Adnan Hadidi, 261–265. Amman: Department of Antiquities.

Nehmé, L. 2013. "The Installation of Social Groups in Petra." In *Men on the Rocks: The Formation of Nabataean Petra*, edited by Michel Mouton and Stephan G. Schmid, 113–128. Berlin: Logos Verlag GmbH.

Osterholtz, Anna J. 2014. "Patterned Processing as Performative Violence at Sacred Ridge." 79th Annual Meeting of the Society for American Archaeology, Austin, TX.

Osterholtz, Anna J., Kathryn M. Baustian, and Debra L. Martin. 2012. "Determining the Minimum Number of Individuals (MNI) for Tell Abraq, UAE." 77th Annual Meeting of the Society for American Archaeology, Memphis, TN.

Osterholtz, Anna J., Kathryn M. Baustian, and Debra L. Martin. 2014. "Introduction." In *Commingled and Disarticulated Human Remains: Working Toward Improved, Theory, Method, and Data*, edited by Anna J. Osterholtz, Kathryn M. Baustian, and Debra L. Martin, 1–16. New York: Springer.

Osterholtz, Anna J., Kathryn M. Baustian, Debra L. Martin, and Daniel T. Potts. 2014. "Commingled Human Skeletal Assemblages: Integrative Techniques in Determination of the MNI/MNE." In *Commingled and Disarticulated Human Remains: Working Toward Improved Theory, Method, and Data*, edited by Anna J. Osterholtz, Kathryn M. Baustian and Debra L. Martin, 35–66. New York: Springer Press.

Osterholtz, Anna J., and Ann L. W. Stodder. 2010. "Conjoining a Neighborhood: Data Structure and Methodology for Taphonomic Analysis of the Very Large Assemblage from Sacred Ridge." Poster, 79th Annual Meeting of the American Association of Physical Anthropologists Meetings, Albuquerque, NM.

Parker, S. Thomas, and Megan A. Perry. 2013. "Petra North Ridge Project: The 2012 Season." *Annual of the Department of Antiquities of Jordan* 57: 399–407.

Parker, S. Thomas, and Megan A. Perry. 2017. "The Petra North Ridge Project: 2014 season." *Annual of the Department of Antiquities of Jordan* 58: 287–301.

Parr, Peter J. 1978. "Pottery, People, and Politics." In *Archaeology in the Levant: Essays for Kathleen Kenyon*, edited by R. Moorey and Peter J. Parr, 203–210. Warminster: Aries and Philip.

Patrich, J. 1990. *The Formation of Nabataean Art: Prohibition of a Graven Image among the Nabataeans*. Jerusalem: Magnes Press.

Perry, Megan A. 2002. "Life and Death in Nabataea: The North Ridge Tombs and Nabataean Burial Practices." *Near Eastern Archaeology* 65: 265–270.

Perry, Megan A. 2016. "New Light on Nabataean Mortuary Rituals in Petra." *Studies in the History and Archaeology of Jordan* XII: 385–398.

Perry, Megan A. 2017. "Sensing the Dead: Mortuary Ritual and Tomb Visitation at Nabataean Petra." *Syria* 94: 99–106.

Perry, Megan A., and Jessica L. Walker. 2018. "The Nabataean Way of Death on Petra's North Ridge." In *Death and Burial in the Near East from Roman to Islamic Times:*

Research in Syria, Lebanon, Jordan and Egypt, edited by Christoph Eger and Michael Mackensen, 121–137. Wiesbaden: Reichert Verlag.

Sachet, Isabelle. 2010. "Feasting with the Dead: Funerary Marzeah in Petra." In *Death and Burial in Arabia and Beyond: Multidisciplinary Perspectives*, edited by L. Weeks, 249–262. Oxford: Archaeopress.

Sachet, Isabelle. 2012. "Dieux et hommes des tombeaux d'Arabie Petree: iconographie et aniconisme des elites nabateennes." In *Dieux et deesses d'Arabie: Images et representations*, edited by Isabelle Sachet and C. J. Robin, 225–260. Paris: De Boccard.

Stodder, Ann L.W., and Anna J. Osterholtz. 2010. "Analysis of the Processed Human Remains from the Sacred Ridge Site: Methods and Data Collection Protocol." In *Animas-La Plata Project, Volume XV: Bioarchaeology*, edited by Elizabeth M. Perry, Ann L.W. Stodder, and Charles A. Bollong, 243–278. Phoenix, AZ: SWCA Environmental Consultants.

Stodder, Ann L.W., Anna J. Osterholtz, Kathy Mowrer, and Jason P. Chuipka. 2010. "Processed Human Remains from the Sacred Ridge Site: Context, Taphonomy, Interpretation." In *Animas-La Plata Project, Volume XV: Bioarchaeology*, edited by Elizabeth M. Perry, Ann L.W. Stodder, and Charles A. Bollong, 279–415. Phoenix, AZ: SWCA Environmental Consultants.

Strabo. 1930. *Geography*, Volume VII: *Books 15–16*, translated by Horace Leonard Jones. Cambridge, MA: Harvard University Press.

Wadeson, Lucy. 2013. "The Development of Funerary Architecture at Petra: The Case of the Facade Tombs." In *Men on the Rocks: The Formation of Nabataean Petra*, edited by Michel Mouton and Stephan G. Schmid, 167–188. Berlin: Logos Verlag GmbH.

White, Tim D. 1992. *Prehistoric Cannibalism at Mancos 5MTUMR-2346*. Princeton, NJ: Princeton University Press.

Whitehead, Neil L. 2004. "On the Poetics of Violence." In *Violence*, edited by Neil L. Whitehead, 55–78. Santa Fe, NM: SAR Press.

Whitehead, Neil L. 2007. "Violence and the Cultural Order." *Daedalus* 136 (1): 40–50. doi: 10.2307/20028088.

Wright, G.R.H. 1969. "Strabo on Funerary Customs at Petra." *Palestine Exploration Quarterly* 101: 113–116.

PART 3

Anatomization

10

Dissection as Social Process

Anatomical Settings in the Nineteenth-Century United States

CHRISTINA J. HODGE AND KENNETH C. NYSTROM

"Poetics" understands the *communication* of knowledge as a simultaneous *production* of knowledge by legitimating certain interpretations over others (Moser and Gamble 1997, 185). Some perspectives are naturalized, others precluded. This volume proposes that the poetics of human body-processing function as a nuanced mechanism of social reproduction across cultures and periods. Therefore, we may learn new things about social history through the explicitly theorized study of body-processing as knowledge production. The term "anatomization" is used to describe one such mode of processing: the dissection of human cadavers. A "poetics of anatomization" studies understandings produced and obscured by (1) anatomized human remains as communication tools and (2) the material practices of anatomization itself. In the nineteenth century, dissection, circulation, and discard of bodies and body parts legitimated differential access to power by treating different sorts of bodies differently, while carefully reserving medical authority for those few initiates into its arcane practices (who were usually white, educated, and male). A focus on poetics illuminates the recursive structures of practice and setting that sustained these processes. In America, identity-based social hierarchies normalized by nineteenth-century anatomical practices continue today to support structural racism and moral inflections of poverty and displacement (see de la Cova, chapter 11, this volume). Settings of dissection, and the practices they afforded their human and nonhuman occupants, are not only crucially important, but also susceptible to archaeological and historical investigation.

DOI: 10.5876/9781646420612.c010

Interpretations of anatomical dissection, as a Western scientific pursuit, have, to date, been undertheorized. A handful of scholars explore affective relationships between the living and dead. These emotional impacts are recognized through body treatment (keeping bodies whole) and lingering materialities of life experience (disease, trauma, age, appearance, etc.) (Crossland 2009a, 2009b; Edwards 2015; Hodge, Morgan, and Rousseau 2017; Tarlow 1999, 2005, 2011). Analyses of dissection practices overwhelmingly focus on clarifying medical history (Blakely and Harrington 1997; Mitchell 2012; Mitchell et al. 2011) or on exposing structural violence via categories of class, gender, and race (Blakely and Harrington 1997; Sappol 2002). Scholars do not broach these topics through social theory, however (although some contemporary studies do, see for example Fountain 2008). In contrast, in this chapter we explicitly use cultural theory to experiment with the notion of poetics as social process.

We draw most directly on Foucauldian discourse analysis and phenomenology, united through the poetics of heterotopic settings. Neil L. Whitehead's performative notion of poetics helps us to populate these settings. In his influential studies of the social effects of violence, he makes a case for the didactic qualities of aggression as "socially constructive cultural performance" (Whitehead 2004, 60). He explores physical contact between antagonist, victim, *and audience*. We are inspired by this three-part model and extend it to include things as actors alongside living humans. We consider not only the direct participants in anatomical acts (corpses and anatomists), but also the student audiences who witnessed dissections and benefited from the circulation of anatomical specimens. We remain mindful of a fourth constituency: the broader public, excluded from these discourses yet pressuring them through normative value systems. Finally, the items and settings involved in anatomization also shaped these encounters. Tempered by a sense of object agency taken from materiality studies, the frameworks of poetics and phenomenology usefully advance our goal of interpreting archaeological evidence of nineteenth-century human anatomization in a theoretically rigorous manner.

Poetics are a component of what is broadly termed "discourse." Discourses are those social rules and dispositions recognized through "systematically organized sets of statements [textual, visual, sensory, and/or material] which give expression to the meanings and values of an institution . . . A discourse colonises [sic] the social world imperialistically from the point of view of an institution" (Kress 1989, 6). Michel Foucault's formulations of discourse theory recognize these patterned material practices as acts of power, which simultaneously introduce and reproduce hierarchical social structures (Diaz-Bone et al. 2008; Powers 2007). These structures, in turn, are intended recursively to stabilize, perpetuate, and legitimate social institutions. Discourses of nineteenth-century dissection illuminate broader political relationships. On the one hand, there are those institutionally sanctioned individuals producing their own medical/social authority by doing dissections. On the other, there are those persons institutionally disenfranchised by being dissected and circulated as anatomical specimens or returned to a normative memorial space via cemetery burial.

As this summary suggests, setting proves fundamental to the workings of historic regimes of power (Foucault 1972, 1973, 1995). Space/place is not neutral, but rather actively participates in social reproduction, manifesting its own poetics, which are perceived through human bodies (Ashmore 2004; Bachelard 1994). This phenomenological lens ameliorates Foucault's top-down concern with setting by incorporating bottom-up practice, experience, and materiality into discourses of place (as public vs. hidden, theatrical vs. memorial, sacred vs. secular, etc.). Foucault's notion of "heterotopias" more specifically models the ways specialized settings—including hospitals, schools, cemeteries, ships, museums, libraries, and many other Enlightenment and modern institutions—functioned as alternate sites of social reproduction and (dis)empowerment (Foucault 1984b, 2002). Collectively, these sites posited an idealized hierarchical social order derived from Enlightenment values and based on capitalism and imperialism. Conceptualizing sites of anatomization as heterotopias opens new interpretive potential.

Foucault (2002, xix) emphasizes heterotopias' disruptive capacities: "Heterotopias are disturbing . . . because they destroy 'syntax' [discourse or habituated rules of meaning] in advance . . . syntax which causes words and things (next to and also opposite to one another) to 'hold together.'" They are "a space of difference, in which ordinary cultural emplacements are brought together and represented, contested, and reversed. Sacred and forbidden spaces, 'crisis' spaces, and spaces for holding deviant individuals are included in this definition. Heterotopias are spatially isolated places that juxtapose incompatible objects and discontinuous times" (Lord 2006, 3). As Beth Lord's explication suggests, settings of anatomical dissection were part of a distributed network of cooperative institutional heterotopias that included almshouses, medical schools, hospitals, and cemeteries. For much of its history, human dissection was by no means widely accepted as a rational societal good. Rather, it was heavily contested—clandestinely operating on the fringes of legality and beyond the pale of polite morality—including throughout the nineteenth century (Blakely and Harrington 1997; Nystrom 2017; Sappol 2002). Therefore, to transgress the boundaries of a cadaver via dissection was to act outside the boundaries of the normal world, requiring an alternative space.

Archaeological case studies from the first and second halves of the nineteenth century afford a diachronic, comparative view of these "anatomical heterotopias." Holden Chapel in Cambridge, Massachusetts, was once part of the Harvard Medical

School. In 1999, excavation in its cellar produced evidence of instructional anatomization and disposal dating to the first half of the nineteenth century. Recovered remains and contextual sources emphasize body fragmentation and the undoing of personhood (Hodge 2013; Hodge, Morgan, and Rousseau 2017). These finds also illuminate the ways poetics of anatomical knowledge (especially anatomical specimens) and the settings in which this education was transmitted (the classroom theater and the storeroom) consolidated early medical authority within certain populations. Human remains recovered from the Erie County Poorhouse Cemetery, founded in 1851, reveal comparable anatomical acts but distinct poetics and phenomenology (Nystrom 2014; Nystrom et al. 2017). The architectural designs of the poorhouse and hospital located power in institutional authorities. Simultaneously, they presented impoverished and ailing bodies as appropriate subjects for control and scrutiny. These relations in life primed unclaimed bodies to serve as instructional cadavers in death. Anatomical dissection at Erie extended institutionalized inequality and manifested structural violence against the poor and vulnerable, establishing notions of dissection as punishment and poverty as criminal. If we accept the overall success of the Enlightenment project, we would expect to find material evidence of increasingly rational scientific inquiry into the workings of the human body over the course of the nineteenth century. We do not.

Post-dissection treatments at these sites prove variable, even contradictory. Dissection was followed by circulation as specimens or discard as refuse at Holden, dating to the early to mid-nineteenth century. Dissection was followed by quasi-normal burial alongside non-anatomized, intact bodies at Erie, active from the mid-nineteenth through early twentieth centuries. Rather than growing more "rational" over time by treating body parts as things to be discarded, the processing of dead bodies continued at times to integrate normative affective relations of identity and memorialization. We find this pattern in the treatment of disempowered individuals at Erie despite the mainstreaming of human dissection that continues to the present day (although that may be changing as gross anatomy classes move away from cadaver use) (McNulty, Sonntag, and Sinacore 2009; Moosman 1980). These findings suggest that, while dissection continued to discipline the bodies of society's most vulnerable populations throughout the nineteenth century, personhood adhered strongly to human remains.[1]

[1] See de la Cova, chapter 11 of this volume, for a case study from the next period of anatomization, the end of the nineteenth into the third quarter of the twentieth century. She describes the continued erasure of personhood among vulnerable populations. Yet the scrupulous preservation and association of personal identifiers such as name, age, and cause of death, maintained both with curated remains and derivative specimens, suggests complex negotiations of anatomized personhood persisted into the postmodern period.

ANATOMIZATION IN THE NINETEENTH CENTURY

The history of anatomization in the United States is grounded in a complex web of social welfare reform, utilitarian philosophy, racial and class politics, and "the creation of a distinctively bourgeois social order and culture" (Sappol 2002, 10). Dissection for the purposes of anatomical study began in the United States as a form of postmortem punishment. Reserved for convicted criminals, the supply of bodies was small, though during the seventeenth and eighteenth centuries this source was generally sufficient to meet demands (Sappol 2002)—although not always. A messy 1775 grave robbery in Boston prompted John Warren (founder of the Harvard Medical School) to write, "where the necessities of society [to conduct dissections] are in conflict with the law, and with public opinion, the crime consists . . . not in the deed, but in permitting its discovery" (Warren 1874, 233). Beginning in the early half of the nineteenth century, the number of medical schools in the United States began to increase significantly. Influenced by medical education in Europe, the burgeoning medical profession in the United States sought to emulate their counterparts and dissection and gross anatomy courses became the *sine qua non* of the medical professional. Due to this increase in demand, medical schools relied upon the illegal resurrection of corpses to supply their gross anatomy courses. These bodies were commonly derived from cemeteries of groups that lacked the political and economic power to stop it, namely African Americans, Native Americans, immigrants, and the poor.

The institution of the almshouse, or poorhouse, expanded in the first decades of the nineteenth century as the increasing number of poor was perceived to be an emerging "social problem, a potential source of unrest and the proper object of a reform movement" (Rothman 1971, 156). Previous attempts to administer "outdoor" relief (i.e., relief that occurred outside the walls of an institution) were considered to only exacerbate and encourage pauperism. In contrast, the controlled, institutional space of the almshouse offered the chance not only to provide for those poor who truly needed and deserved assistance, but also to reform those considered to be intentionally or constitutionally indolent.

Early nineteenth-century institutions appear to have been succeeding in their mission (Katz 1986), but ultimately incompetent administration, overcrowding, and inadequate sanitation exacerbated the vulnerability of the poor. Simultaneously, macroscale political economic forces and changing societal perception of poverty were setting the stage for the emergence of anatomy bills that legalized the anatomization of unclaimed bodies of almshouse inmates.

The utilitarian philosophy of Jeremy Bentham linked poor-law reform and anatomical study and influenced the framing and passage of anatomy laws in the United States and Britain (Richardson 1987; Sappol 2002). This philosophy holds that a person's value is based on that person's contribution to society and the public good. Bentham and his supports also argued that poorhouses should be punitive in nature and should intentionally dissuade people from seeking public assistance (Sappol 2002). Those individuals who did obtain assistance were in society's debt, and therefore, upon their deaths, their bodies could justifiably be used to cancel that debt "because a dead body should only be valued based on its usefulness to the living" (Sappol 2002, 118). Beginning in the 1820s, states began to debate anatomy laws that would allow medical schools to acquire unclaimed bodies from almshouses, and in 1831 Massachusetts became the first state to pass such legislation. There were two key aspects of these bills. First, dissection was framed as a means for advancing medical science, the benefits of which would accrue and ultimately benefit everyone. Second, they played upon the public's fear of grave robbing for dissection. In fact, the 1854 anatomy bill passed by New York was called *The Act to Promote Medical Science and Protect Burial Grounds*. While by this point in time dissection as a form of punishment had a deep history, the intertwining of social welfare reform and medical science succeeded in reframing dissection as a deterrent against indigence and as a means of social control.

During this time, the science of anatomy was couched in heroic terms, as a "centuries long battle between reason and superstition," of "light" versus "darkness," in which "the natural horror which attends meddling with human dead bodies" (Sappol 2002, 77) was overcome. The body itself was conceptualized as dangerous and corrupting, manifesting as both physical (in the form of toxic gases emanating from it) as well as moral dangers (e.g., necrophilia). By conquering the body, the medical student emerged into a new, elite social identity. Dead bodies, whether resurrected or legally acquired from the almshouse, were commodified, their value determined by the market of supply and demand. These bodies were high-value goods that were transformed into teaching tools, curated and displayed as specimens, or treated as trash.

While medical students were entering a new community of elite social status of the burgeoning medical profession, many of the individuals appropriated for dissection were removed from their communities and thus isolated from the social process of memorialization. Further, their postmortem treatment reinforced contemporary sociopolitical inequalities. The presence of the dead body thus transformed the dissection laboratory into a closed, restricted space, accessible to a select group of individuals. Into this darkness comes the medical student, the novitiate who fights back the cultural ignorance and fear surrounding dissection to gain knowledge.

During the post-Enlightenment period, emerging professional medicine worked to rationalize understandings of the body and its operations. Simultaneously, forces of modernity and capitalism individuated Western personhood, including through the elaboration of mortuary ritual and economies of memorialization (Tarlow 1999, 108–146). Shifting Euro-American ontologies of identity increasingly valued the individual and romanticized their loss through death (Buchli and Lucas 2001; Faust 2008; Tarlow 1999). Given the broader cultural context of commemorative death, nineteenth-century anatomists took extreme measures to justify their clinical violation of personhood and emotional detachment. They engaged materialities, corporealities, and phenomenologies to secularize and rationalize the human body (Starr 1982).

This work occurred through a variety of interrelated discourses, which reproduced scientific authority via new bodily relationships expressed in examination, operation, exploration, experimentation, dissection, curation, and disposal. These performances were carried out in specifically appointed settings that expressed *variable* phenomenological qualities—well-lit anatomical theater versus low-ceilinged cellar versus manicured graveyard, for example—with *coherent* affective qualities of taboo (or their inversion through clinical authorization and/or "gallows humor"). The authority to perform anatomical dissection became more restricted as medicine professionalized and dissection became less clandestine and more visible to the public (Hodge 2013). It continued to be more difficult to justify for some populations (wealthy, white, male) than others (poor, black, foreign, criminal) (Nystrom 2014; Sappol 2002), sustaining oppressive structural practices based on social identity categories. The complex histories exemplified by recovered human remains and physical settings of Holden Chapel and the Erie Poorhouse underscore the contextual, improvisational nature of these seemingly homogenous developments.

AN ARCHAEOLOGY OF BODILY FRAGMENTATION: DISTINGUISHING BETWEEN DISSECTION AND AUTOPSY

Much of the discussion in this chapter hinges on our ability to distinguish between dissection and autopsy in the archaeological record. Although it is well established that the social significance of these two processes are distinct, bioarchaeologists do not always enjoy such clear distinctions when attempting to differentiate the procedures. Nevertheless, patterns of treatment on well-contextualized collections, alongside robust historical sources, can allow us plausibly to deduce the modes of fragmentation represented within a given collection.

It is generally agreed that the more extensive the fragmentation of the skeleton/bones, the more likely this represents dissection (Cherryson 2010; Crossland 2009b). The presence of "unusual" cuts, such as knife marks on unopened crania (Dittmar and Mitchell 2015), trephination (Grauer, Lathrop, and Timoteo 2017), bone sectioning (Nystrom et al. 2017; Owsley et al. 2017), longitudinal or sagittal cuts through elements (Western 2012), or evidence of specimen preparation (Novak 2017) are indicative of dissection. Alternatively, autopsies are considered to be more limited; historical anatomy texts focused principally on opening the cranium, thorax, and abdominal cavities (Dittmar and Mitchell 2015). Given this evidence, craniotomies and thoracotomies have a closer association with autopsy (Chamberlain 2012; Cherryson 2010; Dittmar and Mitchell 2015; Waldron and Rogers 1988).

Archaeological indications of dissection can involve duplication of elements or individuals (Crist, Mooney, and Morrell 2017; Davidson 2007) or the retention of elements (Nystrom et al. 2017). It is also necessary to consider the context in which the remains are recovered. Individuals recovered from non-mortuary contexts, such as basements (Blakely and Harrington 1997), privies (Mann, Owsley, and Shackel 1991), and dry wells (Hodge 2013; Hodge, Morgan, and Rousseau 2017; Owsley et al. 2017) are more commonly considered to have been dissected.

Interpretation of evidence of postmortem examination recovered from formal cemeteries is more ambiguous. In these instances, it is necessary to consider the social context in which the procedure occurred. For instance, remains with craniotomies, and thus suggestive of a "limited" autopsy, have been recovered from three African American cemeteries: the Newburgh Colored Burial Ground (Nystrom 2011), New York African Burial Ground (Blakey and Rankin-Hill 2004), and the Eighth Street First African Baptist Church (Angel et al. 1987). Similarly, individuals with craniotomies have been recovered from almshouse cemeteries (Nystrom 2014; Nystrom et al. 2017). Although the osteological evidence may point towards autopsies in these cases, and there are no other archaeological clues to suggest otherwise, we also know that blacks, the poor, and people with mental challenges or intellectual disabilities were specifically targeted for dissection because of their vulnerable position in society.

HOLDEN CHAPEL: A SETTING OF BODILY FRAGMENTATION

Holden Chapel at Harvard University is an excellent site through which to pursue an explicitly theorized mortuary archaeology. When built in 1744, Holden was supposed to serve Harvard College as its first dedicated chapel (Batchelder 1921) (figure 10.1). It was quickly put to other uses and, between 1800 and around 1862, it was dedicated to the growing Harvard Medical School and undergraduate instruction in anatomy and chemistry. It also held a collection of anatomical specimens, natural history curiosities, and scientific apparatuses. These historical functions were far from obvious during a 1999 renovation, until grading in Holden's dirt-floored cellar exposed a circular, sand-bottomed dry well, 1.75 m in diameter, packed 0.65 m deep with noxious debris (Hodge 2013; Sexton 2000). Several layers

Figure 10.1. Late nineteenth-century lantern slide of Holden Chapel, facing northeast. (Courtesy of Special Collections, Fine Arts Library, Harvard University, 1898L.0081.)

of an organic matrix yielded 2,748 fragments of faunal remains, scientific glassware, domestic artifacts like bottles, shoes, buttons, and ceramics, and 907 fragments of human bones. Several of these had cut marks, saw marks, iron pins, pigment, and chemical residues: evidence of use as anatomical specimens (Hodge, Morgan, and Rousseau 2017, 134–136). The fill was capped ca. 1850 per artifact manufacture dates, most likely during an 1850 renovation (Bunting 1985, 27; Hodge, Morgan, and Rousseau 2017, 120).

Holden Chapel illuminates understudied areas of early American anatomization: the anatomical theater as a heterotopic setting affording certain discourses of power. Archaeological and documentary evidence indicates that human remains recovered from the basement of Holden Chapel were not just remnants of anatomical dissection. Rather, many resulted from the systematic production and use of teaching specimens to supplement, augment, or replace human bodies (Hodge, Morgan, and Rousseau 2017). The assemblage touches on mortuary archaeology's common themes of personhood and memorialization. But it is most relevant to understanding dissection as fragmentation; that is, as a redefinition of death and the body through the selective dismemberment and preservation of body parts in a specialized, restricted setting. This process was facilitated through phenomenological experiences of the anatomical theater and materialities (or corporealities) of human remains processed there. At the individual level, they redefined personhood via the fragmentation of human bodies. At a societal level, these discourses aligned with disruptive Enlightenment values pulling authority away from the powers of religion, superstition, and spirituality and toward those of humanism and science.

Anatomical Theater as Setting

In 1782, Harvard started its medical school and requested a library, "complete anatomical and surgical apparatus, a set of anatomical preparations with a proper theater, and other necessary accommodations for dissections and clinical operations" (Harrington 1905, 81). The Board of Overseers also agreed that "the Professors [will] demonstrate the anatomy of the human body on recent subjects if they can be procured; if not, on preparations duly adapted to the purpose" (Harrington 1905, 81–82). In 1801, the Harvard Medical School (HMS) renovated and moved into Holden Chapel (Harrington 1905, 288). The chapel was renovated again in 1814 to improve lighting in the anatomical theater, adding conical skylights to the roof and lengthening the windows. An 1850 renovation added another skylight and additional seating for 150 to the second floor, as well as glass cases to the first floor for the Holden "museum" of human and comparative anatomical specimens, preparations, and curiosities (Bunting 1985, 27) (figure 10.2). The theater was typical of the period and featured curved rows of tiered seats around a large, U-shaped dissection table. The space afforded heightened visibility, hierarchical proximity (with the body at the center, the instructor at/inside the body, and a select audience in orderly rows around), and separation from the public sphere. The needs of anatomy instruction directed changes to Holden's structural fabric, making it a more effective heterotopic space.

The poetics of this educational space mattered. Any structure is inherently exclusive, more so within a closed university setting. Only faculty and young men legitimized through student status were allowed to enter Holden Chapel (Hodge 2013, 140–141). Furnishings in its anatomical theater further ordered an embodied discourse of sensory privilege. Privileged access to the central dissected body was enforced, especially through sight and touch, both highly valued within post-Enlightenment scientific sensual regimes (Howes 2005).

Dissection's embodied set of human/nonhuman relations inverted normative commemorative treatment of the dead in favor of scientific understandings of the human body (Tarlow 2005). Privilege was constructed at HMS through access to

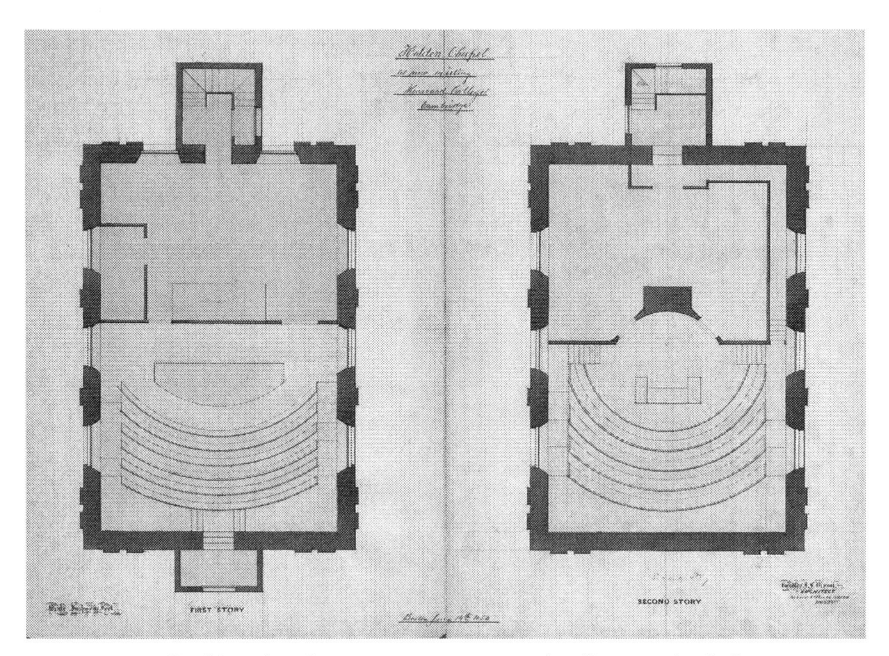

FIGURE 10.2. *"Holden Chapel as Now Existing, Harvard College, Cambridge." Drawing,* J. Gidley and F. Bryant, c. 1850, showing the 1814 floor plan prior to 1850 renovations. Anatomy lectures were held on the second story; note the U-shaped tables configured in the south room and the curved seating. The Holden Chapel dry well was contemporary with this layout and likely filled c. 1850, soon after this drawing was made. (Courtesy of the Harvard University Archives, UAI.15.10.3 Pf.)

the Holden space and the corpses processed there, as well as through the internalized regimes of knowledge produced in this setting (Carr 2010; Foucault 1972). These poetics make sense within the framework of Foucauldian heterotopias. Holden was designed to disrupt the "real" order of things in favor of an alternative order in which anatomical knowledge could be more freely produced.

Fragmentation, Order, and Disorder

A connection exists between anatomical preparations and deep histories of the disordered/disordering body within Western traditions (Hall 1989; Tarlow 1999). Euro-American and other ontologies have long treated relics and deformed body parts as otherworldly signs and wonders (Crossland 2009b; Hall 1989; Tarlow 2011). Nineteenth-century personhood was primarily recognized (and protected) through named, complete, fleshed bodies (Buchli and Lucas 2001; Tarlow 1999,

2011); official absenting of vulnerable people as identified individuals within documentary records is but one manifestation of this process. Susan Stewart (2007, 131) argues that material "projections of the body—the grotesque, the miniature, and the microcosm—reveal the paradoxical status of the body as both mode and object of knowing." To this list we add anatomical preparations. Teaching props played with color, texture, scale, permanence, and juxtaposition. Anatomical specimens were circulated among and produced by Harvard students and displayed at the Holden "museum."

Anatomical specimens' role as didactic objects drew on older discourses of relics and body parts, but they were intended as signs of science rather than as wonders (St. George 2000). Arguably, they also exacerbated disjunction between persons and body parts, as they selectively exaggerated physical properties. Through specimen preparation, anatomists asserted scientific control by imposing an artificial order/stability onto a disordered/diseased/corruptible human body. The creation of these "non-bodies" was an embodied act of modernity (Hodge 2013). Dissected specimens, produced and circulated within anatomical heterotopias, were significant participants in anatomical poetics and the broader Enlightenment project they supported. Yet, even the most careful preparation could only approximate, never replicate, a living human system. This limitation existed even when specimens were fashioned from actual body parts, as were those discarded below Holden Chapel—and excluded from the Erie County Poorhouse cemetery.

ERIE COUNTY POORHOUSE AND CEMETERY: A SETTING OF BODILY INTEGRITY

Both almshouses and cemeteries are quintessential heterotopias per Foucauldian theory (Foucault 1984b, 1995, 2002), "social spaces whose functions are different or even the opposite of others" (Foucault 1984a, 252). The roles of almshouses are well explored archaeologically (Beisaw and Gibbs 2009; Nystrom et al. 2017). They served as extensions of the state apparatus of control, especially putative control of those who challenged its emerging rationalist and capitalistic values of productivity and self-sufficiency. The role of cemeteries is more ambiguous. As Foucault (1984b, 5) envisions it,

> This cemetery housed inside the sacred space of the church has taken on a quite different cast in modern [Enlightenment and post-Enlightenment] civilizations, and curiously, it is in a time when civilization has become "atheistic," as one says very crudely, that western culture has established what is termed the cult of the dead . . . from the moment when people are no longer sure that they have a soul or that the

> body will regain life, it is perhaps necessary to give much more attention to the dead body, which is ultimately the only trace of our existence in the world and in language. In any case, it is from the beginning of the nineteenth century that everyone has a right to her or his own little box for her or his own little personal decay.

This ambiguous concept of "attention" encompasses both scientific scrutiny and spiritual care. That, in Erie County, poorhouse and cemetery spaces were entangled through the processing of anatomized bodies highlights the tensions inherent in post-Enlightenment understandings of the social roles of the vulnerable dead.

Evidence of Anatomization

Between its opening in its Buffalo Plains location in 1851 and its closing in 1926, the Erie County Poorhouse provided a reported 181,894 individuals with assistance. In addition to the poorhouse, the institution also featured an insane asylum, a children's ward and school, and a hospital with maternity and consumptive wards. The Erie County Hospital, which started in one wing of the poorhouse, served the poor and working class of Buffalo in addition to poorhouse inmates (Higgins 1998; Raines 2014).

Burial in the associated cemetery likely began soon after the poorhouse opened at the Buffalo Plains location, with Erie County Poorhouse Hospital Mortality Registers indicating that interment ceased in 1913 (Higgins, Raines, and Montague 2014). The hospital remained in use for over 60 years. The recovered remains represent not only the unclaimed bodies of poorhouse inmates but those individuals who died at the hospital. To give a sense of the number of people who sought assistance at the poorhouse or were treated at the hospital, over a 30-year period (1880–1910) over 42,000 people were in the institution. Further, between 1880 and 1913, of the 7,186 individuals who died at the hospital, just over 44 percent ($n = 3,198$) were unclaimed and buried in the poorhouse cemetery (Higgins, Raines, and Montague 2014).

There are a number of recorded disturbances of the cemetery associated with road construction and/or campus improvement projects. Archaeological excavations of the cemetery occurred in 2009 during a series of improvements to the university's child daycare facilities and again in 2011 during installation of a sewer line. In 2012, the first controlled, large-scale excavation occurred in 2012 in advance of major infrastructure improvements to the entrance to the University at Buffalo's South Campus. Ultimately, approximately 20 percent of the cemetery was excavated, resulting in the recovery of 376 individuals.

Of the individuals excavated from the Erie Poorhouse cemetery, 20 (5.3%) exhibited evidence of anatomization. The most common form of postmortem examination were craniotomies, observed in a total of 12 individuals. Sectioned or transected long bones were observed in four individuals. There is evidence for thoracotomies (transection of sternum or sternal ends of ribs) in two adult males, while a single adult male exhibited evidence of a laminectomy (transection of the vertebral spinous processes). While most of the anatomized remains were "complete," in that the cut bone was recovered in the grave, evidence suggests that the left elbow of one person may have been retained. While the left proximal humerus and distal radius and ulna were recovered during excavation in this grave, the intervening bone was missing. This pattern suggests that the elbow was preferentially removed, possibly to retain it as a teaching specimen. That, at Erie, evidence for specimen preparation was an exception proving a rule. In contrast to treatment at the earlier Holden Chapel site, the preservation of bodily integrity was a common part of anatomical practice at the Erie County Poorhouse Hospital and cemetery—at least if the bodies remained within this setting. The fate of bodies circulated to other heterotopic settings—medical schools—is less clear.

As discussed elsewhere (Nystrom et al. 2017), outstanding questions about the bodies recovered from the Erie County cemetery remain. It is not yet known if people were anatomized at the poorhouse itself or at the Erie County Hospital. While both likely had the facilities, there is no documentary evidence for concluding one way or the other. However, it is known that between 1897 and 1913 the Erie County Hospital transferred the remains of 469 individuals to medical schools in the area to be used as dissection cadavers. There is virtually no information on what happened to these anatomized remains; records indicate that only a single body was ever returned for burial at the poorhouse cemetery. As it stands, while it may not be possible to identify exactly who was anatomized or where, we do know that poorhouses were significant sources of anatomical specimens during this period (Halperin 2007; Richardson 1987; Sappol 2002) and that the remains most likely represent the poor and working class of Buffalo and the surrounding region.

Material evidence, including coffin orientation and spacing, artifacts, condition, and construction materials, suggests that there is an internal division within the cemetery. Graves in the older section have an east–west orientation and are generally not as well preserved, with coffins that used older machine-cut nails (used roughly from the 1790s through the 1830s) (Wells 1998). Graves in the newer section have a northeast–southwest orientation. Graves in this section are more tightly and more regularly spaced, with coffins constructed with wire-drawn nails (post 1830s). The graves that yielded evidence of anatomized remains are found in both sections, suggesting that autopsies/dissections occurred throughout the history of the cemetery. Therefore, cemetery interment of complete, anatomized cadavers (with a single known exception) occurred at Erie both during and after the period when body parts and preparations were being thrown away as waste below HMC's

Holden Chapel. Although the process of anatomization worked against the social personhood of the dead, qualities of individuality lingered (Crossland 2009a, 2009b; Hodge 2013; Hodge, Morgan, and Rousseau 2017). These qualities seem more salient at some heterotopias than others; in this case, at the Erie Poorhouse and Cemetery as opposed to HMS.

Examples in which anatomized remains were accorded "normal" burial have also been observed in several other almshouse/poorhouse cemetery sites, including the Albany County Almshouse Cemetery (Lusignan Lowe 2017), the Milwaukee County Poor Farm Cemetery (Dougherty and Sullivan 2017; Richards et al. 2017), and Dunning Poorhouse (Grauer, Lathrop, and Timoteo 2017). This is not always the case, though. While some of the remains recovered from the Blockley Almshouse were individually interred, there were several clusters scattered throughout the cemetery that contained boxes of anatomized commingled remains mixed with medical waste (Crist, Mooney, and Morrell 2017).

The facts of anatomization at Erie, when compared with those at Holden Chapel, suggest that both period (as it is a later site) and setting (as it was a poorhouse and hospital, not a medical school) significantly shaped the poetics of dissection there. That is, anatomized remains' material properties of completeness and fragmentation, alongside their material practices of restoration, burial, discard, and distribution, posited different values based on the different settings in which they worked. Holden and Erie were two among multiple anatomical heterotopias forwarding alternative visions of world order. The production of specimens at each setting proves crucially important.

CONCLUSIONS

Anatomical Heterotopias

Both Holden Chapel and Erie Poorhouse and Cemetery reinforce notions of dissection arenas as heterotopic spaces, where the dangers of moral/physical corruption could be conquered by privileged medical initiates. Heterotopias in general were crucial to the Enlightenment project to "categorize, classify, and order the world into a totality universal in scope and universally intelligible" (Lord 2006, 2). This role was especially significant for anatomical heterotopias. They posited transgressive relations between living and dead. Enlightenment scientific values proved contradictory to normative values that respected corpses as both sanctified and corrupting (Tarlow 2011). The fact that human anatomization demanded heterotopic settings indicates broad recognition that, despite justifications via scientific rationalism (e.g., Davis et al. 1831), dissection was perceived as an abnormal ordering of society per values of the time.

Anatomical practices made Holden Chapel and the Erie almshouse and cemetery into heterotopias in two ways. First, through their paradoxical simultaneity as things and people, dissected remains destabilized seemingly stable ontological categories like: self/other, subject/object, living/dead, and body/non-body. At both sites, persistent semiotic relationships between cadavers and living persons ensured that, despite their undeniable materiality, dead bodies were never just things (for Piercian semiotics in archaeology, see Knappett 2005). Second, spaces of body-processing—including anatomical theaters, examination rooms, disposal features, and cemeteries—were experienced as sites of experimental discourse. They permitted practitioners to engage in transgressive—and even illegal—behaviors in a protected environment (openness about body snatching, dissection, callous treatment of the dead, handling unclothed corpses, examination of removed organs, disposal of body parts with common trash, etc.).

There is a temporal component to these shifts as well as an ideological one. The earlier site, Holden Chapel, had anatomized body parts discarded as trash while, at the later Erie cemetery, they were buried within a recognized memorial space. We suggest that nineteenth-century tensions between rational and emotional notions of personhood were partially resolved via restoring some qualities of social identity to dissected remains via pseudo-normal burial practices (perhaps also via the preservation of names and other identifiers in scientific collections; see de la Cova, chapter 11, this volume). Bodies in both institutional contexts served the larger project of modernity, however. They were put to work in a new narrative of ordered medical knowledge to which a growing class of largely white, male, professional, formally educated medical practitioners had near-exclusive access. The products of this knowledge, consumed and circulated in restricted medical settings, further naturalized their authority. The poetics of anatomical knowledge ensured this outcome and depended on the processing of—the participation of—dead bodies.

Holden and Erie were two of myriad heterotopias that "participated in the exercise of power through the categorization and controlled deployment of knowledge" in the nineteenth century (Lord 2006, 2). We stop short of claiming that the Enlightenment was unsuccessful. The dramatic differences between the poetics of body-processing recovered at these two sites, however, illuminate just how surprisingly uneven the Enlightenment project proves to have been when it is investigated bottom up, rather than top down.

Reflections

Whitehead's model of poetics, which centers contingency and refuses to take violence for granted, is an appropriate one for a history of American anatomization

(Whitehead 2004). Nineteenth-century dissection consistently operated as an extension of violence and as a manifestation of contemporary socioeconomic and political structures, although the material discourses underpinning these values varied across the century. Through a focus on the poetics of processing dead bodies, we learn that investigators should concern themselves not only with body products and their flows, but also with the resolution of these flows through practices of disposal and discard. The ways bodies were taken out of social spaces and relegated to realms of memory are at least as important as the techniques of processing themselves.

Nineteenth-century body-processing communicated anatomical knowledge through both production and circulation (of lectures, specimens, doctors, etc.). These anatomical poetics brought the inside out in a symbolically charged act of bodily exposure over which anatomists held substantial, but not complete, power (Hodge 2013, 128; Hodge, Morgan, and Rousseau 2017, 132; Stewart 2007, 127). While obviously less than individual persons, specimens simultaneously became more than human bodies: more knowable, more stable, more perfect, easier to control (sensu Stewart 2007, 122–124). The illusory nature of this ordering of flesh and time introduced paradox into science-based processes of knowing. Resulting instability is manifested in historic discomfiture with—or outright rejection of—anatomical dissection, as well as in its practical exploitation of marginalized people (Blakely and Harrington 1997; Capozzoli 1997; Crossland 2009a; Davidson 2007; Fabian 2010; Nystrom 2017). While seeking approximations to living flesh, anatomists further distanced processed remains from their former personhood. This practice reconceived an older narrative of body parts as inherently disordered, inverting their significance. Serving the larger project of modernity, specimens were put to work in a new narrative of ordered medical knowledge to which a growing class of largely white, male, professional, medical practitioners had near-exclusive access. These poetics comprised a material discourse that reinforced emergent claims to medical authority, hence social power.

ACKNOWLEDGMENTS

KCN would like to thank Joyce Sirianni, Jennifer Muller, Jennifer Byrnes, Rosanne Higgins, Doug Perrelli, Jennifer L. Liber Raines, and the rest of the research team for giving him the opportunity to examine the Erie County Poorhouse collection. CJH thanks her former Peabody Museum colleagues Michèle E. Morgan and Jane Lyden Rousseau for their expertise and collaborative coauthorship of an earlier study of the Holden Chapel site. Thanks also to the volume editor and anonymous reviewers for inviting and strengthening this contribution.

REFERENCES

Angel J. L., J. O. Kelley, M. Parrington, and S. Pinter. 1987. "Life Stresses of the Free Black Community as Represented by the First African Baptist Church, Philadelphia, 1823–1841." *American Journal of Physical Anthropology* 74 (2): 213–229.

Ashmore, Wendy. 2004. "'Decisions and Dispositions': Socializing Spatial Archaeology." *American Anthropologist* 104 (4): 1172–1183.

Bachelard, Gaston. 1994 [1964]. *The Poetics of Space*. Translated by Maria Jolas. Boston, MA: Beacon Press.

Batchelder, Samuel F. 1921. "The Singular Story of Holden Chapel." *Harvard Alumni Bulletin* 23 (18): 405–416.

Beisaw, Amy, and James Gibbs, eds. 2009. *The Archaeology of Institutional Life*. Tuscaloosa, AL: University of Alabama Press.

Blakely, Robert L., and Judith M. Harrington, eds. 1997. *Bones in the Basement: Postmortem Racism in Nineteenth-Century Medical Training*. Washington, DC: Smithsonian Institution Press.

Blakey, Michael L., and L. M. Rankin-Hill, eds. 2004. *The New York African Burial Ground Skeletal Biology Final Report*, Volume 1. Washington, DC: General Services Administration and Howard University Press.

Buchli, Victor, and Gavin Lucas. 2001. "Bodies of Evidence." In *Archaeologies of the Contemporary Past*, edited by Victor Buchli and Gavin Lucas, 121–125. New York: Routledge.

Bunting, Bainbridge. 1985. *Harvard: An Architectural History*. Cambridge, MA: Belknap Press of Harvard University Press.

Capozzoli, Maureen McCarthy. 1997. "A Rip into the Flesh, a Tear into the Soul: An Ethnography of Dissection in Georgia." In *Bones in the Basement: Postmortem Racism in Nineteenth-Century Medical Training*, edited by Robert L. Blakely and Mark R. Harrington, 313–339. Washington, DC: Smithsonian Institution Press.

Carr, E. Summerson. 2010. "Enactments of Expertise." *Annual Review of Anthoopology* 20 (56): 17–32.

Chamberlain, A. 2012. "Morbid Osteology: Evidence for Autopsies, Dissection and Surgical Training from the Newcastle Infirmary Burial Ground (1753–1845)." In *Anatomical Dissection in Enlightenment England and Beyond Autopsy, Pathology and Display*, edited by Piers D. Mitchell, 23–42. Farnham: Ashgate.

Cherryson, A. 2010. "In the Pursuit of Knowledge: Dissection, Post-Mortem Surgery and the Retention of Body Parts in 18th- and 19th-Century Britain." In *Body Parts and Bodies Whole*, edited by Katharina Rebay-Salisbury, Marie Louise Stig Sørensen and Jessica Hughes, 135–148. Oxford: Oxbow Books.

Crist, Thomas A., Douglas B. Mooney, and Kimberly A. Morrell. 2017. "'The Mangled Remains of What Had Been Humanity': Evidence of Autopsy and Dissection at Philadelphia's Blockley Almshouse, 1835–1895." In *The Bioarchaeology of Dissection and Autopsy in the United States*, edited by Kenneth C Nystrom, 259–278. New York: Springer.

Crossland, Zoë. 2009a. "Acts of Estrangement: The Post-Mortem Making of Self and Other." *Archaeological Dialogues* 16 (1): 102–125.

Crossland, Zoë. 2009b. "Of Clues and Signs: The Dead Body and Its Evidential Traces." *American Anthropologist* 111 (1): 69–80.

Davidson, James M. 2007. "'Resurrection Men' in Dallas: The Illegal Use of Black Bodies as Medical Cadavers (1900–1907)." *International Journal of Historical Archaeology* 11: 193–220.

Davis, J. B., G. Willard, A. Hutchinson, L. W. Humphreys, and J. B. Flint. 1831. *Report of the Select Committee of the House of Representatives, on So Much of the Governor's Speech, June Session, 1830, as Relates to Legalizing the Study of Anatomy*. Vol. 4. House of Representatives. Boston, MA: Dutton and Wentworth.

Diaz-Bone, Rainer, Andrea D. Bührmann, Encarnación Gutiérrez Rodríguez, Werner Schneider, Gavin Kendall, and Fransisco Tirado. 2008. "The Field of Foucaultian Discourse Analysis: Structures, Developments and Perspectives." *Historical Social Research/ Historische Sozialforschung* 33 (1.123): 7–28.

Dittmar, J. M., and P. D. Mitchell. 2015. "A New Method for Identifying and Differentiating Human Dissection and Autopsy in Archaeological Human Skeletal Remains." *Journal of Archaeological Science: Reports* 3: 73–79.

Dougherty, Sean P., and Norman C. Sullivan. 2017. "Autopsy, Dissection, and Anatomical Exploration: The Postmortem Fate of the Underclass and Institutionalized in Old Milwaukee." In *The Bioarchaeology of Dissection and Autopsy in the United States*, edited by Kenneth C Nystrom, 205–235. New York: Springer.

Edwards, Elizabeth. 2015. "Anthropology and Photography: A Long History of Knowledge and Affect." *Photographies* 8 (3): 235–252.

Fabian, Ann. 2010. *The Skull Collectors: Race, Science, and America's Unburied Dead*. Chicago, IL: University of Chicago Press.

Faust, Drew Gilpin. 2008. *This Republic of Suffering: Death and the American Civil War*. New York: Alfred A. Knopf.

Foucault, Michel. 1972. *The Archaeology of Knowledge and the Discourse on Language*. Translated by A. M. Sheridan Smith. New York: Pantheon Books.

Foucault, Michel. 1973. *The Birth of the Clinic: An Archaeology of Medical Perception*. New York: Pantheon Books.

Foucault, Michel. 1984a. *The Foucault Reader*. New York: Pantheon Books.

Foucault, Michel. 1984b [1967]. "Of Other Spaces: Utopias and Heterotopias." *Architecture /Mouvement/ Continuité*: 1–9.

Foucault, Michel. 1995. *Discipline and Punish: The Birth of the Prison*. Translated by Alan Sheridan. New York: Vintage Books.

Foucault, Michel. 2002 [1970]. *The Order of Things: An Archaeology of the Human Sciences*. New York: Routledge.

Fountain, Thomas Kenneth. 2008. "A Matter of Perception': Rhetoric, Embodiment, and the Visual Practices of Anatomy Laboratory Education." PhD Dissertation, University of Minnesota.

Grauer, Anne L., Vanessa Lathrop, and Taylor Timoteo. 2017. "Exploring Evidence of Nineteenth Century Dissection in the Dunning Poorhouse Cemetery." In *The Bioarchaeology of Dissection and Autopsy in the United States*, edited by Kenneth C Nystrom, 301–313. New York: Springer.

Hall, David D. 1989. *Worlds of Wonder; Days of Judgment: Popular Religious Belief in Early New England*. Cambridge, MA: Harvard University Press.

Halperin, Edward C. 2007. "The Poor, the Black, and the Marginalized as the Source of Cadavers in United States Anatomical Education." *Clinical Anatomy* 20: 489–495.

Harrington, Thomas F. 1905. *The Harvard Medical School: A History, Narrative and Documentary, 1782–1905*. New York: Lewis Publishing Company.

Higgins, Roseanne L. 1998. "The Biology of Poverty: Epidemiological Transition in Western New York." PhD Dissertation, Department of Anthropology, State University of New York at Buffalo.

Higgins, Roseanne L., J. L. Raines, and N. L. Montague. 2014. "Confirming Burial Location in the Erie County Poorhouse Cemetery using Death Certificates and Mortality Records from 1880–1913." *American Journal of Physical Anthropology* 153 (S58): 141.

Hodge, Christina J. 2013. "Non-Bodies of Knowledge: Anatomized Remains from the Holden Chapel Collection, Harvard University." *Journal of Social Archaeology* 13 (1): 122–149.

Hodge, Christina J., Michèle E. Morgan, and Jane Lyden Rousseau. 2017. "Teachings of the Dead: The Archaeology of Anatomized Remains from Holden Chapel, Harvard University." In *The Bioarchaeology of Dissection and Autopsy in the United States*, edited by Kenneth C Nystrom, 115–142. New York: Springer.

Howes, David, ed. 2005. *Empire of the Senses: The Sensual Culture Reader, Sensory Formations Series*. New York: Berg.

Katz, Michael B. 1986. *In the Shadow of the Poorhouse: A Social History of Welfare in America*. New York: Basic Books, Inc.

Knappett, Carl. 2005. *Thinking through Material Culture: An Interdisciplinary Perspective. Archaeology, Culture, and Society*. Philadelphia: University of Pennsylvania Press.

Kress, Gunther R. 1989. *Linguistic Processes in Sociocultural Practice*. 2nd ed. New York: Oxford University Press.

Lord, Beth. 2006. "Foucault's Museum: Difference, Representation, and Genealogy." *Museum and Society* 4 (1): 11–14.

Lusignan Lowe, Kim. 2017. "A Historical and Osteological Analysis of Postmortem Medical Practices from the Albany County Almshouse Cemetery Skeletal Sample in Albany, New York." In *The Bioarchaeology of Dissection and Autopsy in the United States*, edited by Kenneth C Nystrom, 315–333. New York: Springer.

Mann, R. W., D. W. Owsley, and P. A. Shackel. 1991. "A Reconstruction of 19th Century Surgical Techniques: Bones in Dr. Thompson's Privy." *Historical Archaeology* 25: 106–112.

McNulty, John A., Beth Sonntag, and James M. Sinacore. 2009. "Evaluation of Computer-Aided Instruction in a Gross Anatomy Course: A Six-Year Study." *Anatomical Sciences Education* 2 (1): 2–8.

Mitchell, Piers D., ed. 2012. *Anatomical Dissection in Enlightenment England and Beyond: Autopsy, Pathology, and Display*, edited by Andrew Cunningham and Ole Peter Grell, *The History of Medicine in Context*. Burlington, VT: Ashgate.

Mitchell, Piers D., C. Boston, A. T. Chamberlain, S. Chaplin, V. Chauhan, J. Evans, L. Fowler, N. Powers, D. Walker, H. Webb, and A. Witkin. 2011. "The Study of Anatomy in England from 1700 to the Early 20th Century." *Journal of Anatomy* 219 (2): 91–99.

Moosman, Darvan A. 1980. "A Surgeon's View: The Decline and Perhaps the Fall of Gross Anatomy Instruction." *The American Journal of Surgery* 140: 266–269.

Moser, Stephanie, and Clive Gamble. 1997. "Revolutionary Images: The Iconic Vocabulary for Representing Human Antiquity." In *The Cultural Life of Images: Visual Representation in Archaeology*, edited by Brian Molyneaux, 184–212. New York: Routledge.

Novak, Shannon A. 2017. "Partible Persons or Persons Apart: Postmortem Interventions at the Spring Street Presbyterian Church, Manhattan." In *The Bioarchaeology of Dissection and Autopsy in the United States*, edited by Kenneth C Nystrom, 87–111. New York: Springer.

Nystrom, Kenneth C. 2014. "The Bioarchaeology of Structural Violence and Dissection in the Nineteenth-Century United States." *American Anthropologist* 116 (4): 765–779.

Nystrom, Kenneth C, ed. 2017. *The Bioarchaeology of Dissection and Autopsy in the United States*. New York: Springer.

Nystrom, Kenneth C. 2011. "Postmortem Examinations and the Embodiment of Inequality in 19th Century United States." *International Journal of Paleopathology* 1 (3–4): 164–172. doi: 10.1016/j.ijpp.2012.02.003.

Nystrom, Kenneth C, Joyce E. Sirianni, Roseanne L. Higgins, Douglas J. Perrelli, and Jennifer L. Liber Raines. 2017. "Structural Inequality and Postmortem Examination at the Erie County Poorhouse." In *The Bioarchaeology of Dissection and Autopsy in the United States*, edited by Kenneth C Nystrom, 279–300. New York: Springer.

Owsley, D. W., Kari Bruwelheide, Richard Jantz, Jodi L. Koste, and M. Outlaw. 2017. "Skeletal Evidence of Anatomical and Surgical Training in Nineteenth-Century Richmond." In *The Bioarchaeology of Dissection and Autopsy in the United States*, edited by Kenneth C Nystrom, 143–164. New York: Springer.

Powers, Penny. 2007. "The Philosophical Foundations of Foucaultian Discourse Analysis." *Critical Approaches to Discourse Analysis across Disciplines* 1 (2): 18–34.

Raines, J. L. 2014. "The Importance of Documentary Evidence in Understanding Demographic Patterns at the Erie County Poorhouse (1851–1926)." *American Journal of Physical Anthropology* 153 (S58): 216.

Richards, Patricia, Catherine R. Jones, Emily Mueller Epstein, Nicholas W. Richards, Brooke L. Drew, and Thomas J. Zych. 2017. "'You Couldn't Identify Your Grandmother If She Were in that Party': The Bioarchaeology of Postmortem Investigation at the Milwaukee County Poor Farm Cemetery." In *The Bioarchaeology of Dissection and Autopsy in the United States*, edited by Kenneth C Nystrom, 237–257. New York: Springer.

Richardson, Ruth. 1987. *Death, Dissection and the Destitute*. London: Routledge and Kegan.

Rothman, David J. 1971. *The Discovery of the Asylum*. Boston, MA: Little, Brown and Company.

Sappol, Michael. 2002. *A Traffic of Dead Bodies: Anatomy and Embodied Social Identity in Nineteenth-Century America*. Princeton, NJ: Princeton University Press.

Sexton, Rachel. 2000. "Holden Chapel: An Archaeological Window into Harvard's Medical History." *Senior Honors Thesis, Anthropology, Harvard University*, Cambridge, MA.

St. George, Robert Blair. 2000. *Conversing by Signs: Poetics of Implication in Colonial New England Culture*. Chapel Hill, NC: University of North Carolina Press.

Starr, Paul. 1982. *The Social Transformation of American Medicine: The Rise of a Sovereign Profession and the Making of a Vast Industry*. New York: Basic Books.

Stewart, Susan. 2007. *On Longing: Narratives of the Miniature, the Gigantic, the Souvenir, the Collection*. 10th paperback ed. Durham, NC: Duke University Press.

Tarlow, Sarah. 1999. *Bereavement and Commemoration: An Archaeology of Mortality, Social Archaeology*. Malden, MA: Blackwell Publishers.

Tarlow, Sarah. 2005. "Death and Commemoration." *Industrial Archaeology Review* 27 (1): 163–169.

Tarlow, Sarah. 2011. *Ritual, Belief, and the Dead Body in Early Modern Britain and Ireland*. New York: Cambridge University Press.

Waldron, Tony, and J. Rogers. 1988. "Iatrogenic Paleopathology." *Journal of Paleopathology* 1 (3): 117–130.

Warren, Edward. 1874. *The Life of John Warren, MD, Surgeon-general During the War of the Revolution; First Professor of Anatomy and Surgery in Harvard College; President of the Massachusetts Medical Society, etc.* Boston, MA: Noyes, Holmes and Company.

Wells, Tom. 1998. "Nail Chronology: The Use of Technologically Derived Features." *Historical Archaeology* 32 (2): 78–99.

Western, A. G. 2012. "A Star of the First Magnitude: Osteological and Historical Evidence for the Challenge of Provincial Medicine at the Worcester Royal Infirmary in the Nineteenth Century." In *Anatomical Dissection in Enlightenment England and Beyond Autopsy, Pathology and Display*, edited by Piers D. Mitchell, 23–41. Farnham, Surrey: Ashgate.

Whitehead, Neil L. 2004. "On the Poetics of Violence." In *Violence*, edited by Neil L. Whitehead, 55–78. Santa Fe, NM: SAR Press.

11

Processing the Destitute and Deviant Dead

Inequality, Dissection, Politics, and the Structurally Violent Legalization of Social Marginalization in American Anatomical Collections

CARLINA DE LA COVA

This volume has examined the various ways in which anthropologist Neil Whitehead's poetics model can be applied to bioarchaeology. Just as present groups have a moral and cultural ethos that dictates the burial, disposal, or postmortem processing of the dead, so did past cultures. Whether it be rituals tied to warfare or beliefs about the afterlife, the postmortem treatment of individuals is often related to, or symbolic of, their social positions within their respective cultures during their lives. Thus processing, or postmortem treatment, becomes in Whitehead's (2004, 60) words a "socially constructive cultural performance" that is exerted by the living upon the dead to reinforce sociocultural beliefs that form one of many integral fibers of a society. As Anna Osterholtz indicates in the introduction to this book, manipulating the dead is a "discursive act, communicating cultural information through actions that create social identity and memory." Postmortem processing can also serve as a tool to reconstruct, or even erase, the identity and memory of a particular individual or group of persons whose beliefs or perceived behaviors are not in agreement with societal norms. Ultimately, as Osterholtz indicates, the physical body is transformed into a social tool that can be manipulated to transform, reestablish, or reinforce the relationships that exist between the living and the deceased as well as cement social stratification and power.

Previous chapters in this book have focused on these issues amongst archaeologically excavated bodies. However, this work differs. Instead of examining individuals recovered via archaeological methods, this chapter investigates the relationship

DOI: 10.5876/9781646420612.c011

between history, social status, and the poetics of processing in the Hamann-Todd and Terry anatomical collections. The persons who were comprised within these series were not buried, nor were they provided the option of a final cemetery resting place where their loved ones could visit and commemorate their lives. On the contrary, structurally violent dissection laws demanded, due to their social position and unclaimed nature at death, that they be non-consensually anatomized, which ultimately resulted in the erasure of their identities and social memories. This chapter addresses these issues and argues how, via postmortem processing, the bodies of those who make up anatomical collections were utilized as social tools to reinforce and cement social stratification in late nineteenth- and twentieth-century American society.

THE HAMANN-TODD HUMAN OSTEOLOGICAL COLLECTION AND THE ROBERT J. TERRY ANATOMICAL SKELETAL COLLECTION

The Hamann-Todd and Robert J. Terry osteological collections are mostly composed of impoverished, unclaimed persons who died in the very late nineteenth to mid-twentieth centuries. Anatomists, anthropologists, and surgeons have researched aspects of these persons for decades. Their skeletons were integral to creating standardized methods for human identification that remain a vital part of bioarchaeology. Furthermore, their bodies have been used to study variation and aging, and to aid in orthopedic research. As I have indicated in previous publications, despite the knowledge and methods generated from these collections, few anthropologists have examined the complete skeletons or investigated the origins of the peoples who compose these samples, including the paths their lives took that resulted in their dissection and preservation (Cobb 1935; de la Cova 2010, 2011, 2012, 2014; Hunt and Albanese 2005; Muller 2006; Muller, Pearlstein, and de la Cova 2017; Pearlstein 2015; Watkins 2007; Watkins and Muller 2015). Most were of low socioeconomic status (SES), were unclaimed morgue bodies, or expired in public or state institutions funded by the taxpayer, including public hospitals, state mental institutions, city poorhouses, and homeless shelters. State anatomical legislation stipulated that persons who died in these state-funded institutions had to be claimed within 36 to 72 hours. If not, and if they were to be interred at taxpayer expense, then the state's anatomical board distributed the body to a medical or mortuary school for instruction.

The Hamann-Todd Human Osteological Collection, referred to as the Hamann-Todd Collection, is curated at the Cleveland Museum of Natural History and comprises the skeletons of over 3,500 individuals born between 1825 and 1910 who died in Cleveland, Ohio. Documentary information, including photos, somatological data, a morgue record, and an inventory sheet with notes taken by Todd, or his assistants, exists for most subjects. Personal information, like name, sex, age, race, birthplace, occupation (if available), cause of death, and unique pathologies observed during dissection are recorded; some individuals also have clinical histories.

Carl A. Hamann, professor of anatomy at Western Reserve University (WRU), now Case Western Reserve University, started the collection in 1893 (Cobb 1959). After his promotion to dean of the medical school in 1912, British anatomist T. Wingate Todd was hired as Hamann's replacement (Jones-Kern 1997). During Todd's 26 years at WRU, he expanded the Hamann Comparative Anatomy Collection "into the world-renowned Hamann-Todd Osteological Assemblage" (Jones-Kern 1997, 173). Ohio Code, Sections 1713.34–1713.42 and 1713.99 (discussed later in this chapter), indicated that the superintendents of regional mortuaries, city hospitals, charity institutions, city infirmaries, mental hospitals, and the Cleveland Workhouse had to notify Todd of unclaimed bodies in their possession (Jones-Kern 1997). If Todd desired these decedents, they were delivered to WRU for dissection. Thus, the Hamann-Todd Collection is composed of impoverished individuals and state wards that were unclaimed at death.

Like Hamann-Todd, the Robert J. Terry Anatomical Skeletal Collection, referred to as the Terry Collection, originated in the Midwest. Dr. Robert J. Terry, professor and later chair of anatomy at St. Louis's Washington University School of Medicine (WUSM), began his collection in 1910. Upon his retirement in 1941, Dr. Mildred Trotter, a colleague and friend of Terry's at WUSM, expanded the series until her 1967 retirement (Hunt and Albanese 2005). The collection contains 1,728 individuals born from 1822 to 1943, whose sex, age, pathologies, cause of death, and place of death are known (Hunt and Albanese 2005; Trotter 1981). The series was later transferred to the Smithsonian Institution's National Museum of Natural History.

Each individual has a file that includes demographic data, place of birth, occupation, clinical diagnoses, anatomical measurements, and an inventory of the bones and teeth present (Hunt and Albanese 2005). Others have medical histories, including autopsy reports and photographs. Most were unclaimed dead who expired in St. Louis's segregated public city hospitals, city infirmary, homeless shelters, state mental institutions, nursing homes, and other taxpayer-funded establishments. In accordance with Missouri's anatomical acts, their bodies were sent to state medical and mortuary schools for dissection.

A BRIEF HISTORY OF DISSECTION, LEGISLATION, AND THE ORIGINS OF THE ANATOMICAL DECONSTRUCTION OF IDENTITY

To comprehend the relationship between processing, dissection, and social stratification in the Hamann-Todd and Terry collections, we have to understand the history of anatomical legislation, dissection, and medicine's reliance on the poor and

Other for advancement (which some argue persists into the present day). Written anatomical laws have existed for over 700 years and reflect cultural attitudes toward particular social classes of the dead, especially those deemed socially "deviant," such as the poor, the criminalized, and the insane. The earliest anatomical acts date to 1238, when Frederick II granted one human dissection every five years in Salerno, Italy, on executed criminals (Hildebrandt 2008). Over a hundred years later in 1387 Florence, an annual number of three executed bodies was approved (Ball 1928; Hildebrandt 2008). However, the most important legislation for the development of American anatomy, medicine, and attitudes about dissection came from Britain, as our nation's anatomical acts were an extension of those in the United Kingdom.

Like Italy, Great Britain relied on the bodies of criminals to assuage the needs of anatomists. As early as 1506, James IV permitted one executed criminal to be given to the Edinburgh Guild of Surgeons and Barbers annually (Sappol 2002). In 1726, George II gave all executed bodies to English anatomists (Ball 1928). This practice continued in Britain throughout the remainder of the eighteenth and early nineteenth centuries. The Bloody Code (1723–1820), which allowed death-penalty sentencing for over 50 different crimes (some of which were misdemeanors), including murder, increased the number of bodies anatomists had access to. However, it was the 1752 Murder Act that intimately tied execution to dissection as a form of postmortem punishment to reflect society's disdain of criminals. The Murder Act emphasized that those guilty of the "heinous Offence" of murder needed "some further Terror and peculiar Mark of Infamy" in addition to death (Statutes at Large 1786, 604–605). Therefore, sentencing was "pronounced in open Court immediately after the Conviction . . . in order to impress . . . Horror in the Mind of the Offender" and those present "of the heinous Crime of Murder" (1786, 604–605). The law stipulated that interment was disallowed until anatomization was completed. Thus, anatomization and dissection became intimately linked to capital punishment and humiliation (Hildebrandt 2008; Richardson 1987; Sappol 2002). British medical historian Elizabeth Hurren (2013, 302) contends that there were "three distinctive penal stages: first, a death penalty (legal death, to be hanged); second, a sentence to be anatomized (medical death) to look at the major organs expiring; and finally, dissection (post-mortem punishment)." Execution by hanging did not always guarantee death. According to Hurren (2013, 302), "the uncomfortable reality was that it was the surgeon, and not the hangman alone, who ensured that the condemned became legally, socially, and medically dead," ultimately violating the Hippocratic Oath.

Due to the Murder Act of 1751, public dissection became synonymous with legalized humiliation as the law encapsulated the final act of indignity toward one's remains. Not only did it erase an individual's existence amongst the living (as some of those dissected did not have final resting places and were curated by anatomists, or included in their anatomical closets), but it violated religious beliefs. Anatomization became a form of punishment that "represented a gross assault upon the integrity and identity of the body and upon the response of the soul, each of which—in other circumstances—would have been carefully fostered" (Richardson 1987, 76). Dissection was the ultimate desecration, steeped in structural violence, as it targeted criminals, tampered with a body, and destroyed identity after death, thereby hindering resurrection in the afterlife (Halperin 2007). Thus, dissection became a state-sponsored performance to communicate the societal disdain of those who broke the law. The criminal body was transformed into a social tool that could be manipulated and destroyed by elites in a manner that extended beyond the physical world into the afterlife, resulting in complete erasure of one's identity. Soon, however, it would not be solely delimited to criminals. It would be extended to the poor, the insane, and the "lesser" classes of society.

These early anatomical laws and beliefs made their way across the Atlantic as most early medical educators in the American colonies were British. During the seventeenth through nineteenth centuries, the only bodies surgeons and physicians could legally dissect in the United Kingdom and the United States were executed criminals. The first American dissection act was a 1647 resolution passed in Massachusetts indicating that students studying "physick or chirurgery have liberty to reade anotomy [sic] and anotomize once in foure yeares some malefactor in case there be such as the Courte shall allow of" (General Court of Massachusetts 1647). By the eighteenth century, Massachusetts (1784), New York (1789), and New Jersey (1796) had legalized anatomization of executed criminals, or in the case of Massachusetts, dead duellists (Hartwell 1880, 361).

Whilst this legislation on both sides of the Atlantic legally provided anatomists and medical students with bodies for anatomization, demand exceeded supply, resulting in the practice of grave-robbing. In New York City, tensions were strained between the public, the anatomists, and Columbia College medical students, who grave-robbed the Negro Burying Ground and Pauper's Cemetery mere blocks away from the medical school. These graveyards were targeted "chiefly because large numbers were buried together, frequently without coffins, making the procurement of cadavers infinitely easier" (Ladenheim 1950, 26). The most outspoken protests came from those whose final resting places were disturbed by elite anatomists: the marginalized poor, enslaved, and people of color (Ladenheim 1950). Plundering of the city's African Burial Ground especially upset New York's Free Black community, who complained in 1787 that "dissection should be limited to people convicted of capital crimes, the traditional source of bodies" (Sappol 2002, 107). When no action was taken, they petitioned the metropolis's Common Council on February 3, 1788 (de Costa and Miller 2011).

These protests fell on deaf ears until anatomists began to target elite church cemeteries outside of the realm of the poor. On February 21, 1788, a white woman's body interred in Trinity Church's graveyard was stolen (Sappol 2002). When no punishment was levied and medical students continued to plunder graves, animosities exploded into the nation's first riot, the "Doctor's Mob" or "Doctor's Mob of April 13, 1788" (de Costa and Miller 2011). The stimulus of the event remains unclear. On Sunday afternoon, April 13, 1788, boys playing outside the City Hospital obtained a ladder, climbed it, and observed active human dissections. One of the children, whose dead mother had recently been buried, ran home and told his working-class father what he witnessed (Ladenheim 1950). The father, upon returning to his wife's burial site, discovered that her body was missing. Enraged, he and a group of friends broke into the New York Hospital, retrieved partially dissected bodies and displayed them to the public, then destroyed the rooms, books, and anatomical collections in the building (Sappol 2002). The expanding crowd outside of the hospital, enraged by the anatomized remains, stormed the structure in search of the "imbecilic physician, Hicks by name, who is said to have precipitated this affair" by waving body parts at the boy (Ladenheim 1950, 30). Hicks escaped, but four of his colleagues were captured and assaulted by rioters until authorities intervened, incarcerating the anatomists for their protection. The next morning, a large group began searching the city for medical students, physicians, cadavers, and Dr. Hicks. Ultimately a "crowd numbering three to four hundred assembled in front of the jail," shouting to release the prisoners (Ladenheim 1950, 32). Political elites requested that the mob peacefully disperse, but they refused, and grew in number. Eighteen armed men were summoned to protect the jail, but were chased off (Sappol 2002). An additional twelve men were mobilized amidst escalating tensions (Ladenheim 1950; Sappol 2002). The crowd grew more belligerent as the standoff extended for hours. Ultimately, the Governor called the militia with disastrous results. The mob became enraged, throwing rocks and bricks, which resulted in the militia's firing into the crowd. By the next day the riot was quelled with six dead, including three rioters and three militiamen, and six wounded (Sappol 2002).

Within a year of the riots, "An Act to Prevent the Odious Practice of Digging up and Removing for the Purpose of Dissection, Dead Bodies Interred in Cemeteries or Burial Places" was passed, making New York the first state to legally punish grave-robbing. The law indicated that any person who intended to dig up, remove, or carry away a dead body from its burial place within the state for the purpose of dissection would be convicted, punished, and fined. Furthermore, according to the New York statutes (1792), "in order that Science may not in this respect be injured by preventing the dissection of proper subjects . . . when any offender shall be convicted . . . of murder, arson or burglary, for which he or she shall be sentenced to suffer death, may, at their discretion, add to the judgment, that the body of such offender shall be delivered to a surgeon for dissection." Thus, following the 1647 Massachusetts legislation and the British Murder Acts, dissection became entangled with capital punishment in New York. However, it did little to impede anatomists. Almost four years after the Doctor's Riot, "body snatching for the purposes of dissection had resumed" (Sappol 2002, 109) due to the limited number of executions after the state overturned capital punishment for burglary and treason.

Congress passed an act similar to New York's legislation in 1790, which allowed federal judges to add dissection to death-penalty verdicts (Sappol 2002). Vermont followed in 1870 (Sappol 2002). However, during the remainder of the eighteenth and through the nineteenth century, dissection remained illegal in many states, despite the growing number of medical schools and increasing demand for bodies to anatomize. Britain experienced similar pressures during this time, which led to an increased reliance on resurrection men to grave-rob decedents. According to medical historian Ruth Richardson, social disapproval of "bodysnatching was so fierce" that risks associated with grave-robbing in the UK "pushed prices so high as to provide an incentive to murder" (Richardson 2012, 1637). Ultimately, it *was* cold-blooded murder (the William Burke and William Hare killings in Edinburgh, Scotland, and the copycat London Burkers in London) that resulted in British reforms to anatomy laws that would reach beyond the UK to America for generations.

William Burke and his accomplice William Hare murdered sixteen people and sold them to Dr. Robert Knox's dissecting rooms in Surgeon's Square, Edinburgh, in 1828. Upon their capture, Hare turned King's evidence against Burke, who was sentenced in 1829 to death by hanging and subsequent dissection. Burke's skeleton was then rearticulated and exhibited at the University of Edinburgh Anatomy Museum; it still remains on public display. The London Burkers, John Bishop and Thomas Williams, confessed to killing 60 persons including their last victim, a 10-year-old Italian boy named Carlo Ferrari (Richardson 2012). They were found guilty and sentenced to death and postmortem dissection. Burke, Hare, and the London Burkers murdered to profit off the increasing demand of anatomists for fresh bodies. Their crimes, combined with the increase in grave-robbing, spurred Westminster to pass the 1832 Warburton Anatomy Act. The law dictated that the bodies of persons who died in workhouses, prisons, hospitals, and other institutions supported by the taxpayer, and were unclaimed at death or lacked funds for burial, were to be given to anatomists and medical schools for dissection. Ultimately, the 1832 Anatomy Act shifted anatomization from a form of punishment associated with murder to one tied to poverty (Richardson 1987, 2012). Thus, "the poor dying in hospitals and workhouses would provide a new source of fresh corpses so cheap and plentiful that the existing market for corpses was undermined," ending the need for resurrection men, body snatching, and grave-robbing (Richardson 2012, 1637). It was now the bodies of the law-abiding, powerless, and institutionalized poor, not criminals, that drove medical education. This would become a consistent theme in British and American medical education until the late twentieth century as the Warburton Anatomy Act, and its cultural and medical stigmatization of the impoverished, the criminal, and the Other made its way across the Atlantic.

In the United States, bodies remained difficult to obtain for dissection as the practice remained illegal in most states, barring those previously mentioned. Massachusetts was the first to pass legislation similar to the 1832 Warburton Anatomy Act in 1831, one year before Parliament approved the law (McCullough 2011). This legislation, only applicable in Boston, criminalized body-snatching and legalized the use of unclaimed bodies buried at public expense for dissection, thus limiting dissection to the indigent, imprisoned, and insane (Sappol 2002). Other states in the North, such as Connecticut (1833), New Hampshire (1834), Michigan (1844), New York (1854), Pennsylvania (1867), and Maine (1869) followed with similar laws (McCullough 2011; Sappol 2002).

American medical education also underwent an ideological revolution and expanded during the nineteenth century due to a national increase in the number of medical schools. Eighteenth-century Enlightenment ideals transformed medicine, discarding a humoral-balanced approach centered on bile, phlegm, or blood and heroic medical practices (bleeding, purging, or cupping) for a scientifically and clinically based discipline. During this transition, many of the nation's initial anatomists and physicians studied abroad in Europe at epicenters of medicine like Edinburgh, London, Paris, and Germany, where emphasis was placed on dissection, observation, empirical knowledge, and application of the scientific method (Warner 1998). Enlightenment-period anatomists, like Scottish brothers John and William Hunter, and the Parisian school encouraged active learning approaches to medicine and clinical diagnosis through empirical analysis and visual observation (Warner 1998). For nineteenth-century Americans, training with eminent Parisian anatomists and physiologists conveyed knowledge of the latest medical theories, methods, and practices. It also signaled social status and guaranteed respect within the medical hierarchy (Warner 1998).

Parisian medicine ethically conflicted with some Americans, who grew disenchanted with French doctors that objectified their disadvantaged patients (Warner 1998). Students were shocked by the cheapness and insignificance French physicians placed on human life, especially those of the lower class, as they investigated illness by experimenting and withholding curative treatments to see how diseases progressed (Warner 1998). When patients died in publicly funded health establishments, they were considered institutional property and subsequently dissected. Augustus Kinley Gardiner, a physician who studied in Paris, commented in 1848 that access to clinical material, including "bodies of the living and the dead was unrivaled . . . 'every patient who enters a hospital is, in a certain degree, Government property, and not only through life, but even after death, is subject . . . to the control of the physician.'" (Warner 1998, 42).

Despite these attitudes, American anatomists embraced Parisian empirical and clinical approaches. However, whilst Parisian laws created an abundance of clinical subjects as the government subsidized medical care and exerted control over poor bodies, this was not the case in America. The United States was experiencing a boom in number of medical schools, resulting in an increased demand for cadavers as these institutions competed to attract students who wanted the dissection and clinical experiences touted by the British and Parisian methods. For a medical school to succeed, it had to supply students with abundant clinical material, or "living patients for medical and surgical demonstrations as well as cadavers for anatomical dissections and pathological examinations" (Savitt 1982, 333). Even the prestigious Harvard Medical School was forced to move from Cambridge to Boston in 1810 as the institution could not obtain bodies in Cambridge (Sappol 2002). Relocating to Boston placed the school closer to a larger supply of "teaching materials" at the Boston Almshouse.

To educate students, teaching clinics and hospitals were opened in conjunction with medical schools that "arranged with local authorities to treat patients in poor houses or city hospitals" (Savitt 1982, 334). These individuals, targeted as "clinical material" for medical teaching and experimentation, were mostly the poor and the Other, who disliked submitting their bodies to the prying eyes of physicians and medical students who objectified them and consumed their ailments whilst disposing of their humanity.

Regional emphases also impacted medical study, especially in the sectional nineteenth-century South where doctors touted the concept of "southern distinctiveness." Southerners argued that due to the environmental and cultural differences of the South, with its hotter, humid climate, noxious swamp miasmas, large enslaved population, and predominately agrarian economy, the region was afflicted with different diseases and disorders than the North (Savitt 1978). To lure potential students, many institutions advertised in medical journals, newspapers, magazines, and circulars, describing the clinical materials they offered, which comprised poor whites, immigrants, and free and enslaved Blacks. The Medical College of the State of South Carolina, now the Medical University of South Carolina, wrote in 1841 that it had established a hospital for both white and Black patients and "had little trouble filling beds" as Charleston's slave population and its neighboring plantations furnished "ample materials" for clinical instruction (Savitt 1982, 335). Students observed diseases, participated in operations, and experimented on the local slave population (Savitt 1982). This was commonplace in the antebellum (1812–1861) South, where the legal invisibility of freedpeople and the enslaved allowed medical researchers, physicians, and students to use Black bodies for dissection, surgical demonstrations, and experimentation to advance their medical, anatomical, and surgical skills. Poor whites and immigrants were also utilized in a similar manner, but given their lack of status in society, and in the case of Blacks, lack of ownership over their own bodies, they had no power to object. Thus medicine "capitalized on the need of the indigent and the helpless for medical care" (Savitt 1982, 333). When bodies could not be obtained from poorhouses, public hospitals, or slaveholders, then medical professors relied on resurrection men and grave-robbing.

It is believed the majority of bodies used in medical experimentation and dissection in the South and parts of the North were Black (Savitt 1978, 1982; Washington 2007). Southern medical historian Todd Savitt (1978, 1982) asserts that African-descended individuals were anatomized more than whites. Kentucky's *Transylvania Journal of Medicine and the Associate Sciences* (1828–1839) reported a total of 24 "autopsies" by Southern physicians. Of these about 79 percent (n = 19) were performed on Black bodies whilst the remaining five were done on whites, "in a state where the white population far exceeded the black" (Savitt 1982; 338). These "autopsies" were really dissections performed as teaching and learning exercises to benefit students and advance their knowledge of medicine, not as a means of informing one's next of kin about their loved one's cause of death. Records from Johns Hopkins University (the same institution that harvested the cells of Henrietta Lacks without consent[1]) indicate that, between 1898 and 1904, two-thirds of the 1,200 cadavers the university received were Black (Humphrey 1973). Even into the

[1] In 1951 Henrietta Lacks, a poor African American woman, was initially hesitant to seek medical help due to the deeply entrenched mistrust and fear in the African American community of hospitals and white, experimenting doctors. Nevertheless, she went to Baltimore's Johns Hopkins University, the area's only institution that treated African American patients, in regard to a lump in her womb. A biopsy was taken, resulting in a diagnosis of cervical carcinoma. Lacks was treated with radium tube inserts and X-ray therapy. During her treatments, tissue samples were extracted from her cervix without her consent and given to Dr. George Gey, a cancer researcher and director of the Tissue Culture Laboratory at Johns Hopkins. Gey had been attempting to discover an immortal cell line and succeeded with Henrietta's cells, which became known as the HeLa immortal cell line. Given the resilience of these cells, they led to numerous medical breakthroughs for vaccines, such as polio, and drugs to treat an array of health ailments. Whilst medical corporations profited from Henrietta's cells, her name and non-consensual contribution to medical advancement remained unknown; her family lived in abject poverty. Journalist Rebecca Skloot (2010) would be the first share Henrietta's story with the world and unsilence the role she played in medical and pharmaceutical advancement.

twentieth century, body-snatchers continued to ship the bodies of dead southern Black men to desperate anatomy professors in the North (Humphrey 1973).

By the early 1880s, 14 additional states passed laws that allowed for unclaimed bodies to be used in medical training (Humphrey 1973). The twentieth century introduced anatomical legislation that mirrored the Warburton Anatomy Act to every state and district in the continental United States, permanently eliminating the need for grave-robbing (Humphrey 1973). However, in its place a legalized and state-sanctioned tie between dissection and destitution would be permanently forged in America and, as in the United Kingdom, poverty, the inability to afford burial expenses, and insanity were now punished via dissection (Hurren 2012; Richardson 1987; Sappol 2002). Contemporary newspapers and the words of anatomists attest this. An article in the *New York Times* (1860, 8) indicated that dissection "was the fate held in reserve for all who died under the jurisdiction of the Almshouse Department of our City." The *St. Louis Globe-Democrat* (1887, 25) also discussed anatomization and cadaver acquisition in August of 1887, when Professor Curtis, Secretary of the Faculty of the New York Medical College, indicated that

> the law allows the use of bodies at the morgue unclaimed after twenty-four hours, and the bodies of those who die in the charity hospitals provided that the friends of the deceased are too poor to give it a private burial, and provided also that the deceased himself did not express a distinct wish to be buried without undergoing dissection.

This journey from a human being to a dehumanized medical commodity was a fear held by most poor persons during the nineteenth century. Many avoided infirmaries and hospitals as illness was equated with income loss and transformation from a person to a dehumanized test subject that was medically objectified (Rosenberg 1987; Savitt 1978). Furthermore, a very real fear existed that physicians would perform medical experiments that would induce death for autopsy or dissection (Savitt 1978). In African American folklore that dates from the antebellum period into the twentieth century, it was believed that Night Doctors, which often included medical students, would kidnap an individual and experiment on their bodies, or kill them to anatomize their remains (Savitt 1978).

Individuals who submitted their bodies to hospital care and had no local social networks or family were at a disadvantage. Without anyone to claim their remains, anatomical laws dictated that their bodies be sent to medical institutions for dissection. The above history is important in understanding the mentality behind the creation of anatomical collections, as it illustrates the consistent pattern in which medicine and anatomy training in Europe and the United States preyed on the bodies of those considered by elites to be socially and biologically deviant:

criminals, the poor, and people of color. The selective anatomization of these "deviants" became part of a larger performance that reduced their bodies to tools that communicated social status and biological superiority and devalued the poor and the Other, ultimately erasing their social identities and memories. The medical profession saw no societal value in these individuals, apart from the inner workings of their physical corpus, which, if pathological, became a collector's item. The public was also not too terribly concerned with the plight of these individuals as their dissections paid their debt to society or further illustrated their perceived biological inferiorities and divergences.[2] This pattern of targeting the poor, the voiceless, African Americans, and other marginalized groups would remain (and, some argue, remains) a consistent staple in American medicine into the twentieth century and would be the ultimate fate of most of the persons in the Hamann-Todd and Terry anatomical collections.

THE POETICS OF PROCESSING IN THE HAMANN-TODD AND TERRY ANATOMICAL COLLECTIONS

History is often the result of many factors linked together to create events that become critical turning points in a subject's development. The influence of the British and Parisian schools in American medicine, combined with the Warburton Anatomy Act, created a catalyst for future anatomical legislation in America that spurred postmortem class discrimination and racism. As the nineteenth century became the twentieth, most states had passed laws that legalized the anatomization of the unclaimed poor. It was this legislation that allowed for amassing the anatomical collections biological anthropologists have relied on for the creation of identification methods and standards in the field. As bioanthropological scholars move into a more ethically conscious field, especially those associated with the new bioarchaeology, we must recognize that these collections exist because of discriminatory anatomical legislation that preyed, and continues to prey, upon the poor, the mentally ill, and the socially and culturally marginalized. This is especially true of the Hamann-Todd and Robert J. Terry collections. Laws governing the "disposal" of paupers' bodies that allowed for amassing these giant samples are still in effect. For example, in Missouri, where the Terry Collection was amassed, the state's 2013 Revised Statutes (Chapter 194, Death—Disposition of Dead Bodies, Section 194.150, Disposal of Paupers' Bodies) indicate:

> Superintendents or wardens of penitentiaries, houses of correction and bridewells, hospitals, insane asylums and poorhouses, and coroners, sheriffs, jailers, city and

[2] See also Hodge and Nystrom, chapter 10, this volume.

> county undertakers, and all other state, county, town or city officers having the custody of the body of any deceased person required to be buried at public expense, shall be and hereby are required immediately to notify the secretary of the [anatomy] board, or the person duly designated by the board or by its secretary to receive such notice, whenever any such body or bodies come into his or their custody, charge or control, and shall, without fee or reward, deliver, within a period not to exceed thirty-six hours after death, except in cases within the jurisdiction of a coroner where retention for a longer time may be necessary, such body or bodies into the custody of the board and permit the board or its agent or agents to take and remove all such bodies, or otherwise dispose of them; provided, that each educational institution receiving a body from the board shall hold such body for at least thirty days, during which time any relative or friend of any such deceased person or persons shall have the right to take and receive the dead body from the possession of any person in whose charge or custody it may be found, for the purpose of interment, upon paying the expense of such interment. (Missouri 2013)

Similarly, revised code 1713.34 from Ohio, where the Hamann-Todd Collection was amassed, which is titled "Medical colleges or embalming board may receive bodies for study or dissection—procedure," states:

> Superintendents of city hospitals, directors or superintendents of city infirmaries, county homes, or other charitable institutions, directors or superintendents of workhouses, founded and supported in whole or in part at public expense, superintendents or managing officers of state benevolent institutions, boards of township trustees, sheriffs, or coroners, in possession of bodies not claimed or identified, or which must be buried at the expense of the state, county, or township, before burial, shall notify the professor of anatomy in a college which by its charter is empowered to teach anatomy, or the secretary of the board of embalmers and funeral directors of this state, of the fact that such bodies are being so held. If after a period of thirty-six hours the body has not been accepted by friends or relatives for burial at their expense, such superintendent, director, or other officer, on the written application of such professor, or the secretary of the board of embalmers and funeral directors, shall deliver to such professor or secretary, for the purpose of medical or surgical study or dissection or for the study of embalming, the body of any such person who died in any of such institutions from any disease which is not infectious. The expense of the delivery of the body shall be borne by the parties in whose keeping the body was placed.

These laws have changed very little and would have been similar to the contemporaneous legislation Robert J. Terry and T. Wingate Todd utilized to amass their collections. Thus, we know not only the medical ideology these respected historical figures in our discipline were trained in, but we also know how they received decedents for dissection. How can we link this information to the Whitehead's poetics model? Given the historical nature of anatomical legislation, including the laws that allowed for amassing the Hamann-Todd Human Osteological Collection and the Robert J. Terry Skeletal Anatomy Collection, it becomes clear that twentieth-century legislation embodied the same cultural beliefs as those reflected by both the law and anatomists in the eighteenth and nineteenth centuries. Dissection was relegated to the poor, the imprisoned, and the insane, or those viewed as financially and socially deviant in society. The poor and mentally ill, both young and old, were especially trapped, as their reliance on public alms and assistance relegated them to non-consensual dissection to cheaply dispose of their mortal remains and resolve the debt owed to the taxpayer for their maintenance. In the case of the persons that make up the Hamann-Todd and Terry anatomical collections, little religious or commemorative ritual was associated with their deaths. Demise often occurred at overcrowded and poorly maintained state and taxpayer-funded institutions such as public hospitals, city infirmaries (poor houses for the impoverished elderly), and state mental institutions (de la Cova 2012, 2014).

Upon death, individuals were removed to the establishment's morgue or a holding facility maintained for the deceased. If the person was not claimed within the hours required by law, the state anatomical board was notified and would determine, based on state legislation, which institutions needed "corpses" for dissection. These schools were contacted; if they accepted the unclaimed bodies, they paid a transfer and delivery fee to receive the remains. There is little spirituality or ritual involved in this process. The person, now stripped of their name and identity, becomes a number that proceeds through a bureaucratic system. No service, commemoration, or burial is provided to remember the individual. Instead the body is placed in the morgue, prepared for transportation, then unceremoniously shipped as an object for delivery—in this case, to WRU and WUSM for dissection. Thus, as the bodies transition from death to an anatomical object owned by the state, they are effectively disappeared from social memory.

Once the body, now objectified as a "cadaver" and "teaching materials," arrives at the university it is further processed and prepared for dissection. Blood is removed; formalin, preservatives, and dyes are injected into the arteries and veins to deter decay. Whilst T. Wingate Todd did not leave behind a complete account of the postmortem path a person took from the anatomical board to the Hamann-Todd Human Osteological Collection, Robert J. Terry explained the journey a body made from the Missouri Anatomical Board to the storage space that held his skeletal collection. According to Terry, at the height of his collecting in the 1910s–1940, "material" for study was "secured through the State Anatomical Board of Missouri.

Between 100 and 123 cadavers, of which approximately half are negroes, are brought annually to the laboratory" (Terry n.d.). Males exceeded females; Black women outnumbered white ones. Most "white cadavers are above 45 years of age; cadavers under 21 years are very seldom received . . . at the present time the average age of negro cadavers is much lower than that of white, and bodies in the second decade, women as well as men, are not uncommon; a circumstance explained by the recent immigration of strangers into the community and by hard times" (Terry n.d.). During this era, the Great Migration was expanding the African American population of St. Louis. Poor living conditions exacerbated the health of these in-migrants, resulting in high mortality rates. Previous studies have linked the Great Migration to the Terry Collection, illustrating that many of the African Americans within the series were southern-born; marginalized due to race and work ethic, they died miles away from friends or family who could claim their bodies (de la Cova 2011, 2014).

Individuals reached Terry's lab "as soon as forty-eight hours after death and occasionally as late as six days" (Terry 1913, n.p.). Upon arrival, all persons were identified based on their death cards, which recorded ancestry, age, sex, date, and cause of death, and the hospital in which demise occurred. If Terry needed further information, he directly contacted the morgue, clinic, hospital, coroner's facility, or the Missouri institution that the individual died in.

Once all death-card data was verified, a serial number tag was tied to the individual's wrist and the body was then "placed in a Lysol solution for surface disinfection" (Terry n.d.). From this point forward, the person was referred to only by serial number. Once sterilization was completed and prior to embalming, photographs were taken of the body standing, including anterior and side positions (Terry n.d.). Headshots also captured the front and profile of the face. A battery of anthropometric measurements and somatic data was also taken. The body was weighed, a plaster death mask created, and hair and skin samples extracted. Individuals utilized in class studies were "embalmed with carbolic acid, glycerine and alcohol. The brain injected with strong formaline [sic] and a color mass sent into the arteries" (Terry n.d.). In 1913, Terry indicated preservatives injected in the common carotid and femoral arteries were composed of "equal parts, by volume, of carbolic acid . . . crude glycerine and 95% alcohol" (Terry 1913). Formaldehyde was utilized with "water, half and half, for injecting bodies that are to be sectioned for the work in topographical anatomy" (Terry 1913).

All bodies, "by agreement among the anatomists of the State" were held for "one month in the school morgues pending possible claim for burial. After the lapse of one month material is stored awaiting investigation" (Terry n.d, n.p.). In 1913 bodies were held in "make-shift" tanks "constructed of wood lined by heavily galvanized iron" that measured "8 x 6 feet x 4 feet deep" and held "about a dozen bodies"

(Terry 1913, n.p.). Individuals were "completely covered by a 3% watery solution of carbolic acid" (Terry 1913, n.p.). However, Terry would later shift to concrete, then steel tanks, which had similar measurements as his original tanks, but were waterproof. He "put no more than six bodies in one of these tanks" (Terry 1913, n.p.).

Any data taken from the body, including metrics, photographs, hair and skin samples, and death masks, were labeled and stored with the individual's accession number. Terry also kept a meticulous chain of custody for individuals and their dissected body parts so remains would not be lost or stolen but could be easily reassociated. According to Terry (n.d., n.p.), "A cadaver, or parts of it . . . commonly pass through the hands of a number of persons," which made it necessary "to be certain of the identity of the parts and remains that an almost automatic system of labelling of parts and recording of transfers be maintained."

Dissection was performed based on explicit instructions given by Terry, which avoided as much damage as possible to the underlying skeleton. A WUSM pathologist also examined the body and recorded his findings (Terry n.d.). The remainder of the body was then passed to the osteology laboratory where it was further processed. In Terry's words, the "soft parts" were cremated separately and the skeletons were prepared by a trained technician (Terry n.d.). Once clean, dry, and degreased, skeletons were "transferred to the numberer, who first checks them from missing or damaged parts, and for pathological evidence, then numbers each bone with the original number of the cadaver" (Terry n.d.). Once this task was complete, the individual officially entered the collection.

Thus, by their very nature, anatomical collections comprise individuals who are physically and emotionlessly processed by anatomists. However, instead of undergoing mortuary preparations for being laid to rest, these persons are handled, caressed, shaved, cut, sliced, disemboweled, hemisected, and macerated, resulting in complete anatomical deconstruction. Prior to willed body laws, those dissected may not have desired this fate. In the nineteenth and early twentieth centuries, anatomization conflicted with religious beliefs about the violation, completeness, and purity of the body for resurrection in the afterlife. Anatomical deconstruction was tantamount to the erasure of one's memory and social identity in the living and postmortem realm.

By non-consensually physically processing and dissecting one's mortal remains, the anatomist exerts power and control over the powerless poor, ultimately determining their postmortem fate. Historian Michael Sappol (2002) has described dissection as a ritualistic initiation into the world of medicine and social class for nineteenth- and early twentieth-century anatomists and medical students (Sappol 2002). The student, usually (but not always) a white male, learns his place and social power in the medical world through the dissection and clinical study of the impoverished, the minority, and the Other. The anatomist also learns to dehumanize these individuals, who become the literal embodiment of their diseases or anatomical features; their identities do not extend beyond their respective illnesses or corpora. Upon death and subsequent dissection, the individual is no longer a person but a "corpse," or, in the words of Robert J. Terry, "materials," "flesh," or an "it." As illustrated in the above, Terry often objectified individuals. For example, in December of 1912, he contacted the National Incinerator Company in New York City, indicating that he wished to purchase an incinerator for "the disposal of remains from my anatomical laboratory." He was "desirous of information" about "the time required by one of your incinerites, say for example your portable No. 4, for the destruction of three and one-half bushels of damp material such as flesh" (Terry 1912, n.p.). Again, the individual is no longer a person, but materials and flesh. The person's identity has been separated from their remains.

In Western society, people's postmortem treatment is often symbolic of their social position amongst their kin and within their respective culture and community during their lifetime. Applying Whitehead's (2004, 60) poetics model to the postmortem processing of individuals in the Hamann-Todd and Terry collections illustrates how anatomization was a "socially constructive cultural performance" by the living to reinforce sociocultural beliefs about the dead, or as Anna Osterholtz indicates in the introduction to this book, a "discursive act, communicating cultural information through actions that create social identity and memory." The dissection of the persons that make up the Hamann-Todd and Terry collections, and their inclusion in these series when coupled with the structurally violent nature of anatomical acts, speaks volumes about the public's attitudes toward the indigent, the criminal, and the insane (Hodge and Nystrom, chapter 10, this volume; Nystrom 2014). They were not individuals that society wanted to remember. Their identities, like their bodies, were completely dissected and deconstructed, and ultimately disappeared. Recognizable tissues were stripped, removed, and macerated. No religious or social rituals that celebrated these persons in life were performed. The last vestige of their humanity, their names, were replaced with specimen numbers labeled on each of their bones, as one labels property. Thus, anatomical legislation and the way in which these individuals were processed postmortem came to embody societal attitudes of disdain directed at the destitute and "deviant" dead. The dissection and processing of individuals for medical learning or to amass in anatomical collections certainly subconsciously reinforced the social status of the poor, whilst simultaneous coalescing the power of medical elites. Consequently, the physical bodies of the destitute, deviant dead were dissected to illustrate social stratification and power.

Dissection was also a ritual for the anatomists, who utilized "social deviants" to advance their research agendas. However, it should be noted that Robert J. Terry and T. Wingate Todd were products of their times. Whilst they engaged in behavior that would be considered ethically questionable today, they did not break the law (legislation they often helped create). Much like their anatomical forebears, described earlier in this chapter, both men behaved in a manner consistent with contemporary anatomists of social position. The disconnect of identity from one's mortal remains was an integral part of their own anatomical education and speaks to broader issues of structural violence and oppression during the times in which these men studied and practiced anatomy. However, both Terry and Todd are redeemable in the sense that they pushed the boundaries of physical anthropology. They sought to comprehend the relationship between environment and biology and are among the first in the discipline to use a biocultural approach. Terry especially was interested in African American biology from an integral cultural and environmental perspective, something few modern biological anthropologists give him credit for. Terry and Todd's reliance on discriminative anatomical acts was a common practice by *all* anatomists during this era, regardless of race. Even William Montague Cobb, the nation's first black biological anthropologist, relied on similar legislation in the District of Columbia to amass his mostly African American anatomical collection.

CONCLUSIONS: RECONSTRUCTING IDENTITY AND ETHICALLY ENGAGING ANATOMICAL COLLECTIONS

Today, American anatomists are trained differently. Modern dissection does not bear the same cultural meanings and contexts that it did in the past. Nineteenth- and early twentieth-century medical students lived in a society in which ethical behavior was tied to social position and class; the impoverished lower classes, persons of color, and immigrants were not entitled to the same ethical treatment as those of the upper classes.

Gross anatomy still encompasses a rite of passage, as it is usually taken the first year of medical school. If the student has never seen a decedent, they confront this reality during the first week of class. They must learn to touch, cut, break, remove, hold, and comprehend every anatomical aspect of their donor/patient. However, unlike past pupils, modern medical students at most institutions are trained how to ethically engage with the individuals whose bodies will be the foundation of their anatomical knowledge. Instead of calling persons cadavers, they are referred to as donors or patients. Some programs encourage students to name their donors and appropriate ethical behavior is consistently reinforced in regard to handling and dissection of the individual. Furthermore, many medical schools now have memorial ceremonies that commemorate the donor's life and are attended by both students and family members, where stories are shared about how the donor impacted their lives.

If anatomy can change, certainly biological anthropology can do so as well. As the discipline moves forward, we must recognize that our anatomical collections comprise the most vulnerable, impoverished, and mentally ill citizens within their respective cities. These individuals, although legally dissected, did not consent to the anatomization of their bodies. The use of the poor, mentally handicapped, and other social deviants speaks to broader issues in American society tied to class and structural violence. Structural violence not only occurred at the level of legislation, but also with the physical act of dissection. As bioarchaeologist Kenneth Nystrom (2014, 1) has argued, "conceptualizing dissection as a manifestation of structural violence extends the concept to encapsulate postmortem manifestations of social inequality." He aptly points out that although a dead body is no longer living, that does not mean that a deceased individual should be void of a social identity, as the dead can still exist in a culture's social network (Hallam, Hockey, and Howarth 1999; Nystrom 2014). In many cultures, including those within America, death does not destroy identity (Scheper-Hughes 2011). Thus, to ethically engage with anatomical collections means to restore some form of identity to the individuals who make up these series. We must remember to acknowledge who they were and how their social origins resulted in their dissection. To silence the identities and experiences of these individuals continues the cycle of structural violence initiated over one hundred years ago. As bioarchaeologists, we are uniquely positioned to connect past injustices and disparities to current inequalities and be strong advocates for social justice. Anatomical collections should not be precluded from this. The ways in which these persons were processed provides us with insight into past power dynamics in American culture. However, the stories of individuals in anatomical collections also inform the political present as the social marginalization and structural violence they experienced still exists in American society. The anatomical laws that allowed for amassing these individuals are still in effect and continue to target the poor, criminals, and the mentally ill. Furthermore, for over 40 years, non-consensual harvesting of easily accessible body organs under presumed consent laws also disproportionately affect these vulnerable individuals. Presumed-consent legislation allows the state to assume that a person agreed to posthumous organ donation unless the individual or their family members objected prior to death (Orentlicher 2008). This legislation primarily targets persons whose bodies pass before medical examiners and coroners, especially those who die in accidents and homicides. Thus, by default, this legislation disproportionately targets African Americans, Latinos, and other vulnerable groups such as the homeless, especially in inner cities where these individuals are at greater risk of violent crimes, increasing the likelihood that their bodies will be presented to medical examiners or coroners (Goodwin 2001; Sharp 2002; Weinmeyer 2014). Leslie Sharp notes that 20 percent of organ donors in the United States are victims of violence, homicide, or suicide. The majority of organs that are harvested from minorities, low income, and at-risk groups are transplanted into middle- and high-income white individuals (Sharp 2002). Perhaps most alarming is the idea that young men of color are viewed as donors who can redeem their social worth by donating their body parts to valued members of society who are close to death (Sharp 2002). Unfortunately this illustrates that the social beliefs medical elites and the upper classes hold in regard to the poor, criminals, and the Other have not changed in over 200 years; their bodies continue to be exploited for anatomical capital. This is why it is important to reconstruct the identities of those in the Hamann-Todd and Terry collections, share their stories, and illustrate how their past informs our present as their experiences still resonate in the medical world today amongst minority and impoverished groups. Medicine can learn much from anthropology and anatomy, especially in regard to engaging with poor and disadvantaged groups who often mistrust medical professionals due to a consistent history of exploitation. Most important, in our own discipline of bioarchaeology, we should acknowledge these ethical issues as we move into a new social bioarchaeology, not only for our discipline, but as a means of social justice for those who are silenced and non-consensually dissected in the present day.

REFERENCES

Ball, John M. 1928. *The Sack-'Em-Up Men: An Account of the Rise and Fall of the Modern Resurrectionists*. London: Oliver and Boyd.

Cobb, William Montague. 1935. "Municipal History from Anatomical Records." *Scientific Monthly* 40 (2): 157–162.

Cobb, William Montague. 1959. "Thomas Wingate Todd, MB, ChB (Eng.), 1885–1938." *Journal of the American Medical Association* 51 (3): 233–246.

de Costa, Caroline, and Francesca Miller. 2011. "American Resurrection and the 1788 New York Doctors' Riot." *Lancet* 377 (9762): 292–293.

de la Cova, Carlina. 2010. "Cultural Patterns of Trauma among 19th-Century-Born Males in Cadaver Collections." *American Anthropologist* 112 (4): 589–606.

de la Cova, Carlina. 2011. "Race, Health, and Disease in 19th-Century-Born Males." *American Journal of Physical Anthropology* 144 (4): 526–537. doi: 10.1002/ajpa.21434.

de la Cova, Carlina. 2012. "Patterns of Trauma and Violence in 19th-Century-Born African American and Euro-American Females." *International Journal of Paleopathology* 2 (2): 61–68. doi: 10.1016/j.ijpp.2012.09.009.

de la Cova, Carlina. 2014. "The Biological Effects of Urbanization and in-Migration on 19th-Century-Born African Americans and Euro-Americans of Low Socioeconomic Status: An Anthropological and Historical Approach." In *Are Modern Environments Bad for Human Health? Revisiting the Second Epidemiological Transition*, edited by Molly K. Zuckerman, 243–266. Hoboken, NJ: Wiley-Blackwell.

General Court of Massachusetts. 1647. Records. ii, 175. Session beginning October 27, 1647.

Goodwin, Michele M. 2001. "Deconstructing Legislative Consent Law: Organ Taking, Racial Profiling and Distributive Justice." *Virginia Journal of Law and Technology* 6 (2): 2–49.

Hallam, Elizabeth, Jenny Hockey, and Glennys Howarth. 1999. *Beyond the Body: Death and Social Identity*. London: Routledge.

Halperin, Edward C. 2007. "The Poor, the Black, and the Marginalized as the Source of Cadavers in United States Anatomical Education." *Clinical Anatomy* 20: 489–495.

Hartwell, Edward M. 1880. "American Anatomy Acts." *Boston Medical and Surgical Journal* 103 (16): 361–363. doi: 10.1056/NEJM188010141031601.

Hildebrandt, Sabine. 2008. "Capital Punishment and Anatomy: History and Ethics of an Ongoing Association." *Clinical Anatomy* 21 (1): 5–14.

Humphrey, David C. 1973. "Dissection and Discrimination: The Social Origins of Cadavers in America, 1760–1915." *Bulletin of the New York Academy of Medicine* 49 (9): 819–827.

Hunt, David R., and John Albanese. 2005. "History and Demographic Composition of the Robert J. Terry Anatomical Collection." *American Journal of Physical Anthropology* 127 (4): 406–417. doi: 10.1002/ajpa.20135.

Hurren, Elizabeth T. 2012. *Dying for Victorian Medicine: English Anatomy and Its Trade in the Dead Poor, 1832 to 1929*. London: Palgrave Macmillan.

Hurren, Elizabeth T. 2013. "The Dangerous Dead: Dissecting the Criminal Corpse." *Lancet* 382 (9889): 302–303.

Jones-Kern, Kevin F. 1997. "T. Wingate Todd and the Development of Modern American Physical Anthropology, 1900–1940." PhD Dissertation, Department of Anthropology, Bowling Green University, Bowling Green, OH.

Ladenheim, Jules C. 1950. "The Doctors' Mob of 1788." *Journal of the History of Medicine and Allied Sciences* 5 (1): 23–43.

McCullough, David 2011. *The Greater Journey: Americans in Paris. New York*: Simon and Schuster.

Missouri. 2013. Missouri Revised Statutes, Chapter 194, Death—Disposition of Dead Bodies, Section 194.150.1, Disposal of Paupers' Bodies.

Muller, Jennifer L. 2006. "Trauma as a Biological Consequence of Inequality: A Biocultural Analysis of Washington DC's African American poor." PhD dissertation, Department of Anthropology, State University of New York at Buffalo.

Muller, Jennifer L., Kristen E. Pearlstein, and Carlina de la Cova. 2017. *The Bioarchaeology of Dissection and Autopsy in the United States*, edited by Kenneth C. Nystrom, 185–201. New York: Springer.

New York. 1792. *Laws of the State of New York Comprising the Constitution, and the Acts of the Legislature, since the Revolution, from the First to the Fifteenth Session, Inclusive in Two Volumes, Vol. II*. New York: Thomas Greenleaf.

New York Times. 1860. "City Poor Given up to Dissection by David Lynch." November 5, 1860.

Nystrom, Kenneth C. 2014. "The Bioarchaeology of Structural Violence and Dissection in the Nineteenth-Century United States." *American Anthropologist* 116 (4): 765–779.

Ohio. 1994. "Medical Colleges or Embalming Board May Receive Bodies for Study or Dissection—Procedure." Code 1713.34, effective 10-06-1994. Ohio Revised Code.

Orentlicher, David. 2008. "Presumed Consent to Organ Donation: Its Rise and Fall in the United States." *Rutgers Law Review* 61 (2): 295–331.

Pearlstein, Kristen E. 2015. "Health and the Huddled Masses: An Analysis of Immigrant and Euro-American Skeletal Health in 19th Century New York City." PhD Dissertation, Department of Anthropology, American University, Washington, DC.

Richardson, Ruth. 1987. *Death, Dissection and the Destitute*. London: Routledge and Kegan.

Richardson, Ruth. 2012. "Recruiting the Unclaimed." *Lancet* 380: 1637–1638.

Rosenberg, Charles E. 1987. *The Care of Strangers: The Rise of America's Hospital System*. New York: Basic Books.

Sappol, Michael. 2002. *A Traffic of Dead Bodies: Anatomy and Embodied Social Identity in Nineteenth-Century America*. Princeton, NJ: Princeton University Press.

Savitt, Todd Lee. 1978. *Medicine and Slavery: The Diseases and Health Care of Blacks in Antebellum Virginia*. Urbana: University of Illinois Press.

Savitt, Todd Lee. 1982. "The Use of Blacks for Medical Experimentation and Demonstration in the Old South." *Journal of Southern History* 48: 331–348.

Scheper-Hughes, Nancy. 2011. "Dissection: The Body in Tatters—Dismemberment, Dissection, and the Return of the Repressed." In *A Companion to the Anthropology of the Body and Embodiment*, edited by Frances E. Mascia-Lees, 172–206. Malden, MA: Wiley-Blackwell.

Sharp, Lesley A. 2002. "Denying Culture in the Transplant Arena: Technocratic Medicine's Myth of Democratization." *Cambridge Quarterly of Healthcare Ethics* 11: 142–150.

Skloot, Rebecca. 2010. *The Immortal Life of Henrietta Lacks*. New York: Crown Publishing Group.

Statutes at Large. 1786. Statutes at Large from the Ninth Year of the Reign of King George the Second, To the Twenty-fifth Year of the Reign of King George the Second. London: Charles Eyre and Andrew Strahan.

St. Louis Globe-Democrat. 1887. "Students and 'Stiffs': How Dissecting Material Is Utilized in a New York Medical College." April 3, 1887.

Terry, Robert J. 1912. Robert J. Terry to the National Incinerator Company, December 16, 1912. In *Robert James Terry Papers*, edited by Missouri History Museum Archives. St. Louis, MO: Missouri History Museums.

Terry, Robert J. 1913. "Title." Robert James Terry Papers, St. Louis, MO.

Terry, Robert J. n.d. "Title." Robert James Terry Papers, St. Louis, MO.

Trotter, Mildred. 1981. "Robert J. Terry (1871–1966)." *American Journal of Physical Anthropology* 56 (4): 503–508.

Warner, John Harley. 1998. *Against the Spirit of System: The French Impulse in Nineteenth-Century American Medicine*. Baltimore, MD: Johns Hopkins University Press.

Washington, Harriett A. 2007. *Medical Apartheid: The Dark History of Medical Experimentation on Black Americans from Colonial Times to the Present*. New York: Anchor Books.

Watkins, Rachel J. 2007. "Knowledge from the Margins: W. Montague Cobb's Pioneering Research in Biocultural Anthropology." *American Anthropologist* 109 (1): 186–196. doi: 10.1525/aa.2007.109.1.186.

Watkins, Rachel J., and J. Muller. 2015. "Repositioning the Cobb Human Archive: The Merger of a Skeletal Collection with Its Texts." *American Journal of Human Biology* 27 (1): 41–50. doi: 10.1002/ajhb.22650.

Weinmeyer, Richard. 2014. "The Racially Unequal Impact of the US Organ Procurement System." *Virtual Mentor* 16 (6): 461–466.

Whitehead, Neil L. 2004. "On the Poetics of Violence." In *Violence*, edited by Neil L. Whitehead, 55–78. Santa Fe, NM: SAR Press.

12

Conclusion

Poetic Amplifications and Extensions, How to Process the Dead

ERIC J. HAANSTAD

In my first conscious memory, I am an observer and participant in a kinship-based social death-processing event. The funeral of my great grandmother, "Gammy" Inga Jordeth, initiated my processual consciousness. In the summer of 1978 at three years old, I am standing on the steps of the Goodhue Church in the North Dakota plains where my great grandfather served as a pastor before his death from pneumonia in 1923, leaving Inga to raise six children before her death. The apocryphal country church among the wheat fields featured in the *November Rain* Guns N' Roses' video is a hyperreal simulation of the Goodhue's sacred architecture. I am observing Gammy's open-casket visitation service as my cousin asks her mother, "Is she dead?" I do not remember the specific appearance of my great grandmother's body, but I remember her presence, mirroring Beth Scaffidi's observation in this volume (chapter 2) that "the dead body is agentive in its own right." My aunt quietly affirms my cousin's inquiry with a nod, confirming to us what death looks like as an embodied possibility.

Inga Jordeth's finished wooden casket then lowers into the ground by a mechanistic system of pulleys. This fleeting snapshot series of initiating memories documents a family death ritual. Before this moment, I presumably had experiences, but I am not aware of them in my present memories. After this potent event of processing our dead kin, my sentient experience of life began. As a searing social event, this funeral is both meaningfully profound and culturally reflective of American death-processing as highly preservative and mechanistic in its core practices. In this way, it offers a contemporary extension of Dilpreet Basanti's analysis that, "the

DOI: 10.5876/9781646420612.c012

sarcophagus we see here suggests an understanding of Christian mortuary treatment that privileges the preservation of the individual body over the creation of social memory" (chapter 6, this volume). Although Inga's funeral diverges from this analysis in that it created strong social memories in addition to preserving an individual Christian body, it confirms that the body transcends its mere shell. The realities generated by her presence as kin, ancestor, immigrant, Norwegian, American, and Dakotan emerge from her resonant social body.

The contributors to this volume demonstrate this vital generation of social and individual memory and meaning through the potent presence of the dead. These archaeologists and bioanthropologists reveal vast diversities of mortuary processing across time. They analyze bodies that are both configurable canvases in poetic practice (Roselyn Campbell, chapter 7) and active agents in the creation of shared cultural meaning (Scaffidi, chapter 2). As powerful and contested mediations of cultural performance, human remains reflect multiple, often contradictory, approaches to individual life and social death (Kyle Waller and Adrianne Offenbecker, chapter 3; Basanti, chapter 6). The violent cacophony of cut marks, binding, burning, evisceration, anatomizing, embalming, mutilation, disarticulation, dismemberment, decapitation, defleshing, scalping, trophy-taking, blunt trauma, and ritual sacrifice insists that method matters in mortuary processing (Campbell, chapter 7). These choreographies of death generate shared litanies of meaning and create vibrant linkages in warfare, exchange, politics, kinship, cosmology, architecture, materiality, symbolism, and other culturally specific systems (Debra Martin and Anna Osterholtz, chapter 5). Concepts of poetics readily demonstrate the extraction of social meaning from violent practice. Crucially, these poetics also amplify and extend the cultural impact of shared meaningful violence. To reflect on the overarching question addressed by the contributors to this volume, "why do we manipulate bodies?" the chapters offer a united demonstration of the key extensions and amplifications of meaning encoded in the poetics concept. In this often-overlooked operant definition, Whitehead specifies that the poetics of violence is about "mapping how cultural conceptions of violence amplify and extend the social force of violent acts and how these acts produce shared violent meanings" (2007, 6). As a generative social performance, the poetics of body-processing amplify shared meaning and extend meaningful death across space and time.

CREATION, PRESERVATION, AND DESTRUCTION: THE *TRIMŪRTI* OF BODY-PROCESSING

The myriad practices of mortuary-processing described in the preceding chapters are manifested in both corporeal and symbolic forms. The symbolism of processing death, like violent symbolism, tends to juxtapose themes of order and disorder. These poetics extend the communicative potency of death-processing and increase the cultural impact of violent practice. In this way, processing the dead produces meaning while simultaneously intensifying the force of its social messages. For example, in the Andean ethnohistoric conceptions described by Scaffidi, heads and hands contain the essence of personhood while eyes, tongues, and mouths are powerful venues for enemy spirits. Inserting, manipulating, or destroying these bodily locations harness them for cultural creation, maintenance, and destruction (Scaffidi, chapter 2). I focus here on the cyclical roles that generate, preserve, and dismantle the social order, the *Trimūrti* of death-processing.

As a socially generative performance, violent poetics amplify how processing the dead creates new cultural forms. In this volume's most recent case studies, Megan Perry and Anna Osterholtz (chapter 9) describe how a new medical elite class emerged from anatomical interventions on cadavers. The creation of new medical schools and initiatory rituals created the Hamann-Todd collections from the institutionally dehumanized and dissected poor. The emergence of the new medical elite prompted the relocation of Harvard Medical School from Cambridge to Boston in search of a larger supply of conveniently available bodies from the city's Almshouse (Carlina de la Cova, chapter 11). Through scientific willingness to meddle with the dead, this socially generative moment paraded as a cosmological triumph by depicting the emergent social elite as heroic conquerors over dark superstition. In a related case, Scaffidi's analysis in chapter 2 of the Peruvian Majes Valley depicts the taking and making of feline trophy heads as socially generative across physical and spiritual realms. The ritual production and image creation of trophy heads transformed warrior victims into culturally productive agents for trophy-taking communities.

In this way, violent performances that accumulated feline heads and manipulated the dead created new social meaning through the generative act of bodily reconfiguration. The violent poetics of these acts and imagery amplified the cultural force of these new forms of meaning. Simultaneously, trophy-processers reinforced and extended messages of political dominance while mediating the liminality of the living and the dead (Scaffidi, chapter 2). In other contexts, violent spectacles of dismembered sacrificial burials and the social performance to public crematory rites also expanded the social order. The regenerative properties of mass killing, bodily destruction, and trophy-taking highlight violent performances as culturally renewing extensions of a groups' dominance over others (Martin and Osterholtz chapter 5).

In conjunction with the socially generative capacities of these burial trophies, feline iconographs, and corpse fragmentations, body-processing also sustains cultural orders. As violent performance, processing the dead reinforces and maintains the social order through poetic acts that extend this preservative role. At this second vertex of the processing *Trimūrti*, ritual modification and violent performance can sustain social groups threatened by resource scarcity (Kristin Kuckelman, chapter 4). Similarly, through intensified crematory investment in southern Arizona and the proxy houses of the dead in Çatalhöyük, Turkey, mortuary rituals reinforce social ties through performative expansion of daily practice (Marin Pilloud et al., chapter 8). As demonstrated in these repositories of memory, postmortem processing amplifies meaning among shared social structures (Basanti, chapter 6; Pilloud et al., chapter 8). It harnesses sensory difference and intensifies cooperative practice, fostering inclusivity among social groups. Such processing deemphasizes individual importance while it expands group networks across regional space. The poetic amplification of mortuary processing maintains and expands social ties through acts of dynamic cohesion.

Beyond social reinforcement, the poetics of processing provides vital augmentations of social control. This conjoined controlling dualism is clearly evident in Waller and Offenbecker's account (chapter 3) of the two cooperative and political death cults in Paquimé, Mexico. In this case, the aggrandizing rituals of a political cult operated in tandem with an agricultural fertility cult to maintain community norms and reinforce elite status. Violent spectacles of bodily trauma and mortuary manipulation institutionalized inequality. Haphazard public offerings of defleshed and dismembered enemies were dropped on top of venerated elite burials. These performances of symbolic dominance and political terror served as a potent source of social control. In this way, political ancestral cults and cooperative fertility rituals worked in tandem to enforce social orders through death-processing. The amplifying attributes of death poetics extended the cultural force of performative spectacles that normalized and maintained social hierarchy.

While maintaining social control, these preservative death poetics pervaded cultural and political life. In the Puebloan worlds described by Martin and Osterholtz, warfare, violent performance, and witch-killing is integral to enforcing social conformity. As a perceptual production, violence and warfare amplify the connective intimacy between perpetrators, victims, and witnesses. It blurs distinctions among this triangular relationship while reinforcing hierarchies of control (Martin and Osterholtz, chapter 5). Canvases of human bodies, even when encased in sarcophagi, enact the social order and extend its meanings (Basanti, chapter 6). In ancient Egypt, divine sacrifice, punitive display, and public execution maximized the social control of ruling authorities. The "smiting Pharaohs" punished enemies of the state with foot-beating, drowning, burning, flaying, impaling, and beheading in calculated public displays that amplified their social, political, economic, and cosmological will. Using the human body and violent imagery as media, these criminal-justice displays preserved the social orders of the ruling cults and extended them into the afterlife (Campbell, chapter 7).

As a putative apparatus that reinforces social control, death-processing also appears in nineteenth-century US anatomy laws that link poverty to punishment. The American legal apparatus transformed medical-school grave-robbers into legal beneficiaries of social welfare reform by bringing a steady supply of cadavers from the poorhouse to the dissecting table. As a crime deterrent, anatomical dissection marked the bodies of the poor with visible signs of their indigence. Medical dissection extended Bentham's putative model and sustained the American political economic order (Perry and Osterholtz, chapter 9). The structural violence against almshouse inmates and the dehumanizing desacralization of African Americans ushered medical students through dissection as a rite of passage that preserved the elite medical social order (Christina Hodge and Kenneth Nystrom, chapter 10). In Neolithic Anatolia, mortuary treatments also reinforced cultural stability over time through ritual repetition before social groups fragmented and abandoned these sustaining death practices (Pilloud et al., chapter 8).

Just as the sustaining role of body-processing reinforces the social order among perpetrators, victims, and witnesses, this triangular relationship also links its preservative, degenerative, and regenerative capacities (Kuckelman, chapter 4). As cultural destroyer, the third vertex of the processing *Trimūrti* expresses the amplification of violent communication through symbolic overkill and extreme violence. Like magic and sorcery, the non-monolithic category of violence is simultaneously regenerative and destructive (Martin and Osterholtz, chapter 5). Extreme processing creates social memory through the violent destruction of Others, linking this triangle's vertices through multifaceted and interrelated poetics. State-sanctioned violence amplifies bodily destruction through overkill and traumatic mass spectacles. From contemporary tragedies in Rwanda, Bosnia, and Sierra Leone to the archaeological, osteological, and historical horrors of this volume, violent body-manipulation inspires mass fear and extends the social force of collective destruction (Campbell, chapter 7).

As witnessed in the Sacred Ridge bodies, where only a single articulated joint remained, the complete annihilation of the dead through systematic disassembly demonstrates the totalizing political amplification of extreme violence (Martin and Osterholtz, chapter 5). The kratophanic witch-killings of Puebloan and Athapaskan groups required similar complete bodily destruction, creating decapitated, traumatized, and fragmented skeletons that ensured the annihilation of the socially aberrant dead through the sanctioned multiplication of abhorrent acts (Waller and Offenbecker, chapter 3). These symbolic performances and violent spectacles were specifically designed to engender mass trauma in survivors and witnesses, with acts such as eye mutilation that symbolically showcased and simultaneously embodied the total domination of enemy groups. As Neil Whitehead repeatedly told his students, "just because it's symbolic, doesn't mean it's not real" (personal communication, 2001). This profound double-negative directly applies to the traumatic symbolism of violent eye-mutilation and the extreme violence represented in this volume.

AMPLIFYING THE DEAD ACROSS SPACE, MATERIALITY, AND TIME

From the extreme violence of complete disarticulation to the social transformations of crematory ritual, death poetics amplify shared social meaning across space and time. Multiscalar communication of meaningful violence and mortuary practice extends across social distance between individuals, households, communities, and regional groups (Waller and Offenbecker, chapter 3). Widespread transformation from burial to intensified cremation shifted funerary variability to widespread homogeneity across Southwestern regional networks. Similar transregional expansions occurred as interpueblo warfare, trophy-taking, and performative assault intensified (Kuckelman, chapter 4). These regional amplifications also crafted stronger alliances capable of summoning hundreds of neighboring warriors to decimate entire villages (Martin and Osterholtz, chapter 5). Through totalizing mass attacks, widespread execution spectacles, or subtle social transformations from Neolithic to Chalcolithic burials, many of the practices described in this volume represent vital transregional extensions of meaning across space (Martin and Osterholtz, chapter 5; Pilloud et al., chapter 8).

These spatial projections are mirrored in material architecture from effigy mounds to T-shaped ballcourts, great kivas, reused tomb-spaces, and other ritual buildings that reinforced and intensify shared meaning across communities and regions (Waller and Offenbecker, chapter 3; Kuckelman, chapter 4; Perry and Osterholtz, chapter 9). Emergent forms of ritual architecture or allegiances to regional sacrificial cults amplified the shared resonance of death practices in material space. The almshouse, dissection theater, and anatomical museum extended the state's corporeal control through architecture while the cemetery extended the individualized embalmed death cult by spatial design. The anatomical theatre with its dissection table and arc lighting provided a public space to transcend Victorian taboos about sacred bodily integrity (Perry and Osterholtz, chapter 9). As Basanti (chapter 6) writes, following Mol (2002), the dissecting table bifurcated bodily reality into corpses that are simultaneously social beings and malfunctioning machines. Similarly, the vaulted skylights, glass cases, and public architecture of the Holden museum extended the visibility of the state's anatomical specimens while intensifying the hierarchical separation between the public sphere and medical elite (Perry and Osterholtz, chapter 9).

The proliferation of ritual spaces, sacred structures, and defensive architectures work in tandem with other forms of material design to amplify the communicative capacities of death manipulation. In an example from the northern San Juan, Kuckelman (chapter 4) associates violent performance with the inconsiderate placement of altered skull fragments outside of a special-use doorway. These placements exemplify the conjoining of architecture and body-processing in material poetics. Alternate architectural and processing poetics are also present in elite offerings, such as the robust male placed deliberately in symbolic sexual congress on a specialized wooden shelf in the House of the Dead in Paquimé, Mexico (Waller and Offenbecker, chapter 3). Similarly, widespread investigations of the Northern Stelae Field, based on the proliferation and persistence of the Aksum stelae, are a testament to the ability of potent architectural forms to amplify other practices of death-processing (Basanti, chapter 6).

Poetic amplifications through material design, space, and architecture are also evident in the phalange necklace, trophy skulls, and musical remains placed in Paquimé's unique cross-shaped ritual space. The circular drill holes designed for ceiling suspension found in these remains further enhance the visibility of the meaningful confluences of architecture, materiality, and body-processing (Waller and Offenbecker, chapter 3). Radical variability in the material design of corpse manipulation demonstrates the enduring vibrancy of these poetics. In San Juan, trophy scalps were designed for portability and durability, maximizing the shared symbolism of military prowess and regional prestige in cosmological projections of cultural dominance (Kuckelman, chapter 4). The shamanic warrior belts of feline hunters also demonstrate these material amplifications, extending the social presence of trophy-makers beyond their victims' villages and into the afterlife (Scaffidi, chapter 2).

The transmutations of trophy-takers into ancestral heroes and spiritual beings at Uraca amplified the social and cosmological force of their acts through mergers of ritual processing and material design. These Andean design components incorporated practical and ritual considerations, such as the sealing of the mouth, which enhanced the trophies' portability while simultaneously reversing continence and containing avenging spirits within the head. The removal of the eyes might also signal similar ritualized practicalities of trophy-head processing's materiality. This symbolic broadcast may represent the proliferation of the red-glowing eye themes prevalent in the mythic spotted felines of Nazca art and cosmology (Scaffidi, chapter 2). The trophy heads' multivalent design and the symbolic power provides ample demonstration of the subtly agentive corpse. Like Basanti's opening reference (chapter 6) to the Thai abbot's observations in Burdett's (2007) detective fiction, the constant transformation of materiality and personality is actively present in all bodies, living and dead. Many emic realities present in this volume posit the living material sentience of the dead.

In this way, the processing of the dead is a ritual technology mediated through material practice. Marshall McLuhan conceptualizes media as any technology that extends human perception (1994). Scaffidi's analysis (chapter 2) of Uraca trophy-head ritual highlights their ability to transform human users, access extrasensory abilities, and broadcast cultural forces of shared meaning across time and space. Like McLuhan's typefaces and telegraphs, the heads and the technologies described in the preceding chapters are media. Their mediated extensions of perception are sources of amplifying poetics.

These mediated productions can include execration rituals involving statuaries, figurines, and images that enact violence and death-processing through expressive representation, amplifying the shared meaning of material acts into social imaginaries (Campbell, chapter 7; Pilloud et al., chapter 8). The reinforcement of social memory through the recirculation of remains extends the shared meaning of burial rituals across time. In Pilloud and her colleagues' account (chapter 8) of neolithic Anatolia, this amplification maintained social houses through a living archive that extends the shared remembrance of the dead through time. In monumental productions like the Royal Tomb at Ur, sacrificial killings were deliberately designed to generate potent temporal moments reverberating into eternity (Campbell, chapter 7). The material production and design of mausoleums included rock symbolism, ritual ware, and inscribed stelae, and extended the Aksumite ancestral house across time into the present through perpetual regenerations of the living and the dead (Basanti, chapter 6).

Forms of performative violence including trophy-taking, corpse mutilation, and bodily display extend pervasively and persistently across time (Kuckelman, chapter 4). The symbolic tableaus of body-processing and violent spectacles create lasting messages, reinforcing their cultural logics across multiple generations (Campbell, chapter 7; Martin and Osterholtz, chapter 5). Unique forms of corpse fragmentation resonated as regional codes across the American Southwest with minimal variation over vast temporal periods (Martin and Osterholtz, chapter 5). This extension through time informs the emotionally meaningful resonance of specific violent acts, transmitting social memory through persistent mortuary practice (Pilloud et al., chapter 8). This temporal amplification into the afterlife often serves as the primary reason for burial processing, sacrificial violence, and divinely mandated punishment (Campbell, chapter 7).

As these examples from the American Southwest to the Egyptian valleys indicate, death-processing extends across time and beyond the terrestrial. These metaphysical amplifications routinely originate in the physical, as in the Northern San

Juan region, where ritual architecture and the disposal of enemy remains amplified Puebloan regional authority to influence supernatural worlds (Kuckelman, chapter 4). Similarly, through ancestral veneration rites, Aksumite social houses persisted not only across time, but also into dream realms and across thresholds of life and death (Basanti, chapter 6). Cosmological extension to extraphysical realms could reciprocate intervention back to the terrestrial as divine rainfall or supernatural favor (Kuckelman, chapter 4). Culturally meaningful violence could also reach across eternity into spiritual realms as perpetual punishment that precluded victims' transit into the afterlife (Campbell, chapter 7). From the "otherworldly signs" of grotesque anatomical specimens to the obliterating permanency of definitive massacres, these bodily manipulations amplify shared meaning across time, space, and dimensions beyond (Martin and Osterholtz, chapter 5; Perry and Osterholtz, chapter 9).

WHY DO *KANAIMÀ* MANIPULATE BODIES AND DID ED GEIN EAT THE DEAD?

The interdimensional properties of death-processing indicate its potency and suggest reasons for its practice. Action, imagery, and materiality in protracted violent engagement create experiential exchange between perceived social distinctions of victim, perpetrator, witness, ancestor, human, and animal (Scaffidi, chapter 2). Corporeal domination of enemies through ritual modification reciprocally extends the communicative exchange of protracted warfare to vast non-corporeal audiences (Kuckelman, chapter 4). Poetic amplifications encompass the social imaginary, as the practical folklore of the Night Doctors who kidnap African Americans for medical experiments illustrates (de la Cova, chapter 11). The entrenched social logic of these nineteenth-century imaginaries in physical reality is similarly evident in mortuary ritual. Petra's funerary feasts, for example, link the living kin of the *marzēḥā* to the deceased in intimate physical performances that intensify the social realities of kinship beyond death (Perry and Osterholtz, chapter 9).

Nevertheless, as the *kanaimà* complex referred to in the introduction to this volume shows, much of our death-processing is not about the dead at all and is clearly focused on manipulating the living. In Whitehead's last interview, he continues to connect his impending death directly to occult manipulations of *kanaimà* practitioners who poisoned him in perceived retribution for his archaeological disturbance of a *kanaimà* burial bundle. As Neil said, "they put something in me that I can never take out" (Janik and Whitehead 2012). It is instructive that the *kanaimà* complex incorporates protracted physical violence and assault while the victim is living. The practice includes ritual poisoning and the insertion of a spice packet into the victim's rectum to reverse continence. This process initiates active bodily putrification, which produces the *maba* or "body honey" in the abdomen of a victim after death and burial. These incorporative elements are the means for material production, while the *maba* (sucked through a hollow reed that is inserted into the interred corpse's abdominal cavity) is the ends. Thus, the *kanaimà* complex is also a technology of processing, one that exudes extreme cultural difference in its violent poetics, as dissociatively unpalatable as suicide bombing and serial killing (Whitehead 2002).

As these extreme cases illustrate, the preceding chapters converge thematically on the tension between legitimacy and illegitimacy. Socially legitimate community-based violence provides a temporal and spatial extension of cultural logic through ritualized performances, sacred endorsements, and social sanctions (Kuckelman, chapter 4). Violent communication, including the destructive display of enemy bodies, provides a public venue that amplifies social legitimacy and political authority (Kuckelman, chapter 4). This poetic extension of legitimacy continues in the more recent transformations of anatomization from the transgressive illegal fringe to a state-sanctioned legal marker of the political and economic order (Hodge and Nystrom, chapter 10). Indeed, from the dissected skeletal display of mass murderers to the criminalization of the deviant poor, both the University of Edinburgh Anatomy Museum and the Harvard Medical School benefited from anatomization's legitimizing extensions of social control (Hodge and Nystrom, chapter 10; de la Cova, chapter 11). Physical anthropology emerged from the conversion of social deviance and structural vulnerability into new sources of legitimate intellectual capital. Simultaneously, the state-sanctioned legitimacy of anatomical law transformed the illegitimate moral deviancy of grave-robbing and dissection into the vaunted ritual performance of medical elites (de la Cova, chapter 11).

Like the medical grave-robbers who preceded his contemporary example, the infamous Ed Gein was a much more prolific processor and body snatcher than a mass murderer or serial killer. The prototype for *Texas Chainsaw Massacre*, *Psycho*, *Silence of the Lambs*, and countless other media representations, he confessed to more than forty nocturnal visits to collect bodies of the dead from graveyards of Plainfield, Wisconsin. He also killed two women, whom he decapitated, dressed like deer, and mutilated in dozens of ritually specific bodily manipulations. In this way, Gein is a processor of the dead first and a killer of the living second. His burial desecrations highlight how the poetics of processing, like the poetics of violence, occur within visceral cultural faultlines of legitimacy and illegitimacy. Like the grave-robbing medical practitioners described in this volume's final chapters, the processing of nineteenth-century anatomizers was only transformed from grisly sacrilege to societal sanction via the legitimacy of legal authority. Similarly, the sanctioned and culturally legitimate preparation and preservation processes of contemporary mortuary programs in the United States could be interpreted as illegitimate sacrilege when viewed through other interpretive frameworks of processing death.

Gein's notoriety as a "ravenous cannibal" is also instructive in demonstrating the poetic amplifications that accompany narratives and practices of death-processing. For instance, police investigators found Bernice Worden's entrails on the kitchen floor wrapped in newspaper along with her heart "in a plastic bag in front of Gein's pot-bellied stove" (Schechter 1989). Rather than highlight how closely this evidence of body-processing resembled dressing deer innards prior to disposal, popular folklore and media narratives immediately intensified the case's cannibalistic connotations by incorrectly transferring her heart to a pot on the stove (United Press 1957). Subsequent film characters based on Gein, from Leatherface to Lechter, repeatedly amplify this provocative association of cannibalism with serial killing. Gein's inverted status as a serial killer and cannibal rather than a grave-robber and corpse manipulator thus demonstrates the social predilection for the amplification of death-processing.

This case raises unsettling questions about the historical and contemporary fascination with cannibalism and the evidentiary leaps required to prove its supposed prevalence in the bioarchaeological record. In the cooking, burning, fracturing, and pot polishing of Paquimé death-cult remains, the extent or existence of cannibalistic practices touted by Casserino and others does not necessarily emerge from evidence of extreme violence (2009). In the monstrous example from Plainfield, even if Worden's heart had been found luridly cooking in a pot on a stove rather than in its actual location in a plastic bag on the kitchen floor in front of a pot-bellied stove, would this evidence have proved anthropophagy? Similarly, as some of the contributors in this volume readily point out, cannibalistic practice, particularly its gustatory, survival, and nutritional forms, requires physical evidence that human remains are often unable to provide (Waller and Offenbecker, chapter 3). While contributors to this volume provide admission that evidence of cannibalism is not sufficiently robust or widespread, some are willing to make the evidentiary leap towards its gustatory forms (Kuckelman, chapter 4). Although anthropophagous performances can be ritualized elements of extreme processing, there are key evidentiary differences between extreme disarticulation and dietary consumption (Kuckelman, chapter 4; Martin and Osterholtz, chapter 5). To determine whether archaeological victims are "possibly eaten" might require further introspection among the social imaginaries of more familiar cannibalistic cults of the Western zeitgeist.

Arens's observations are applicable here, that for many Western observers "the obvious preference runs in the direction of transforming those suspected of being cannibals into confirmed ritual endocannibals and, in the twentieth century, into gustatory exocannibals on a grand scale . . . The idea and image of cannibalism expands with time and the intellectual appetite" (1979, 165). While Whitehead also vehemently refuted overzealous archaeological claims of widespread anthropophagy and the vociferous proponents of the "protein debate," this volume admirably extends his ideas beyond the grave. Indeed, some of his last work highlights this transcendental moment beyond terrestrial experience, when we become "human no more" (Whitehead and Wesch 2012). Concurrently, in a 2008 dream, I am among others in an underground Seattle war room. One of my colleagues reluctantly triggers the nuclear button. As the doomed descending sound of an impending missile grows louder, Neil tells us, "You don't want to be eking out a postapocalyptic existence. You want to be here, at ground zero." The dreamworld fades to black and his sonorant disembodied voice says, "There, that's better."

Whitehead would repeatedly say that life is preparation for death. It follows that the act of living is an attempt to process death. In Lakota, *hoka hey* does not mean "it's a good day to die" but rather something closer to "onward." The phrase thus shares more in common with the Heart Sūtra mantra of Mahāyāna Buddhism in Sanskrit, "*gate gate pāragate pārasaṃgate*" ("gone, gone, gone beyond, gone utterly beyond"). Is following this infinite path not how to process death? Like forms of religious ritual and martial practice, death is a doorway. Physical and cosmological manipulations of this portal sustain continual cultural exchange between the living and the dead.

FUTURE TRAJECTORIES: RENDERING, REDUCTION, AND REFLEXIVITY

The preceding chapters' thematic convergence on the amplifying qualities of poetic processing suggest continual trajectories of intensification. Radical expansion compels anthropological researchers to reach further, charting multidimensional future projections. Before exploring how these trajectories show paths to rendering beyond the human, it is useful to track the trajectories of its opposite. What do cases of deamplification, instability, and collapse of death-processing practices suggest about the human and nonhuman future?

Basanti's evocative analysis (chapter 6) of social disruption among the pre-Christian Aksumites presaged by the fall of Stela 1 signals the multidimensional complexities of deamplification as a poetic reversal (7). The stela's vital living connection to the Aksumite social house meant that its material destruction was tied to social death. Its collapse unraveled familial orders, disrupting the pre-Christian burial poetics that extended group relationships through shared performance. During a time of radical social change, the dramatic fall of the stela accelerated the rift between two mutually exclusive burial traditions. The tensions between these competing ways of life and death show how poetic amplification interrelates with its opposite through disruptive upheavals in burial practices.

Dynamic tensions of deamplification as the destructive engines for intensified poetics of death-processing are also seen in this volume's more contemporary cases of anatomization. As anatomical processors continued to pursue greater levels of separation, deconstruction, and numeration, these practices required continual reductions and eventual disappearances of human bodies (de la Cova, chapter 11). From the anatomical table to acid-proof tanks, dissection reduced bodies to cadavers and then to individual "soft parts," bone pieces, and scientific collections. In the process, the intensification of anatomical science erased individual memory and social identity as bodies dissolved and catalogues reduced them to dissected objects (de la Cova, chapter 11). The bureaucratic triumphs of anatomization required equally dramatic reductions in the desecrated bodies of the destitute and deviant.

Like the interdependent relationship of processing poetics where amplification is fueled by active reduction, these chapters also suggest an underlying interdependence of human-animal dynamics. Despite the absence of occurrences of the word "render" as a term of reference in the preceding volume, dialectical interspecies dynamics frequently appear. This thematic reoccurrence indicates the inclusive potential of rendering as an analytic concept along with death-processing. For example, Martin and Osterholtz (chapter 5) present intimate human-animal relationships in death, such as the extreme processing of Sacred Ridge, where dog and human remains were mixed extensively to dehumanize and de-identify the interred (6). These interspecies mergers suggest that rendering could be productively considered along with rendering as a category of practice.

Drawing from examples of deer-mask shapeshifting in Mesolithic Britain, were-jaguars in Amerindian societies, and mortuary bearhood in Upper Paleolithic Siberia, the processed bodies of humans are routinely commingled with the rendered bodies of animals (Conneller 2004; Vivieros de Castro 1998; Losey et al. 2013). These death practices blur distinctions between human-animal categories and bridge divisions between rendering and processing as well. In addition to Jack the Ripper's possible slaughterhouse rendering background, other examples from this vibrant literature include the deliberate mortuary comingling of humans with sharks, foxes, and many other animals (Betts, Blair, and Black 2012; Durgun 2017; Knight and Watson 2017; Maher et al. 2011). Basanti's key social distinctions between the chemically signaled body removal of ant colonies and group-oriented human mortuary rituals begin to appear more fluid as human-animal relationships intertwine. Thus, many of these authors reveal the potential connections between rendering and processing through the blurring of human-animal distinctions and the becoming of nonhuman persons among animals, materials, and landscapes (Basanti, chapter 6).

In a curious moment on the grounds of Santa Fe's School for Advanced Research (also known as El Delirio), I learned that Whitehead purposefully avoided the SAR pet cemetery and the mortuary stone memorials for its breeders and benefactors, the White sisters. In this strange irony of funerary materiality, the Dark Shaman himself would not go there, recalling finding three pennies that surely signaled occult malfeasance in the carved stone mausoleum dedicated to Martha White's memory. This Southwestern cemetery thus contains the confluence of animal-human interaction in the large Irish Wolfhound graves, the mortuary memorialization of carved stone statuary, and the unlikely ritual taboos of a self-professed "student of the dark side" (personal communication, New Orleans, LA 2002).

While assembling this conclusion, productive human-animal linkages in processing and rendering unexpectedly emerged during a recent applicable experience with a plate of spicy crawfish in a local Asian restaurant. Encountering my order of unshelled small crustaceans in a publicly exposed dining location, the waiter asked me to confirm if I knew what I was ordering. Based on previous experience in Southeast Asia, I deferred to social conventions in consuming the inside of each shrimp or crab head, although the taste of crustacean brains was not my favorite. Thus, my American Midwest rendering process was crafted in symbolic response to the waiter and from performative necessity to the crustaceans. I felt a subtle need to honor each crawfish by at least opening its head and making a symbolic gesture towards sucking the brains along with each claw leg. I systematically disassembled each body, breaking it with teeth or technology, although this intense action yielded little to no meat.

At the risk of unintentionally downplaying the historic horrors of human trauma with the routine practices of human carnivorism, I experienced an undeniable resonance with the research in this volume. Cases of extreme processing such as at Sacred Ridge, where "in only one instance was an articulated joint recovered" (Martin and Osterholtz, chapter 5), suggest further questions about intentionality. The Sacred Ridge perpetrators certainly operated on a radically divergent set of symbols, assumptions, and motivations than contemporary settlers like me. Nevertheless, my mundane experience with extreme processing of Midwestern crawfish suggests an overarching attempt to honor the dead. At minimum, these cases seem to both acknowledge our victims' inherent value and meaning through as near complete disassembly as we could accomplish. Simultaneously, we both perhaps shared our social performances as direct and indirect perpetrators with victims and witnesses who also participate in acts of processual rendering.

If poetic amplification is one of the key features that lead us to render the dead, where do these processes lead? All of the bodily, burial, and funerary practices described in this volume culminate in our own participation, witnessing and processing the dead through research and writing. Bioarchaeology is also processing, projecting shared meanings of death into the present. Its methods are coterminous and interrelated with the rendering of death. Just as victims and witnesses share violent productions with perpetrators, anthropological observers and bioarchaeological researchers also produce cultural productions of meaning. Importantly, they amplify and extend these productions into the present across centuries from the moment these acts of violence occurred (Waller and Offenbecker, chapter 3). From the physical variables of cut marks, burned bone, and broken bodies, bioanthropologists invoke the contextually nuanced meanings, exchanges, and symbols that inscribe violent death and extend them into the future (Martin and Osterholtz, chapter 5).

The thousands of individual skeletons from the Hamann-Todd and Terry collections taken from homeless shelters, city hospitals, mental institutions, and nursing homes provide the bulwark of anthropology's physical disciplines. Prior to their ultimate repose in the Smithsonian Institution's Natural History Museum, the structural violence and non-consensual anatomization that processed people into collections also created contemporary bioanthropology (de la Cova, chapter 11). In this example, so uncomfortably close to home, the cultural crucible of processing the dead continues to demonstrate its generative capacities. Writing this chapter is another extension of these processes. In attempting to understand and synthesize my dedicated colleagues' research, I inscribe their symbolic representations into digital images before transforming them into physical ink and paper sheets, cutting them into individual strips of information. On one paper strip, de la Cova (chapter 11) documents the routinized atomization of Robert Terry dissolving the soft tissues of a dozen African Americans in a single concrete tank of carbolic acid. On another, Kuckelman (chapter 4) recounts the final attack on the residents of the Castle Rock Pueblo, their starving, fractured, and burned bodies dropped unceremoniously near their kivas by the neighbors who besieged them.

This chapter represents further processing as I convert these representations of extreme violence and funerary memorialization into strips of cut paper, each itself a fragment of the dead bodies of commingled trees disassembled for industrial processing plants in the North American Midwest. By reassembling the dead—human, plant, and animal—the inscribed representations of this conclusion continue to extend the meanings of death. The dead paper strips extend the living performances they document, and the preceding research upon which I am reliant, into the future. In her introduction to this volume, Osterholtz describes the manipulated dead, a phrase that invokes the temporal mythology of 2001's *Donnie Darko* and its philosophy of time travel. This chain of reference and intertextuality is not as irrelevant as it may seem to more scientifically oriented readers. These chapters engage in time travel. Through reading, acts of violence and practices of death are made present. Through the perceptive faculties of those who read these pages, they die and live again. The performance of bioarchaeological research, writing, and readership extends the encoded meanings of the thousands of deaths shared here into the present. As Whitehead told one of his students after touching the *kanaimà* remains that he ascribed as connected to his own eventual death, "and now, you're tainted too" (personal communication, Madison, WI, 2008).

It is not easy to process the dead. Processing death often requires communal, personal, apocalyptic, and cosmological alignment. It often leaves few archaeological traces. In an experiential example from the recent summer, I tried to determine where I could encounter the American Total Solar Eclipse (TSE) of 2017, which unexpectedly became a transformative ritual of death-processing. With a mundane work schedule pending and crushingly limited time to inhabit the path of totality, an eclipse map showed that Carbondale, Illinois, was not only mere miles away from the eclipse's longest duration, it is also the "Eclipse Center of the United States" with another TSE converging there in 2024. It just so happens that in the early 1970s, my parents lived in Carbondale while my dad went to graduate school in psychology. He nearly went to military service in Vietnam after US Marines ROTC officer training. In a brief break from fieldwork in 2003, I flew back to my parents' house, got nostalgic, and viewed some slide cubes from our old-school family photo collection. Over various idyllic summers, we would routinely watch these as a kinship event. Encountering a cube of slides that I had never seen, I quickly understood why my parents were not inclined to show it often: this box consisted of a set of images from summer of 1973. That year my older brother, Mark, died before I was born. He had Down syndrome and died of complications from pneumonia when he was just over a year old.

Many contingencies converged to bring me to existence. One is my dad not dying in Vietnam. And if my brother had lived, my conception in the autumn of 1973 is a low probability as well. Parents in graduate school with two kids, one with Down syndrome, might not have a third child. Thus, in 2003 I realized that I owe my life to my brother's death. In 1973, my parents buried my brother's little casket in Carbondale, moved to the outskirts of Chicago, and created another son. My mom was always good about telling me about Mark, usually on his birthday, later in my life. When I saw that the 2017 TSE longest-duration point was near Carbondale, I was compelled to go. Within days of the event, the compulsion became a desire to keep my brother company during this strange moment. I wanted to be there to protect him, because he might not otherwise understand why it was dark in the middle of the day.

The night before the eclipse, I stayed in the distant enclave of Champaign, Illinois. I left Champaign early in the morning on August 21 and needed every second to arrive before totality. Amid brutal interstate traffic I was still thirty miles from Carbondale. Two hours before the eclipse and the interstate was a parking lot. In an uncertain decision I cut across a large lake bridge and made my way through county backroads, skirting the gathering hordes. I made the shadow of totality with minutes to spare and arrived at the cemetery site my mom had sent pictures of from the last time they visited. I knew the name of the grounds and had a printed photo of the site so I knew that there was a distinctive grave marker and tree nearby. However, I was informed by a group of graveyard security heavies that I couldn't observe the eclipse from within the cemetery. Through a magical set of gatekeeping negotiations, my entry was resolved through human compassion. The scale of the eclipse's presence in Carbondale was clear: the cemetery was circled by the flags of a paid area for viewers who could not, in any circumstances, hang out among the graves.

I still didn't know the exact location of my brother's grave, but the shadows of totality, now fifteen minutes away, were clearly present. Looking at various trees and trying to find a distinctively congruent nineteenth-century tombstone nearby, I found the location from the family photograph ten minutes before totality. I took a few low-quality photos with an elderly camera and sat down. I brushed grass clippings off Mark's tombstone and thanked him for my life. I stayed with him in liminality for as long as I could.

Knowing that mass exodus was imminent, eventually I headed for what should have been a six-hour drive under normal conditions. The first song on an iPod random shuffle of more than 10,000 songs was Curtis Mayfield's "Beautiful Brother of Mine," released in October 1971. Mayfield is also a Chicago child, like myself. Thus began a vehicular return journey that I will remember to my own grave. This eclipse experience, entrained with American mortuary practice, is entirely reliant on commemorative burial in perpetuity. Beyond the grave of my brother, my V-4's carbon trail, and these digital words, little trace of this confluence of meaning in death remains. Without the socially shared poetics of individualized burial and the mediated memorializing of my parents in oral traditions, slide cubes, and digital photography, this recognition of the self in the funerary conditions of my brother would have been impossible. The subsequent disillusion of identity, vibrant reformulation of meaning, and vital recommitment to life emerges from our ability to process the dead.

REFERENCES

Arens, W. 1979. *The Man-Eating Myth: Anthropology and Anthropophagy*. New York: Oxford University Press.

Betts, M. W., S. E. Blair, and D. W. Black. 2012. "Perspectivism, Mortuary Symbolism, and Human-Shark Relationships on the Maritime Peninsula." *American Antiquity* 77 (4): 621–645. doi: 10.7183/0002–7316.77.4.621.

Burdett, John. 2007. *Bangkok Haunts*. New York: Alfred A. Knopf.

Casserino, Christopher Michael. 2009. "Bioarchaeology of Violence and Site Abandonment at Casas Grandes, Chihuahua, Mexico." PhD, Anthropology, University of Oregon, Eugene, OR.

Conneller, C. 2004. "Becoming Deer: Corporeal Transformations at Star Carr." *Archaeological Dialogues* 11 (1): 37–56. doi: 10.1017/S1380203804001357.

Durgun, Pınar. 2017. "Human-Animal Interactions in Anatolian Mortuary Practice." *Chronika* 7: 11–27.

Janik, Tarryl L, and Neil L. Whitehead. 2012. "Sound of Death and the Legacy of Thinking Violence: Notes on a Final Interview with Neil L Whitehead." *Anthropology News* 53 (7): s1-s89. doi: 10.1111/j.1556–3502.2012.53701_s.x.

Knight, Andrew, and Katherine D. Watson. 2017. "Was Jack the Ripper a Slaughterman? Human-Animal Violence and the World's Most Infamous Serial Killer." *Animals: An Open Access Journal from MDPI* 7 (4): 30. doi: 10.3390/ani7040030.

Losey, Robert J., Vladmir I. Bazaliiskii, Angela R. Lieverse, Andrea Waters-Rist, Kate Faccia, and Andrzej W. Weber. 2013. "The Bear-Able Likeness of Being: Ursine Remains at the Shamanka II Cemetery, Lake Baikal, Siberia." In *Relational Archaeologies: Humans, Animals, Things*, edited by Christopher M. Watts, 65–96. London and New York: Routledge.

Maher, Lisa A., Jay T. Stock, Sarah Finney, James J. N. Heywood, Preston T. Miracle, and Edward B. Banning. 2011. "A Unique Human-Fox Burial from a Pre-Natufian Cemetery in the Levant (Jordan)." *PLoS ONE* 6 (1): e15815. doi: 10.1371/journal.pone.0015815.

McLuhan, Marshall. 1994 [1964]. *Understanding Media: The Extensions of Man*. Cambridge, MA: MIT Press.

Mol, Annemarie. 2002. *The Body Multiple: Ontology in Medical Practice*. Durham, NC: Duke University Press.

Schechter, Harold. 1989. *Deviant: The Shocking True Story of Ed Gein, the Original "Psycho."* New York: Pocket.

United Press. 1957. "Farmer Hints He Killed Woman; Police Find 10 Skulls." *United Press*, 18 Nov. https://www.upi.com/Archives/1957/11/18/Farmer-hints-he-killed-woman-police-find-10-skulls/9561510801683/.

Vivieros de Castro, Eduardo Viveiros. 1998. "Cosmological Deixis and Amerindian Perspectivism." *Journal of the Royal Anthropological Institute* 4 (3): 469–488.

Whitehead, Neil L. 2002. *Dark Shamans: Kanaimà and the Poetics of Violent Death*. Durham, NC: Duke University Press.

Whitehead, Neil L. 2007. "Violence and the Cultural Order." *Daedalus* 136 (1): 40–50. doi: 10.2307/20028088.

Whitehead, Neil L., and Michael Wesch. 2012. *Human No More: Digital Subjectivities, Unhuman Subjects, and the End of Anthropology*. Boulder: University Press of Colorado.

Contributors

DILPREET SINGH BASANTI, Northwestern University

ROSELYN A. CAMPBELL, Cotsen Institute of Archaeology, UCLA

CARLINA DE LA COVA, University of South Carolina

ERIC J. HAANSTAD, University of Notre Dame

SCOTT D. HADDOW, University of Copenhagen

CHRISTINA J. HODGE, Stanford University

CHRISTOPHER J. KNÜSEL, Université de Bordeaux

KRISTIN A. KUCKELMAN, Crow Canyon Archaeological Center

CLARK SPENCER LARSEN, The Ohio State University

DEBRA L. MARTIN, University of Nevada-Las Vegas

KENNETH C. NYSTROM, State University of New York at New Paltz

ADRIANNE M. OFFENBECKER, University of Calgary

ANNA J. OSTERHOLTZ, Mississippi State University

MEGAN PERRY, East Carolina University

MARIN A. PILLOUD, University of Nevada-Reno

BETH KOONTZ SCAFFIDI, University of California, Merced

MEHMET SOMEL, Middle East Technical University

KYLE D. WALLER, University of Missouri

Index

Page numbers in italics indicate illustrations.